# AIR DEFENCE GUNNERS AT WAR

# AIR DEFENCE GUNNERS AT WAR

## *India-Pakistan War 1971*

COLONEL MANDEEP SINGH

MANOHAR
2022

First published 2022



ISBN 978-93-91928-79-7

*Published by*
Ajay Jain *for*
Manohar Publishers & Distributors
4753/23 Ansari Road, Daryaganj
New Delhi 110002

*Typeset by*
Ravi Shanker
Delhi 110095

*Printed at*
Replika Press Pvt. Ltd.

*To*

*Harpreet, Prabhleen and Gurleen*

# Contents

# List of Maps

# Acknowledgements

It is often said that writing a book is a lonely and tiresome process but I have been fortunate to have received the support and encouragement of several friends and colleagues while writing this book. It has never been my effort alone but of my family, friends and colleagues. I am grateful to all of them, for without them this work would not have been possible.

I embarked on this journey of writing books on the history of air defence artillery only because of the encouragement and support of Lieutenant Colonel A.S. Bajwa (Baaz) and it is he who has kept me going. For this, I will be forever indebted to him. A special thanks to Baaz, who I am proud to call my friend.

I have always tried to follow the wonderful duo of Jagan Mohan P.V.S. and Samir Chopra whose books on air wars inspired my first book on the India Pakistan War of 1965. As with the first, I owe a debt to them for this book as well. My humble and sincere thanks to them for their books and their words of encouragement that have inspired me.

In the absence of published accounts of the defence artillery per se, the veterans were an invaluable source of information about the conduct of the ADA operations. I met over a score of veterans who shared their experiences with me. I am thankful to each one of them with a special mention of Brigadier Deepak Sharma, Colonels H.S. Sandhu, R.C. Dabral, Yogi Mehta, D.K. Bhandari and H.S. Chaudhary, Lt Col. B.S. Chhetri and Captain Arvind Nautiyal also very graciously guided and mentored me during the writing of this book. A special word of thanks to Lt Gen A.P. Singh, PhD, director-general, Army Air Defence, for his encouragement and advice that immensely helped me in completing this project.

Last but not the least, my thanks and gratitude to my wife, Harpreet, for all the sacrifice, support and help she has given me over the years, while I have been busy with my books. It could not have been possible without her.

*New Delhi* COLONEL MANDEEP SINGH
*15 January 2022*

# Abbreviations

| | |
|---|---|
| AGL | Above Ground Level |
| AEW | Airborne Early Warning |
| AC | Aircraft |
| AWACS | Airborne Warning and Control System |
| AD | Air Defence |
| ADA | Air Defence Artillery |
| ARP | Air Raid Precautions |
| ADDC | Air Defence Direction Centre |
| ADOC | Air Defence Operations Centre |
| AA | Anti-Aircraft |
| AAA | Anti-Aircraft Artillery |
| AADC | Anti-Aircraft Defence Commander |
| AAOR | Anti-Aircraft Operation Room |
| AATC | Anti-Aircraft Training Centre |
| A/Tk | Anti-Tank |
| Armr | Armour |
| Armd | Armoured |
| Arty | Artillery |
| Bty | Battery |
| BC | Battery Commander |
| Bde | Brigade |
| BM | Brigade Major |
| Cantt | Cantonment |
| Capt | Captain |
| COD | Central Ordnance Depot |
| Col | Colonel |
| CAP | Combat Air Patrol |

| | |
|---|---|
| Cdo | Commando |
| Cdr | Commander |
| CO | Commanding Officer |
| C&R | Control & Reporting |
| CW | Continuous Wave |
| Div | Division |
| EW | Early Warning |
| ECM | Electronic Counter Measures |
| ELINT | Electronic Intelligence |
| EW | Electronic Warfare |
| GHQ | General Headquarters |
| GOC | General Officer Commanding |
| GCI | Ground Control Interception |
| GL | Gun Laying |
| GPO | Gun Position Officer |
| GPOA | Gun Position Officer-Assistant |
| Hy | Heavy |
| HAA | Heavy Anti-Aircraft |
| in | Inch |
| IAF | Indian Air Force |
| IST | Indian Standard time |
| JCO | Junior Commissioned Officer |
| Lt | Lieutenant |
| Lt Col | Lieutenant Colonel |
| Lt Gen | Lieutenant General |
| Lt | Light |
| LAA | Light Anti-Aircraft |
| MVC | Maha Vir Chakra |
| Maj | Major |
| Maj Gen | Major General |
| Mk | Mark |
| MT | Mechanised Transport |
| mm | Millimetre |
| MES | Military Engineering Service |
| MOU | Mobile Observation Unit |
| NCO | Non Commissioned officer |
| No. | Number |

| | |
|---|---|
| OC | Officer Commanding |
| Orbat | Order of Battle |
| OR | Other Ranks |
| PAF | Pakistan Air Force |
| PST | Pakistan Standard Time |
| PAD | Passive Air Defence |
| PoW | Prisoner of War |
| Recce | Reconnaissance |
| Regt | Regiment |
| Rdr | Radar |
| RDF | Radio Direction Finding |
| Regt | Regiment |
| RIAF | Royal Indian Air Force |
| 2 ic | Second in Command |
| SM | Sena Medal |
| SP | Self Propelled |
| SC | Shaurya Chakra |
| SOP | Standard Operating Procedure |
| SAM | Surface to Air Missile |
| SEAD | Suppression of Enemy Air Defence |
| Sqn | Squadron |
| SU | Signal Unit |
| TOT | Time over Target |
| TNT | Trinitrotoluene |
| Tp | Troop |
| UN | United Nations |
| UNSC | United Nations Security Council |
| VrC | Vir Chakra |
| VA | Vulnerable Area |
| VP | Vulnerable Point |

# Preface

A news agency reported on 7 December 1971 that an anti-aircraft fire opened up in Bombay (now Mumbai) after radar men reportedly sighted a flight of Pakistani jet planes sweeping in from the Arabian Sea. As the guns opened up and hundreds of anti-aircraft shells burst over the city, air raid warnings were issued and a blackout was enforced. The news agency quoted hospital sources to have reported that fifteen people were wounded by shrapnel from the anti-aircraft guns. Air raid warnings were reportedly sounded in towns and villages in the area around Bombay.[1]

The 'air raid' reportedly lasted for about half an hour. Not many had experienced an air raid before and the sight of tracers streaking across the sky as sirens wailed created mass panic in the city. The anti-aircraft firing continued for well over an hour but there was no air raid that night. Or any other night, for that matter, but the panic that had gripped the city remained for some time. Thankfully, people did not leave the city and there was no migration reported from Bombay after the incident of 6 December. But the situation was more serious at another port city, Karachi. *Dawn* reported that the air raids by the Indian Air force 'created panic among the citizens and many moved houses. The people from upcountry living in Karachi rushed to their hometowns.'[2]

The war was just a couple of days old but the fear of air raids and the 'rain of fire' was spreading in the civil populace. It was never known as to how much of the panic was real or was it just hyped by the press for often there was misreporting as in the case of a sailor accidentally setting off his machine gun at Bombay. As the gunshots were heard, all ships started firing in the direction of the sound of the gunfire. The two reporters on board the ship that had radio communications set up for them ran for that single line but only one could get into the communication room first. Without bothering to cross-check, his single-line flash went out – 'Bombay tonight came under enemy attack for the first time'.

All India Radio (AIR) picked up the flash from the agency. BBC quoted AIR on it and Voice of America (VOA) relayed it from BBC. Radio Pakistan quoted VOA to announce that the Indian Navy had been destroyed and the Pakistan defence establishment seemed to confirm it without cross-checking. It all happened in a day and was simply a work of bad reporting.[3]

Whatever be the truth, it did not seem to matter as 'news' of air raids and enemy attacks spread far and wide and were believed to be true, leading to panic. The fear of air attacks was not something new. It had been so in 1962 when the faulty intelligence on Chinese air capability had convinced the Indian leadership that the Chinese were likely to retaliate massively to any offensive air action. The Indian leadership was not willing to accept any threat to the cities in the plains. This was partly based on an assessment by the Intelligence Bureau (IB) that the PLAAF would be capable of undertaking missions at night as far as up to Madras, without interference, due to our lack of night interceptors.[4]

While it may seem to be an act of overcautious leadership, the fears of panic spreading in the populace in case of an air attack were not misplaced. It had happened so during the Second World War when the Japanese came knocking at India's doors. Imperial Japanese Navy aircraft from a Japanese aircraft carrier bombed Vizag and Madras on 6 April 1942. Two fighter planes came overhead at around 8 a.m. at Vizag. Sensing danger, the air raid wardens sounded the sirens and the people of the town ran for nearby shelters. After a few rounds of scouting the planes disappeared but as they returned around 1 p.m., the Bofors AA guns on American ships in the harbour opened up. The retaliatory fire, combined with the natural protection of the hills on all three sides, did not allow the planes to attack the ships at the inner harbour and forced the Japanese to abort their mission. They made a final attempt around 6 p.m. and had to return almost empty-handed except that they managed to drop a bomb which fell on one of the targeted ships, *Marine Maller*, but it mercifully did not explode.

Thankfully, there were no more air raids as Japan was focused on its operations in Burma. But as Yasmin Khan, in her book, *India at War: The Subcontinent and the Second World War*, mentions, the threat of Japanese air raids caused panic amongst the common people and gave rise to rumours which only further fuelled the panic.[5]

Sulochna Sisadhari, a schoolgirl from a prosperous family, remembered the foreboding atmosphere in the Vizagapatam of her childhood, the blackouts, rations and panic, which now bore some resemblance to the British home front: 'We were scared of war as we were afraid of bombing by enemy countries. We used to live near the sea coast of Vizagapatam. Defence services used to have coastal batteries, anti-aircraft guns and searchlights. Every week they used to practise firing into the sea. We used to watch as we were close by and got scared.

The reaction to the air raids was pure panic. It was not only the civil population that left the towns in hordes but even government offices shifted out of Madras. The High Court of Madras was moved to Coimbatore, the Inspector General of Police to Vellore, the Board of Revenue to Salem and the Secretariat to Ooty with only a skeleton staff remaining at Fort St. George, Madras. Animals at the Madras zoo were shot dead by a platoon of Malabar Police so that they would not try to escape – as it was feared that wild animals running amok could lead to more panic. The animals included three lions, six lionesses, four tigers, eight leopards, four bears and a black panther. The only one to escape this slaughter was an elephant as there were not enough people available to bury it.[6]

The panic soon spread to other parts of India. Jamshedpur saw an exodus of workers, much before the air raid on Calcutta (now Kolkata) later in December. Even Bombay on the west coast was not immune to rumours and several rich business families sent their women and children to Gujarat; much like what happened in London during the Blitz. Six extra trains were run everyday from Bombay to cope with the additional load. But all this without any real raid coming in. It took some time before the panic subsided and people started returning.

Calcutta was famously bombed on Christmas Day in 1942 and

it led to another mass exodus of labourers and workers. The work at docks came to a halt. The factories stopped and markets wore a deserted look.[7] The Japanese returned to Madras in October 1943 when a single aircraft came and dropped a couple of bombs. The earlier panic was not there this time for there were no air raid sirens and the strict censorship meant that the news was never leaked. Ignorance was truly bliss in this case.

The fear of air raids and the *rain of fire and death*, however, remained in the psyche of the populace and there was always an apprehension that an enemy air raid could lead to panic amongst the common populace which could be difficult to control. This was a major reason for keeping the air force out of the war in 1962.

The events in Bombay in 1971 showed that an air raid could still cause panic though much had changed since 1942.

The obvious means of preventing recurrence of such mass migration and panic is to have an effective air defence system in place and it was with this intent that in November 1962 Pandit Nehru had asked President Kennedy specifically for an 'Air Defence umbrella' to include twelve squadrons of all-weather supersonic fighters and a modern radar cover.[8]

Air defence, though, is much more than fighter aircraft and radars. It includes 'all measures taken to reduce or nullify the effects of hostile air action'.[9] It includes anti-aircraft guns, surface-to-air missiles and even passive measures like camouflage and concealment, with aircraft being only one component of the air defence system. The role of the ground-based air defence weapons (GBADWS) in providing effective air defence has, however, been largely overlooked with the focus remaining on the manned aircraft, even though GBADWS have caused greater attrition and deterrence over the years.

During the Second World War, the Allied Air Forces (AAF) lost more aircraft to German Flak than to any other weapon system. The AAF lost 18,418 aircraft in combat against Germany in Second World War of which 7,821 were shot down by AAA with German aircraft claiming 6,800 aircraft.[10] Of the total 1,230 American combat losses in the Korean War, all but 143 were claimed by ground fire while a Chinese source states that more than 90 per cent of US aircraft were downed by AAA during the war.[11] The losses in the Vietnam War were also largely to AAA.

Both these were asymmetrical wars as the United States Air Forces were not opposed by an adversarial air force and it was only the ground-based weapons that offered opposition. This explains the higher losses to AA weapons but the fact remains that the presence of AAA made the aircraft engage the targets from greater distance and height. This reduced the bombing accuracy and degraded the effectiveness of airstrikes. With the GBADWS getting better, a need arose to carry out specialized air defence suppression missions – the packaging of strike missions changed over time and that took away resources that would have been otherwise used for strike missions. The presence of AAA in itself was affecting the performance of the air forces.

Even in symmetrical wars between two balanced air forces, it has been experienced that a large share of aircraft losses is due to the GBADWS. During the Kashmir War 1947-8, the Indian Air Force lost seventeen aircraft of which seven were to anti-aircraft fire.[12] Similarly, of the total 59 IAF aircraft lost during the India-Pakistan War 1965, 11 were shot down by Pakistani AA fire while 14 were lost to Pakistan Air Force.[13] Pakistan, on the other hand, lost a total of 43 aircraft of which 25 were shot down by Indian AA artillery and 18 were claimed by IAF.[14]

The India-Pakistan War of 1971 was no different. Almost half of IAF losses were to Pak AA weapons as India lost 34 of the total 71 aircraft lost during the war to ground fire while PAF shot down 16 Indian aircraft. Similarly, the PAF losses to ADA were more than that to IAF.[15] The reliability of such claims, though, has often been disputed as they are based on regimental records that tend to exaggerate the claims. Two examples should suffice to underscore this point. One Indian AD regiment claims to have shot down seven PAF aircraft during the war, while another claims eleven aircraft in their regimental histories.[16]

Such exaggerations are partly due to how kills are claimed by the regiments/batteries and the absence of corroborating evidence to verify them. It is difficult to verify the loss of an aircraft in case the wreckage reportedly falls in enemy territory as the loss is often denied by the opposing side.[17]

On the other hand, losses to AAA were often explained as having occurred due to accidents and technical reasons by both sides. This practice was followed by both sides and was not restricted to only Pakistan. The B-57 shot down by ADA at Jamnagar on 6 September

1965 was recorded as an accident by the PAF.[18] 'As an over-fatigued crew descended lower and lower to pinpoint its target, the bomber hit the ground and exploded with all its ordnance and the invaluable officers'.

Between the inflated claims by the regiments and denial of any losses by the air forces, the true role of ADA is often overlooked and their contribution is ignored. ADA was not only deployed at the airfields but also served with the field armies, at naval establishments and on strategic national assets. It served well with honour and has much to be proud of. There were occasional misses, too, as was the case with all arms, but in all battles, the ADA gunners always rose to the challenge and acquitted themselves well.

This work has been pieced together from official histories, regimental records, accounts of the air wars and a large number of secondary sources but it also draws on oral histories of the war. A large number of veterans shared their personal experiences and it is their contribution that has made this book possible.

This is their story and this book is for all war veterans.

## NOTES

1. 'Antiaircraft Fire in Bombay', *New York Times*, 7 December 1971 accessed on 10 June 2021 at https://www.nytimes.com/1971/12/07/archives/antiaircraft-fire-in-bombay.html
2. 'A Leaf from the History: When the War Began', *The Dawn*, 8 April 2012, accessed on 12 June 2021 at https://www.dawn.com/news/708855/a-leaf-from-history-when-the-war-began
3. Sujata Anandan, 'Why we Should not be Trigger-happy', *Hindustan Times*, 27 February 2019 accessed on 12 June 2021 at https://www.hindustantimes.com/mumbai-news/why-we-should-not-be-trigger-happy/story-ZBIWRBiQqMnwU3cLro9vlK.html
4. R. Sukumaran, 'The 1962 India-China War and Kargil 1999: Restrictions on the Use of Air Power', *Strategic Analysis*, vol. 27, no. 3, July-September 2003, Institute for Defence Studies and Analyses, New Delhi, 2003, pp. 332-4 quoting B.N. Mullick, *My Years with Nehru: The Chinese Betrayal,* Allied Publishers, New Delhi, 1972, pp. 350-1 accessed at https://idsa.in/system/files/strategicanalysis_sukumaran_0903.pdf
5. Yasmin Khan, *India at War: The Subcontinent and the Second World War*, Oxford University Press, New York, 2015, pp. 171-4.

6. 'And then, Madras was Bombed', *The Hindu*, 5 October 2012, accessed on 10 June 2021 at https://www.thehindu.com/news/cities/chennai/and-then-madras-was-bombed/article3965756.ece
7. Robert H. Farquharson, *For Your Tomorrow: Canadians and the Burma Campaign, 1941-1945*, Victoria, B.C., Canada, 2004, p. 98.
8. The events since the Sino-India war panned out differently though and India never received American aircraft or radars and instead turned towards the Soviet Union for military aid.
   Jeff M. Smith, 'A Forgotten War in the Himalayas', *Yale Global Online*, 14 September 2012, accessed on 5 June 2021 at http://yaleglobal.yale.edu/content/forgotten-war-himalayas
9. Definition of air defence as given in 'AAP-6 NATO Glossary of Terms, 2009'.
10. Kenneth Werrell, *Archie to SAM: A Short Operational History of Ground-Based Air Defense,* Air University Press Maxwell Air Force Base, Alabama, August 2005, p. 30.
11. Werrell, op. cit., p. 76.
12. Jagan Pillarisetti, 'Aircraft Losses in the 47-48 Operations', *Bharat Rakshak*, 11 November 2010 accessed on 5 May 2021 at http://www.bharat-rakshak.com/IAF/history/1948war/1049-losses.html#gsc.tab=0
13. B.C. Chakarvorty, *History of the Indo-Pak War 1965*, History Division, Ministry of Defence, Government of India, New Delhi, 1992.
14. Air Marshal A.K. Tiwary, *Indian Air Forces in Wars*, Lancer, New Delhi, 2013, p. 118.
15. IAF lost 34 of the total 71 aircraft losses to Pak AAA while Indian ADA shot down 15 PAF aircraft as compared to 12 by the IAF. [S.N. Prasad, and U.P. Thapliyal, *India-Pakistan War of 1971: A History*, Natraj Publishers, New Delhi 2014, pp. 236-7.]
16. 26 AD Regiment claims seven aircraft to include three F-104 Starfighter, three Mirage-III, one F-6 and two F-86s while 29 AD Regiment claims eleven aircraft to include five F-6 and six F-86 Sabres. These claims are mentioned in their Regimental histories and also find mention in various press releases issued by ADGPI.
17. During the 1965 war, PAF denied losing any F-86 Sabre to ADA and the standard acknowledgement was that 'the aircraft was hit but managed to return to base'.
18. Sultan Hali, 'B-57 the Intrepid Bomber of PAF', *Defence Journal,* accessed on 4 October 2019 at http://www.defencejournal.com/may99/b-57.htm

# Introduction

The first anti-aircraft (as air defence was then called) artillery unit in India was the 8th AA Battery, Royal Artillery, that arrived in India on 9 November 1926 and was located at Peshawar in North-West India. It was an independent battery and was equipped with eight 3-inch 20 cwt AA guns, organized into a battery headquarters with four sections of two anti-aircraft guns each and had a war establishment of 221 all ranks.[1]

The choice of Peshawar may seem odd today but then the AA battery was meant to defend the North-West Frontier from a possible attack by the then Soviet Air Force, should the threat of a Soviet invasion of India became real. The deployment was based on the appreciation flowing from the Defence of India Plan of 1921 that had been passed by the Legislative Assembly of India in March 1921. The resolution defined the role of the army in India as 'the defence of India against external aggression and the maintenance of internal peace and tranquillity'. For any other purpose, the obligations resting on India were to be optional and self-imposed. This role of the army was accepted by the Government of India and His Majesty's government in the United Kingdom. The next step was drawing up a 'Defence of India' plan. With Soviet Russia as the only (then) major power that was a threat to the British interests in the East, the plan was drawn up against an eventuality of an attack by Soviet Russia on India, through Afghanistan.

As Soviet Russia's Air Force was in no position to pose any serious threat or support its purported invasion with large scale air operations, it was appreciated that one AA battery would be an effective deterrent.

In absence of any AA battery in the army in India, an AA battery of Royal Artillery had thus to be moved to India.[2]

For years, it remained the only AA battery in India and it was only on the eve of the Second World War that major changes took place in the anti-aircraft artillery in India. The modernization committee, under the chairmanship of Major General Auchinleck, was amongst the first to propose major changes in the Indian Army. The Chatfield Committee, which was formed subsequently, in turn, based its recommendations on the report of the modernization committee. Though the existing structure of military commands and districts in India was recommended to be retained, the army in India was grouped under five categories, viz., Frontier Defence Troops, Internal Security Troops, Coast Defence Troops, the General Reserve, and the External Defence troops.

It was at this stage that anti-aircraft artillery was first recommended to be part of the Indian Army as three anti-aircraft batteries were recommended to be integral to the General Reserve. In a departure from the past practices, these batteries were recommended to be a part of Indian Artillery and not borrowed from the Royal Artillery, as had been the norm till date.

The recommendation remained unactioned and there were no Indian AA units when Second World War started. The only AA unit in India in 1939 was 8th AA Battery, RA located at Peshawar. It was not surprising as the defence plans remained focused towards the north-west, so much so that Plan A, prepared as per the directive issued by the Commander-in-Chief, India, on 21 May 1940,[3] was for operations in the north-west. The plan envisaged the total requirement for air defence to be that of three AA regiments. This requirement was later revised to include four more regiments; one heavy mobile anti-aircraft and three light mobile anti-aircraft regiments to serve with the expeditionary force. The requirement of guns for the static defence was also finalized for the first time, with the total requirement coming to be 234 static heavy and 153 static light anti-aircraft guns.[4]

These plans and requirement of AA regiments remained unimplemented and it was the threat from Japan as it came knocking on India's doors that spurred the raising of the Indian AA Artillery.

In July 1937, war broke out between China and Japan. With

Japanese forces sweeping across mainland China, Hong Kong was cut-off from the mainland by October 1938. This was a direct threat to British interests with the situation in the Far East fluid, to say the least. The imperial defences had been neglected for long and were in an abysmal state. Faced with Japanese expansionism, Great Britain decided to send a fleet to the Far East early in 1939 but because of the very serious threat at home from Germany and Italy, only two capital ships could be sent. The coastal defences at Hong Kong were modernized but all it had was two infantry battalions which were grossly inadequate to put up a stout defence. Of greater importance was Singapore – the Gibraltar of the East – that was planned to be reinforced with land and air forces in August 1939. Nearer home, all that Burma had was a very small defensive force called the Burma Auxiliary Force. Its state of preparedness could be judged from the fact that it had one AA regiment but no guns.

India was expected to play a major role in defending imperial interests and provide troops for the war effort in the Middle East and British outposts in the Far East but its large standing army was woefully antiquated as the modernization process was only just taking off. The requirement of troops was, however, so urgent that, India sent the 12th Indian Infantry Brigade Group from the 4th Indian Division, it being the first to be sent to Singapore. The remainder of the division was sent to Egypt in 1940.

After Dunkirk, India was in the process of raising one armoured and five infantry divisions but there was a problem in providing artillery regiments as there was just one unit – the 'A' Field Regiment with four 4-gun horsed batteries located at Bangalore. As the Indian artillery came to be expanded in 1940 to meet the requirement of the new formations, the British War Office decided in August 1940 to create a separate AA branch, also of Indian artillery.

A technical training battery was raised on 15 September 1940 at Colaba with the nucleus provided by 8th AA Battery, RA.[5] It was later used in turn to raise the first AA unit of Indian Artillery – 'R' (Royal) HAA Regiment on 1 October 1940, followed by, 'U' LAA Regiment in January 1941. By 1942, the anti-aircraft branch had grown considerably with a total of eighteen anti-aircraft regiments with an equal number of heavy AA and light AA regiments grouped under three AA brigades. In addition, there was one independent HAA battery and two independent LAA batteries on the order of battle. By the end of 1944, the Indian artillery had a total of thirty-three air defence artillery units making the India Command the second most densely protected area – second only to Great Britain.[6] Interestingly, the Indian Army had more AA regiments than field regiments at one time, though they were mostly deployed for the defence of the homeland. A few AA regiments saw overseas service.

The first Indian AA unit to be operationally deployed was 1 HAA Battery as it was moved to Assam for the protection of the Digboi oilfields. This was followed by 1 Indian HAA Regiment with 5 Indian LAA Battery that was sent overseas to Singapore as part of reinforcements for Malaya Command.[7] The regiment was tragically lost as the Japanese overran Singapore and it became one of the units that surrendered. It was never raised again. The Indian AA Artillery next saw action in Burma where 8$^{th}$ Indian HAA and 3$^{rd}$ Indian LAA Battery formed part of Burma Corps (Burcorps) providing air defence to the Allied troops as they withdrew in face of the Japanese offensive.

The Indian AAA expanded rapidly after the rout in Burma and the AA training centres were hard-pressed to meet the increased demand. Several infantry battalions were then converted to AA regiments. Amongst the changes effected was the raising of AA/anti-tank regiments of which a total of four were raised, though only one saw service as such before being disbanded.[8]

At its peak, AAA had three training centres at Malir Cantt, Deolali and Mehgaon. There was a fourth centre, i.e. the No. 4 AA Training Centre (AATC) that was raised in Calcutta to train Women Auxiliary Corps (India) personnel. These women were used for plotting, radio operation and other AD duties in the AA Operations Rooms (AAOR). With the requirement rather limited, No. 4 AATC was closed down after five months in July 1943. Several British AA brigades and regiments were also moved to India to beef up the anti-aircraft defences in India. Most of the Indian AA regiments were deployed in India Command that included Ceylon (now Sri Lanka), Maldives and Aden. The only exception was 25$^{th}$ Indian LAA Regiment that was raised and deployed in Iraq.

Several Indian AA regiments formed part of $14^{th}$ Army and took an active part in operations as part of its corps and divisions. A couple of regiments even took part in amphibious operations during the race to Rangoon (now Yangon). Even as the operations were going on, several AA regiments were demobilized as the Japanese air threat had greatly lessened by 1944. Later, two LAA Regiments were earmarked and trained for Operation Zipper – the amphibious operation to retake Malaya, but as the operation was subsequently scaled down, only one LAA battery was sent to Malaya.[9]

As part of the demobilization and reorganization process, three regiments were placed in suspended animation on 4 June 1945, followed by the conversion of one LAA and eleven HAA regiments to field/medium/anti-tank units. Once the re-organization of artillery was completed in 1947, only six AA regiments remained on the order of battle.

In the division of assets between the two armies at the time of Partition, India's share was only two LAA regiments with Pakistan getting two HAA and two LAA regiments. However, India was to convert one field artillery regiment to an HAA regiment (making it 2+1 AA regiments) while Pakistan was to convert one HAA regiment to a field regiment and one LAA regiment to an anti-tank regiment (i.e. 1+1 AA regiments).[10] The LAA regiments that came to India were 26 LAA and 27 LAA Regiments. The equipment required to convert one field regiment to an HAA regiment was available with India but rather than convert a field regiment, India raised a new HAA regiment in 1948.

The two AA regiments that went to Pakistan Army were renumbered and designated as 5 HAA Regiment (erstwhile 18 HAA Regiment) and 6 LAA Regiment (erstwhile 25 LAA Regiment).[11]

Post-Independence, the first task given to the Indian AA regiments was to assist in maintaining law and order in the wake of the riots following the Partition. 26 LAA Regiment, placed under 1 Armoured Division, performed its duties creditably in face of daunting odds, with Major Gurcharan Singh and Naib Subedar Dhan Singh awarded Ashoka Chakra Class II (now called the Kirti Chakra) for their act of valour.[12]

No sooner had the riots been brought under control than Pakistan invaded Kashmir in an attempt to annex it by force. Tribesmen led by its Pakistan Army officers in civilian garb crossed over into Kashmir on 22 October 1947. The tribesmen were well-armed with automatic weapons, mortars and flame-throwers. The Maharaja of Kashmir, on 24 October 1947, requested the Indian government for military aid. The Indian government conveyed to the Maharaja that it would be legitimate to send the Indian troops to Kashmir only after Kashmir formally acceded to India. By 26 October, Kashmir looked indefensible and Pakistani militiamen were knocking at the doors of Srinagar and were just 50 km away. At this late stage, the Maharaja of Jammu & Kashmir signed the Instrument of Accession. J&K acceded to India on 27 October 1947 and the unprepared Indian military got sucked into a war.

Within hours of the signing of the Instrument of Accession, the first three Dakotas of No. 12 Squadron, RIAF, took off from Willingdon (Safdarjung) airfield in Delhi at 0500 hours on 27 October 1947 with troops of the 1 SIKH ex-Gurgaon. The first aircraft touched down at 0830h, just in time to save the Srinagar airstrip and the city from being overrun by the militiamen. This was followed by airlifting of an infantry brigade to Srinagar. The Tempests of No. 7 Squadron, RIAF, were soon providing close support to the Army in checking the advance of Pakistani militiamen and carrying out reconnaissance missions.[13]

The RIAF aircraft repeatedly came under hostile ground fire with the aircraft getting hit at times but no casualties were suffered till 1 December 947 when a Harvard flown by Flt Lt U.A. D'Cruz was shot down by the ground fire. D'Cruz was accompanied by P.N. Sharma of *Blitz*, a tabloid, on a reconnaissance-cum-photographic mission over the Akhnoor-Bhimber area, when D'Cruz noticed that the raiders had surrounded a village and set it ablaze. He strafed them and managed to disperse them. Thereafter, he flew to another location where he observed the raiders carrying stores and ammunition on donkeys and camels. As D'Cruz dived to strafe them, his aircraft was shot at by Pathan tribesmen and was damaged. D'Cruz crash-landed at Bhimber and was captured by the tribesmen along with Sharma.[14]

Pakistan deployed detachments of its 5th and 6th AA Regiments along with its field and mountain guns to be used in the ground role.

Four anti-aircraft guns were deployed in Pandu and Chota Kazi Nag sector while two heavy and four light AA guns were deployed in the Uri and Akhnur sectors. An arsenal of 3.7-inch heavy AA guns of 5 Heavy AA Regiment and 40 mm AA guns of 6 Light AA Regiment were also employed in ground role in the Jhelum Valley. To offer some resistance to the RIAF, Pakistani artillery even used its mountain guns for firing airburst shells, notably in the Poonch area. The available records also mention that one AA gun was deployed near Poonch to take on IAF aircraft.[15]

Notwithstanding the paucity of AA guns, the RIAF aircraft regularly faced hostile fire, though it was more from small arms than from AA guns. But such hostile fire also proved fatal at times. On 16 March 1948, Flying Officer Balwant Singh flying a Tempest was carrying out a close support mission in Naushera-Jhangar areas when he was fired at and was 'hit by the ground fire'. Balwant was hit and incapacitated as a result of which he could not pull out of the dive. His Tempest crashed into a hill, killing Balwant instanteously.[16]

In another incident, the RIAF aircraft, came under heavy flak while carrying out strikes against the Kishan Ganga bridge in April 1948. One of the AA gun posts near the bridge was neutralized by the striking aircraft, but another gun deployed west of the international border, managed to hit the leading Tempest. Thankfully, Wing Commander Ranjan Dutt 'managed to limp back to base in his damaged aircraft'.[17]

Pakistan had, by now, deployed AA guns all along the western border, especially in the Tithwal region. They managed to hit the RIAF aircraft on many occasions but failed to shoot down any aircraft. The pilots' luck did not hold for long as Flying Officer K.L. Mathur's Tempest was hit by the AA fire and the controls damaged. He managed to reach back and line himself with the runway, but as he touched down, one of the wheels collapsed. The aircraft swung and hit a building on the side. Mathur was only slightly injured though the Tempest burned away.[18] A total of seventeen RIAF planes were lost during the war, of which eight were either shot down by the Pak AAA or damaged severely, leading to their loss while landing.[19] One of the few aircraft shot down by Pak AAA was a Tempest that was lost in the Tithwal area on 7 October 1948. The pilot, Flying Officer U.G. Wright, baled out and had a harrowing experience during his parachute descent. He was shot at by rifles, light-machine guns and even 3-inch mortars but he made it back to his lines.[20]

The Pakistan Air Force stayed away for the most part during the war and was primarily involved with logistic support operations. The Pak C-47 Dakotas flew 347 sorties dropping 500 tons of supplies at Bunji, Skardu, Gilgit and Chilas without losing any aircraft. The first Siara-i-Jurat of the PAF was awarded to Sqn Leader M.A. Dagar who successfully dodged an Indian Tempest while on a mission in Kashmir.[21]

Even as no missions were undertaken against Indian forces by the PAF, Indian ADA was deployed for the protection of the airbases. Earlier, in the meeting of the Defence Committee of the Cabinet (DCC), an all-out war with Pakistan was not envisaged and the service chiefs did not point out any air threat from Pakistan.[22] 26 LAA Regiment, then at Uruli, had been placed under command of 1 Armoured Division at Jhansi and was earmarked to move to Hyderabad with the formation. In June 1948, one LAA Battery of the regiment was moved to Jammu & Kashmir and its troops placed under 19 and 26 Divisions. The battery-less one troop was deployed at Srinagar airfield while the Troop was deployed at Jammu airfield. This followed the directive issued by the DCC to the service chiefs to take immediate steps to protect the two airfields.[23]

The regimental headquarters of 26 LAA Regiment along with the remaining two batteries moved to Hyderabad with 1 Armoured Division for the likely operations against the Nizam. 27 LAA Regiment at Ambala was ordered to be prepared for operations in the Amritsar-Ferozepur area with 4 Infantry Division standing by for contingency. In April 1948, the first post-Independence raising had been completed as 19 HAA Regiment was raised with 3.7-inch HAA guns at Khadakvasla. One battery of the regiment was moved and deployed at Pathankot airfield. In September 1948, 45 LAA and 46 LAA Regiments were raised at Jhansi under 11 Army Group Artillery and were meant for AD of infantry divisions. These regiments were, however, not employed during the First Kashmir War.

In June 1948, Pakistan inducted four 40 mm Bofors and two 20 mm Oerlikons for air defence of its forces in the Mirpur sector. The guns were deployed in an open area and did not have much camouflage.

In one of the air raids by IAF over the area, a Pakistani 40 mm AA gun was damaged.[24]

With the ceasefire coming into effect from 1 January 1949, the war had ended but the troops of both sides remained dug in facing each other along the Cease Fire Line (CFL). The subunits of 19 HAA and 26 LAA Regiments remained deployed at their operational tasks till August 1951.

In 1949, India enacted the new Territorial Army legislation which paved the way for the raising of new AA Regiments (TA). Four Heavy AA Regiments, viz., 103 HAA, 104 HAA, 105 HAA and 107 HAA Regiments (TA) were raised using the Second World War vintage 3.7-inch HAA guns lying in ordnance depots. Interestingly, they were raised as HAA regiments, not because of the threat assessment but only because there was a ready stock of these guns available at ordnance depots. The heavy AA guns were, however, not suitable for use against the modern jet aircraft with the ideal AA guns considered to be in the range of 20 to 40 mm. It was thus decided to henceforth raise only LAA regiments and, accordingly, the next three raisings were of LAA regiments (TA) in 1951. These were 126 LAA, 127 LAA and 128 LAA Regiments (TA).[25]

With the induction of jet combat aircraft in the subcontinental air forces, there was a need to have a relook at the AA defences and upgrade the AAA to take on the emerging threats. As the mainstay of Indian AAA was still the 40 mm L/60 Bofors AA gun, a search was on to find a radar-controlled AA gun to equip the AA regiments. While the choice of the gun was simpler as Bofors had already developed the 40 mm L/70 AA gun, the search for a suitable fire control radar took a little more time. In the end, four vendors were shortlisted – Contraves of Switzerland, Arenco of Sweden, Aldebaran of Italy and CSF of France. After extensive trials during 1960-1, Radar Superfledermaus of Oerlikon Contraves was selected to be used with 40 mm L/70 guns. An agreement to produce the radars under licence by BEL was signed in June 1961 with the production to commence by 1963.[26]

It was not only the radar-guided AD guns that India was looking at as it sought to further expand into the missile age, and an agreement was signed with Switzerland in 1962 for the development of the intermediate-range surface-to-air missile, codenamed Project Indigo.[27]

Switzerland had a long history of developing and perfecting weapons including missile systems and, as a 'neutral' country, was an obvious choice for a non-aligned country for weapon development. The project, however, did not fructify beyond the preliminary research stage.

While these developments were taking place, China invaded India in October 1962. It was a turning point in more than one sense. A total of six AD artillery units were employed in Assam/Bengal, mainly in the non-AA role. As there were no AA regiments for the mountainous sectors, the LAA regiments with infantry divisions were detached and deployed in the east.[28] 107 HAA Regiment (TA) at Calcutta was also moved to Tezpur and was used in a non-AA role.

The detachment of LAA regiments from infantry divisions was to have long-term implications as they (AA regiments) were never orbatted to the infantry divisions afterwards. They became part of independent AD brigades and this detachment from infantry formations resulted in a chasm that persists to a large extent to date.

The war changed the strategic scenario as India, shocked by the blatant Chinese aggression, turned towards the West, especially the US, for military aid, including an Air Defence umbrella. The US, preoccupied with the Cuban missile crisis, did not respond immediately. On 19 November 1962, Nehru wrote to Kennedy for a more specific aid for an Air Defence umbrella – to include 'twelve squadrons of all-weather supersonic fighters' and a modern radar cover. Before the US could even consider the request and firm up a response, China declared a unilateral ceasefire. With its long-standing aim of containing Communism, the US finally reached out with a proposal of a Military Aid Package (MAP) though its relations with Pakistan, a CENTO and SEATO member, were a factor in deciding upon the quantum of aid. As a result, the initial aid provided was modest: military advisors, ammunition, rifles, mortars and airlift support.[29] Nevertheless, as a follow-up action, a US military mission toured India and recommended joint air defence exercises. The first such exercise took place in November 1963 and was rightly described as precedent-setting. The joint tripartite exercise with the United Kingdom joining in, codenamed 'Shiksha', was aimed to augment, exercise and improve the Indian air defence system, including training Indian air defence personnel. The other aim of the exercise was to familiarize the US and UK personnel with operating conditions in India. One USAF fighter squadron, two mobile USAF radar units and one RAF fighter-interceptor squadron participated in the exercise, with Australia providing some communication personnel and aircraft.[30] Following an outcry in the media against US military personnel being stationed on Indian soil, phase two of the exercise was cancelled and never took place. The exercise, however, brought out some glaring deficiencies in the air defence set-up – more notably, the absence of a radar cover. To help set-up an effective AD system, the US provided Star Sapphire Radar systems with the Project Indigo early warning communications system as a *gift* to be used on the northern borders only.

When India put out a wish list for a military aid package worth Rs. 500 million, the US offered aid worth Rs. 150 million only, with the catch that no combat equipment would be given.[31] In addition, British Bloodhound or Thunderbird missiles were to be offered. Reportedly, trials were also conducted but as the overall MAP was not up to India's desired standard, the proposal fell through. Meanwhile, the Soviet Union came up with a more agreeable aid package, which included MiG-21, SA-2 Surface to Air Missiles (SAM) and the P-35 radar system. It is worth remembering that the Soviet Union had only provided MiG-19s to China by that time. As the Soviet proposal included the local manufacture of MiG-21s, it was a far better option and was taken up by India. The Army made a bid for the SAMs but all the haggling between the Army and IAF came to a nought as the role of AD artillery was limited to providing low-level air defence and the SA-2 system went to the IAF.

The post-1962 period saw the de-induction of 3.7-inch HAA guns and the Indian ADA was left with only the 40 mm AD guns. With only one type of gun system and the revised responsibility of low-level AD, the need to differentiate between HAA and LAA regiments was no longer there and all regiments were now classified as AD regiments.

It was a time of fast-paced changes for air defence. India had acquired and inducted SA-2 and long-range radars though these were with the air force and not the artillery. The 40 mm L/70 AA gun was being manufactured in India[32] as was the Radar Superfledermaus, albeit at a slow pace. New AD regiments had been raised and by the time

India had to again go to war in 1965, India had 21 AD regiments. On the other hand, Pakistan had only 9 AD regiments.

With the induction of Soviet SA-2 SAMs, Project Indigo, for indigenous development of surface-to-air missiles with Swiss aid, was also scrapped.[33]

In a related development, even as ADA was evolving and expanding, the responsibility for the seaward defence was entrusted to the Navy in 1963. The coast batteries, which, till then, were manned by the Army, were taken over by the Navy.[34] Right from the beginning, ADA and coastal artillery have had an umbilical relationship, with a common training establishment (coastal and AA Artillery School at Karachi). This change in responsibility was another break from the past and was to put ADA on an independent trajectory.

## PAKISTANI AIR DEFENCE ARTILLERY

Pakistan AA artillery had a modest beginning as it started with two AA regiments as its share following the Partition of India and Pakistan. These were 18th (earlier 2nd) Indian Heavy AA Regiment with 1, 7 and 8 Heavy AA Batteries and 25th (earlier 3rd) Indian Light AA Regiment with 3, 6 and 7 Light AA Batteries. The regiments were re-numbered soon after, with 18th HAA Regiment now designated as 5th HAA Regiment and 25th LAA Regiment becoming 6th LAA Regiment. Even the batteries were numbered afresh as follows:[35]

| *Indian Designation* | *Pakistani Designation* |
|---|---|
| 5 HAA Regiment | |
| 1 HAA Battery | 12 HAA Battery |
| 7 HAA Battery | 18 HAA Battery |
| 8 HAA Battery | 24 HAA Battery |
| 6 LAA Regiment | |
| 3 LAA Battery | 14 LAA Battery |
| 6 LAA Battery | 20 LAA Battery |
| 7 LAA Battery | 21 LAA Battery |

During the first India-Pakistan War of 1948, both the AA regiments fielded detachments albeit in a ground role. Four anti-aircraft guns were deployed, besides medium and field artillery in Pandu and Chọta Kazi Nag sector, while 2 × Heavy AA guns and 4 × Light AA guns were deployed in the Uri and Akhnur sectors. *History of Pakistani Artillery* by Maj Gen Shaukat Riza notes that an AA gun was deployed near Poonch to try and engage Indian Air Force Dakotas. Firepower from 3.7-inch heavy AA guns ex-5 Heavy AA Regiment and 40 mm AA guns of 6 Light AA Regiment were also employed in ground role in the Jhelum Valley.[36]

In March 1950 Pakistan raised 3 Army Group Royal Pakistan Artillery (AA), its first AA Artillery headquarters. The two AA Regiments were placed under it was entrusted with the responsibility of planning air defence of Pakistan in conjunction with PAF. Shortly afterwards, 13 LAA Regiment was raised in April 1950 – the first AA unit to be raised in independent Pakistan, followed by 45 Independent LAA Battery. With the raising of an Anti-Aircraft Artillery Operations Room (AAOR) on 27 July 1951, Pakistani AAA was getting its AA organization in place.

All the AA units and the AAOR were placed under 3 AGRPA with Lt Col Calver, commanding officer of 6 LAA Regiment, appointed as its first commander. He was succeeded by Brigadier Pinchard in October 1950. While Major Shirazi, a 'fresh off Staff College' officer was appointed as the DAA & QMG, he was soon enough shifted as the brigade major with an infantry officer posted in as the DAA & QMG. One plausible reason for doing so was that there was an acute shortage of qualified artillery officers and the priority was to post them to the field units rather than to headquarters.

The AA regiments raised during the period were:

| | |
|---|---|
| 13 LAA Regiment | April 1950 |
| 19 LAA Regiment | August 1951 |
| 20 HAA Regiment | May 1951 (Converted to LAA Regiment on 1 March 1960) |
| 29 LAA Regiment (SP) | |
| 36 LAA Regiment | |
| 45 Independent LAA Battery | |

The first HQ corps artillery came up in 1951 with Brig J.H. Frowen, DSO appointed as its first commander with 13 LAA Regiment and the 82 LAA Battery forming part of it besides the four 40 mm LAA and two 3.7-inch HAA guns pooled in ex-Artillery Centre. This HQ was designated as HQ 1 Corps Artillery in 1957 (and later as HQ

4 Corps Artillery after the 1965 war, swapping the designation with HQ 4 Corps Artillery that became HQ 1 Corps Artillery).[37]

The year 1954 was a major milestone for Pakistan Army as the US Military Aid Programme (MAP) was initiated that year. Keeping in mind the manpower ceiling of 40,000 laid down as a condition for the implementation of MAP, Pakistan Army went about laying down the details of units to be raised. As regards AA artillery, the MAP resulted in a marginal increase of two LAA regiments and one LAA battery, as elucidated below[38]:

| *Units before MAP (November 1954)* | | *Units after MAP (December 1959)* | |
|---|---|---|---|
| LAA regiments | 3 | LAA regiments | 5 |
| HAA regiments | 2 | HAA regiments | 2 |
| LAA batteries | 2 | LAA batteries | 3 |

With time, the HAA regiments were converted to LAA regiments as the 3.7-inch HAA guns were phased out. Pakistan also received the M24 Twin 40 mm AA Gun 'Duster' from the US. 19 LAA Regiment (SP) was the regiment to be equipped with this mobile gun system. The other change was the induction of 20 mm Quad AA guns.

Both Indian and Pakistani ADA truly came of age in 1965 as the two nations once again went to war with both the air forces used offensively for the first time. For the ADA, it was to be the baptism by fire.

## NOTES

1. Bisheshwar Prasad, *Expansion of the Armed Forces and Defence Organization, 1939-45*, History Division, Ministry of Defence, Government of India, New Delhi (Reprinted and Distributed by Pentagon Press, New Delhi), 2012, p. 436.
2. Some sources mention that the 8th AA battery was raised in India but there is no corresponding corroboration of this claim.
3. Prasad, op. cit., pp. 439-41.
4. Prasad, op. cit., p. 443.
5. The commonly referred to the date of raising is 14 September with No. 1 Technical Training Battery being formed on this date at Colaba. However, the date of raising of the first AA unit as recorded in official documents is 15 September with the place of raising recorded as Karachi and not Colaba, Bombay. (Authority: Statistical Review of Personnel, Army of India, vol. I, I July 1939 to 1 October 1941, Compiled by Statistical Section, GHQ, Delhi, 1941)

6. N.W. Routledge, *History of the Royal Regiment of Artillery: Anti-Aircraft Artillery, 1914-55*, Brassey's, London, 1994.
7. File No. 601/2290/WD, War Diary of 1st Indian HAA Regiment maintained by History Division, Ministry of Defence, New Delhi.
8. Notings of Artillery Directorate on 'Expansion of Artillery 1939-1941' accessed at History Division, Ministry of Defence, New Delhi.
9. File No. 601/2093/WD War Diary of Headquarters 9th AA Brigade, RA maintained by History Division, Ministry of Defence, New Delhi and Judy Dean, *An Easy War in the Royal Artillery (Part 2),* BBC WW2 People's War, 26 May 2005.
10. Partition of Personnel and Units of Armed Forces *Fourth Meeting of Partition Council, Allocation of Armoured Corps and Infantry Units, Partition Proceedings,* vol. 5, p. 44. Accessed on 3 January 2020 at http://shodhganga.inflibnet.ac.in/bitstream/10603/14220/8/08_chapter%204.pdf
    Also, refer to History of Artillery: *Pangs of Partition,* Directorate General of Artillery, accessed on 5 January 2020 at http://indianarmy.nic.in/Site/FormTemplete/frmTempSimple.aspx?MnId=8Z5bhvBfqykVyUp0Sk8YRQ==&ParentID=iyOBZ+iSBXrLmgvH+uj7Iw==
11. 'History of Pakistan Army Air Defence' accessed on 19 March 2019 at http://www.pakarmymuseum.com/exhibits/history-of-air-defense/
12. Gallantry Awards, Ministry of defence, the government of India accessed on 22 April 2021 at https://www.gallantryawards.gov.in/Awardee/gurcharan-singh-0
13. 1947-48 Kashmir Operations, An Air Force Perspective, IAF accessed on 5 May 2021 at https://indianairforce.nic.in/content/1948-ops
14. He remained a prisoner with the tribesmen and later with the Pakistan Army, until December 1948, when he was returned to India under a scheme for the exchange of prisoners of war. Flt Lt U.A. D'Cruz's was later awarded a Kirti Chakra – a first for the Indian Air Force.
    Bharat Kumar, *An Incredible War: Indian Air Force in Kashmir War 1947-48,* KW Publishers, New Delhi, 2007, p. 221.
15. The RIAF records show an extensive AA deployment by Pakistan during the war but there are no mentions of the same in publicly available Pakistani narratives. The history of Pakistan Artillery only mentions the use of AAA in the ground role with one mention of its employment in AA role near Poonch. [Shaukat Riza, *Izzat-o-Iqbal: History of Pakistan Artillery*, School of Artillery, Nowshera, 1980, p. 55.]
16. Bharat Kumar, op. cit., p. 202.
17. Ibid., p. 205.
18. Ibid., pp. 207-8.
19. Jagan Pillaiserati, 'Aircraft Losses in 47-48 Operations', *Bharat Rakshak*, accessed on 5 May 2021 at http://www.bharat-rakshak.com/IAF/history/1948war/1049-losses.html#gsc.tab=0
20. Pakistan does not claim this loss and there is no mention of this in its official history. The Tempest is more likely to have been shot down by small arms fire

and not by AA guns. Jagan Mohan, 'An Overview of the RIAF in the Kashmir Ops', *Bharat Rakshak*, 19 July 2009 accessed on 4 September 2020 at http://www.bharat-rakshak.com/IAF/history/1948war/1000-overview.html#gsc.tab=0

21. 'How PAF fought in the Wars', *The News*, Lahore, 6 February 2018, accessed on 19 March 2020 at https://www.thenews.com.pk/print/364500-how-paf-fought-in-wars
22. Bharat Kumar, op. cit., p. 300.
23. Ibid.
24. Riza, op. cit., pp. 62-3.
25. There is no source(s) in the open domain giving details of raising of all AD regiments which were on the Order of Battle of Indian Army. The dates of the raising of AD units has been collated from various sources like newspaper articles about the Raising Day celebrations of the Regiment(s), Issue of First-day covers and including anecdotal knowledge of veteran AD officers.
26. S. Prabhala, K.V. Koshy and S. Krishnan, *Inside the Solid State: The Story of Bharat Electronics* Westland, Chennai, 2014, p. 34.
27. Timothy V. McCarthy, 'India: Emerging Missile Power', in William C. Potter, and Harlan W. Jencks (eds.), *The International Missile Bazaar: The New Suppliers' Network*, Routledge, New York, 1994, pp. 202-3.
28. The LAA regiments used to be integral to Infantry Divisions till 1962 but due to the emergent requirement of AA regiments in high altitude areas along the border with China, especially in north-east, the AA regiments were taken away from Infantry divisions and deployed separately.
29. Memorandum for the President, 11 October 1963, State Department Archives accessed on 21 September 2020 at https://www.archives.gov/files/declassification/iscap/pdf/2011-056-doc22.pdf
30. Jeff M. Smith, 'A Forgotten War in the Himalayas', *Yale Global Online*, 14 September 2012 accessed on 5 June 2021 at https://yaleglobal.yale.edu/content/forgotten-war-himalayas
31. K. Subrahmanyam, 'Arms and Politics', *Strategic Analysis*, January 2005, vol. 29, issue 1 accessed on 18 July 2021 at http://www.idsa.in/strategicanalysis/ArmsandPolitics_ksubrahmanyam_0305
    Also see 'Memorandum for Henry Kissinger', 26 January 1972, Foreign Relations 1969-76 US Department of State Archives, accessed on 18 July 2021 at https://2001-2009.state.gov/r/pa/ho/frus/ nixon/e7txt/ 49244.htm
32. L/70 production started by Ordnance Factory http://ofbgcf.nic.in/#
    Also http://www.ofbindia.gov.in/units/index.php?unit=gsf&page=about&lang=en, accessed on 8 August 2021.
33. Timothy V. McCarthy, op. cit., and William C. Potter and Harlan W. Jencks, op. cit.
34. Vice Admiral G.M. Hiranandani, *Transition to Triumph Indian Navy 1965-1975*, p. 16 accessed on 28 November 2020 at https://www.indiannavy.nic.in/content/transition-triumph

35. Maj Gen Shaukat Riza, *Izzat-o-Iqbal History of Regiment of Artillery 1947-1971*, School of Artillery, Nowshera, 1980, pp. 16-21.
36. Ibid., pp. 71-80.
37. Ibid., pp. 109-11.
38. Ibid., pp. 114-20.

## CHAPTER 1

# Revisiting 1965

At 0300 hours on 1 September 1965, Pakistan launched Operation Grand Slam intending to capture the vital town of Akhnoor in Jammu to sever communications and cut-off supply routes to Kashmir.[1] The Akhnoor sector was lightly defended by four Indian infantry battalions and a squadron of tanks.

Attacking with an overwhelming ratio of troops and technically superior tanks, Pakistan made gains against Indian forces as the defenders were caught unprepared and suffered heavy losses. Facing heavy odds, the commander of the 191 Infantry Brigade requested close air support at 1100 hours but the request reached Indian air headquarters only at about 1600 hours. Yashwant Chavan, the defence minister, when apprised of the situation, gave the go-ahead without referring the matter to the Cabinet due to the criticality of the request and the paucity of time. Within an hour of the orders being issued, the first aircraft, four Vampires of No. 45 Squadron, IAF, had taken off.[2]

Facing the two Pakistani infantry brigades and two armoured regiments was 3 MAHAR of 191 Infantry Brigade, supported by a squadron of 20 LANCER with AMX-13 tanks. When the first four Vampires came overhead, in a case of mistaken identity, they attacked their own troops causing considerable damage – all artillery ammunition vehicles, three AMX-13 tanks, one armoured recovery vehicle and one tank ammunition lorry were destroyed.[3] The Vampires then turned their attention to Pak armour. As the IAF aircraft started their run over the Pak tanks, the AA guns of 111 LAA Battery/29 LAA Regiment opened fire, knocking off the Vampire flown by Flt Lt S.V. Pathak. The IAF had suffered its first loss in the very first engagement.

The IAF carried out a total of 28 sorties in support of the Army during the day and lost four aircraft; three to PAF Sabres and one to Pak ADA. In addition, several IAF Mystéres in the follow-up waves were hit by ground fire and quite a few of them had 0.50-inch bullet holes to show off.[4] The war had really and truly started for the Air Force and the ADA.

It was to last 22 days but with no clear winner. Both sides claimed victory, but, as a commentator said, it was a war in which Pakistan lost and India did not win.[5]

The claims of inflicting heavy losses on the adversary, especially of losses in the air, have never been officially confirmed. The official history of the war may have been written – but was never made public. A quasi-official history of the Indian Army and the IAF was released but there were no acknowledgements of claims. The role and performance of ADA, though wrongly linked with the number of aircrafts shot down, was mostly ignored and overlooked, but then there was more to ADA during the war than the number of aircraft shot down, and that makes for an interesting narrative.

Pakistan launched Operation Grand Slam on 1 September, but then it was just one part of its overall aim of annexing Kashmir. It was a four-phased plan, of which Operation Desert Hawk launched in the desolate Rann of Kutch was the curtain-raiser. It was intended to bring territorial disputes between India and Pakistan into the international limelight and also to test the new weapon systems acquired from the US since Pakistan had joined the US-led Southeast Asia Treaty Organization (SEATO) and Central Treaty Organization (CENTO). Drawing away Indian troops from Punjab was another intended aim of this operation.

It was only after Pakistan had set-up a post well within the area claimed by India at Kanjrakot, Gujarat, that Headquarters Maharashtra and Gujarat Area (HQ M&G Area) issued its Operational Order No. 1 of 1965 (Operation Kabadi) on 21 February 1965, dispatching 31 Infantry Brigade Group to capture Kanjrakot.[6] The brigade group was provided support elements by HQ M&G Area, including one AD battery of 103 AD Regiment (TA) to be deployed in the forward zone during the operation. The operations in the Rann were a protracted affair that ended in June 1965 with a ceasefire agreement brokered by the British prime minister.

The two air forces had agreed to keep away from the Rann, though Pakistan Air Force did carry out a number of sorties in support of its Army. In a little-known incident, a two F-86 mission of No. 17 Sqn, PAF, was covering the move of Pak Army on 19 April when one of the F-86s, piloted by Flying Officer Waleed Ehsanul Karim, was hit by AA fire. Ehsanul Karim managed to bring his Sabre back to Badin where it was repaired. Karim carried out another sortie in the evening, a reconnaissance mission, when his aircraft developed engine trouble and plunged into the Arabian Sea, about 10-15 miles off the south coast of Karachi. Though the immediate reason for the crash was engine failure, the damage caused by the AA fire during the morning sorties was also a contributory factor leading to the loss.[7] The Indian ADA was not actively involved in further operations except for the occasional use of Indian AD troops in the ground role. Some subunits of Pakistani AAA besides the mobile elements of sector operations centres (SOC) had also been deployed but were not used during the operation.

While Operation Desert Hawk was underway in the Rann, Pakistan had already started rolling out the next phase – Operation Gibraltar. Hundreds of trained Mujhahids infiltrated the Kashmir Valley to recruit locals and incite them to rebel against the Indian government. The plan failed but not before the infiltrators managed to create a great deal of disorder in Kashmir by acts of violence and arson. To stop these infiltrators, the Army decided to block the points of ingress, and in a series of such moves, occupied posts at the Tithwal sector and Kargil. On 28 August, in the boldest counter-insurgency move that the Indian Army had ever taken, 68 Infantry Brigade captured the strategic Haji Pir Pass and, with it, a large chunk of PoK fell into Indian hands. The air forces of both the countries had kept away from any combat employment though the IAF did use modified Mi-4 helicopters as 'gunships' in support of the Army and which proved very effective.

After the start of the standoff in the Rann, India had ordered Operation Ablaze and with it, the embodiment of TA regiments had commenced. As a result, the AD regiments (TA) were at their operational locations when the war started on 1 September. At the time of going to war, India had twenty-one AD regiments, of which fifteen AD regiments, including five TA regiments, were deployed in the western sector and six were deployed in the east.

All AD regiments were equipped with the towed version of 40 mm L/60 AA guns except one, 29 AD Regiment (SP), that had 40 mm L/60 guns mounted on Ford Morris trucks. Also, one battery of 19 AD Regiment was equipped with radar-controlled 40 mm L/70 guns. Pakistan, on the other hand, had nine AD regiments and a more varied equipment profile as the AD weapons included 40 mm L/60 guns, M24 Twin 40 mm Track Mounted AA Gun 'Duster' and 20 mm Quad AA guns. It had only one LAA regiment deployed in East Pakistan.

For the ADA, the priority was the defence of air force bases and installation, with the majority of AD regiments deployed in these tasks. Initially, India had only 29 AD Regiment (SP) as part of a field formation, however, ADA batteries and troops were placed under field formations with the progress of operations. This was the line-up as the operations started.

The deployment of AD regiments in the east was biased towards the Indo-China border to cover for the possible threat from the People's Liberation Army Air Force (PLAAF) of China, with five of the six regiments deployed mainly to defend the airfields in north Bengal and Assam. Kalaikunda, with three combat squadrons, including one of Canberras, did not have any ADA resource when the war broke out and was provided with an AD battery at a later stage on the night of 6/7 September.

In the west, after the hectic air operations on 1 September in the Akhnoor sector, there was a lull on 2 September, with both forces largely remaining on their sides and refining their tactics. The air activity was stepped up by both sides on 3 September and it was on this day that IAF got its first kill. The Indian ADA also claimed its first Sabre as Havildar Perumal C. Perumal's detachment of 27 AD Regiment shot down a PAF F-86 Sabre at Akhnoor bridge.[8] On 5 September, 27 AD Regiment claimed another F-86 Sabre as Havildar Tata Pothu Raja's detachment shot down the aircraft at the Tawi bridge near Jammu. Potha Raj recalls:[9]

We were posted on a hill to protect the bridge. I was in charge of an L-60 gun with a capacity to fire 120 rounds from 7,000 ft. It was quite early in the morning when I noticed a couple of fighter jets swooping down on the bridge.

I was trained to recognize aircraft and I knew they were Sabre jets from their wide mouths. After getting the nod from my commanding officer, I aimed at the target and fired. I hit the target. The aircraft came down in a hail of smoke and fire and the pilot was killed.

India may have been getting its act together in the air and claimed a couple of PAF Sabres but the operations on the ground were not going as Jaurian had fallen to Pakistani forces on 4 September and the Pak Army was just six miles from Akhnoor on 5 September. At this critical stage, India decided to open a new front in Punjab to relieve the pressure off Akhnoor.

In a bold move, India launched a riposte, with the Indian Army crossing the border in the Lahore-Kasur sector on 6 September. 11 Corps under the command of Lt Gen. Joginder Singh Dhillon launched the offensive, attacking three thrust lines – each thrust was by an infantry division, supported by armour and artillery. 15 Infantry Division was in the northern thrust along the Grand Trunk Road to Lahore, 7 Infantry Division in the centre on the Khalra-Burki axis, while the southernmost thrust was delivered by 4 Mountain Division on the Khem Karan-Kasur axis.[10]

Pakistani 1 Corps was responsible for defence in the sector and it had 6 Armoured Division located at Gujranwala, 10 Infantry Division at Lahore, 11 Infantry Division at Bedia-Kasur and 15 Infantry Division at Sialkot.

11 Corps offensive 'Operation Riddle' started at midnight 5/6 September. The progress of 15 Infantry Division on the northern axis was eventful. Its 96 Infantry Brigade had been taken away as Corps reserve, unbalancing the formation from the very start. The divisional artillery was deployed in the night and was not available till one hour after the first light on 6 September. The ADA complement earmarked for the division was not available it had not yet reached up from Dehradun, leaving the division vulnerable to air attack, especially since the formation was told that it could not expect any support from the IAF as it would be occupied in air superiority missions.[11]

The division's advance was being led by 3 JAT which took the first two objectives by 0658 hours. It was then PAF struck. At 0700 hours the first of PAF F-86 Sabres attacked the unit column.[12] The PAF also attacked all along the Grand Trunk Road, including Gharenda where the division headquarters had set up its command post and where the division reserves were located. The Sabres attacked with impunity, knocking off several ammunition vehicles, blocking the main axis and forcing the advancing troops to take the tracks through slushy rice fields. In the air raid, 3 JAT lost five of its six recoilless (RCL) guns and three mortars with their carriers. 54 Infantry Brigade was also badly hit, losing almost all its 'F' echelon vehicles. There was just no opposition to PAF in absence of IAF and ADA.

The PAF raids notwithstanding, 3 JAT, in a brilliant feat of arms, became the first Indian battalion to cross the Ichhogil Canal. It beat back a counter-attack, but the Pakistani Army brought in its armour for the next counter-attack. As the battalion had lost all its RCL guns and had no armour to support it, it could not hold back the Pakistani counter-attack and had to withdraw. The state of the demolished bridge that had been used to cross over to the west bank had influenced the decision to withdraw but the absence of an anti-tank weapon was a more critical factor. It can only be speculated now that, if the formation had an air defence cover and the RCLs had not been lost, would have the battalion held on to its gains. Not catering to air defence for the formation had proved to be a costly mistake.

Overall, PAF could claim partial credit for checking the Indian advance towards Lahore, while IAF was not present anywhere near 11 Corps. It flew a few Mystére sorties in the Chhamb sector and claimed some tanks and vehicles as destroyed but did nothing else to directly support the Army. It did not carry out any counter-air missions to keep the PAF down and prevent any interference with its own ground operations. Even the missions purportedly in support of the Army were rather wasted, as in the case of the Canberras of No. 5 Squadron, IAF, that were tasked to engage a Pak Army Corps headquarters. In the words of Squadron Leader V.C. Goodwin:[13]

> At the briefing, I asked what do we do if we don't see anything across the road, and the CO said 'you will drop your bombs across the road'! My navigator was Flt Lt Mangat and we could see the bombs of Red 1, 2, and 3 bursting across the road. There was no corp HQ or signs of any troops, except open fields, and as per

orders we also dropped our bombs there. The next day in the papers, it said IAF Canberras strike Pakistani Army corp HQ in Gujarat. Nothing but propaganda!!

While the IAF shied away from attacking the Pakistani air bases, the PAF hit the Indian airbases on 7 September and hit them hard.

The PAF had worked out a plan in June 1965 to strike at Indian airbases in the event of an all-out war, designated as the Air War Plan No. 6.[14] On 6 September, it was put into action and it severely tested Indian air defence set up. Keeping in mind the need to maintain a balanced posture, PAF had allocated the following resources for the pre-emptive strikes:

| *Take-off Base* | *Aircraft* | *Target* |
|---|---|---|
| Sargodha | 8 × F-86 F Sabres | Adampur |
| Sargodha | 8 × F-86 F Sabres | Halwara |
| Sargodha | 4 × T-33 | Ferozepur Radar |
| Sargodha | 6 × F-86 F Sabres<br>1 × RB-57 ELINT | Amritsar Radar |
| Peshawar | 8 × F-86 F Sabres | Pathankot<br>Srinagar |
| Mauripur | 8 × F-86 F Sabres | Jamnagar |
| Mauripur | 4 × T-33s | Porbandar Radar |
| Mauripur | 12 × B-57s | Jamnagar |

As Sargodha did not have the required complement of aircraft to carry out simultaneous raids against four IAF bases, PAF had planned to shift 12 F-86 Sabres and six T-33s from Mauripur. The move of these aircraft was delayed so as not to have too many aircraft out in the open on the tarmac but this delay proved costly as four of the 12 Sabres from Mauripur developed defects and had to be put down for repairs. This left only six F-86 Sabres for three targets – Adampur, Halwara and Amritsar Radar. As a concession, Amritsar was dropped as a target and the six F-86 were earmarked for Adampur and Halwara but this was not the only snafu in the PAF plan. It was important for PAF to attack all the targets simultaneously to maintain surprise but here, too, PAF suffered a setback. The 8 × F-86 Sabres escorted by 2 × F-104s from Peshawar earmarked for Pathankot and Srinagar arrived over their target right on the designated TOT of 1740 hours but the first F-86 from Sargodha took off only at 1810 hours for Adampur while the second section earmarked for Halwara took off at 1820 hours. This meant that the element of surprise which was critical to success had been lost. Even so, IAF and ADA were caught unprepared at most of the locations as the PAF struck at the Indian airbases.

The worst affected was Pathankot where PAF destroyed ten IAF aircraft – two MiG-21s, six Mystéres, one Gnat and one C-119 Packet, and damaged three more, including two Gnats and one Mystére.[15] It was a failure of the air defences as, even though the information of the raid was passed to the Pathankot airbase by the P-35 radar at Amritsar, no action was taken. Neither was the combat air patrol, or CAP launched to intercept the raiders nor the ADA at the airfield warned about the raid.[16]

The air defences were better prepared at other bases and PAF failed to achieve much success. The CAP at Halwara intercepted the PAF Sabres, shooting down two of them while the ADA claimed a third. The Pakistani accounts mention only three Sabres of which two were lost to the Indian CAP while the third managed to return to Sargodha.[17] Adampur was not attacked as the PAF Sabres turned back after observing the CAP aborting the mission. It was at Jamnagar that ADA scored as a B-57 was shot down by 129 AD Regiment (TA). This was the first aircraft shot down by a TA regiment during the war and the first B-57 to be shot down by the ADA.[18]

PAF refused to acknowledge that the B-57 was shot down by the ADA and its official version claimed that B-57 crashed due to crew fatigue and spatial disorientation coupled with bad weather. It was only after forty years that PAF accepted the loss of B-57 to ADA. Interestingly, the regiment did not claim any kill for this B-57 and this finds no mention in the ADA history and it never got the credit for the same.

After the PAF strikes on 6 September, IAF responded in strength with raids on PAF air bases, including Sargodha, on the next day. Sargodha was very well-defended with five LAA batteries deployed at the airbase. It had 20 LAA Regiment with one LAA battery each from 13 and 36 LAA Regiments besides some LAA guns manned by PAF personnel as well.[19]

During the raids, IAF lost five aircraft from 31 sorties at Sargodha, one of which was claimed by Pak AAA.[20] There are several accounts of the raid with conflicting claims but all are unanimous about the fact that the airbase was well defended and the raids did not inflict much damage. In a separate account, the LAA guns of PAF in their very first engagement claimed to have hit and damaged one of the IAF aircraft.[21]

A careful reading of the accounts of the losses incurred by the IAF shows that a couple of losses were put down as 'technical loss' or an accident whereas the loss was partly attributable to the damage caused by AA fire. The losses shown as 'technical loss' were that of Flt Lt Kacker's Hunter at Sargodha and Squadron Leader Jasbeer Singh's Mystére at Gujranwala. Pak AAA had hit Kacker's fuel tanks, resulting in a serious loss of fuel. On the way back, the engine, starved of fuel, flamed out and Kacker had to eject.[22] In Jasbeer's case, as he approached, the Mystére was hit by AAA, making it go out of control and plough headlong into the ground, leaving no time for him to eject.[23]

The raids by PAF at Srinagar and Amritsar on the same day, i.e. 7 September, were warded off by the Indian ADA, but the real action of the day for PAF was at Kalaikunda in the east. In the first raid, PAF claimed two Canberras of No. 16 Squadron, IAF and four Vampires of No. 24 Squadron on the ground as it caught the defences by surprise. The second PAF raid was not so lucky and it was picked up by the radar well in time giving enough scope to the air defences to be ready. Two Sabres were shot down by the IAF Hunters while a third was claimed by Naik Madalai Muthu of 28 AD Regiment.[24]

The raids on Kalaikunda were the only serious efforts by PAF in the east and with IAF exercising restraint, the ADA was not tested except for an occasional foray by the Pakistanis. All of these were repulsed by the Indian ADA.

After 7 September, there was a shift in the strategy with regard to the use of air forces. After suffering heavy losses, both IAF and PAF shied away from attacking each other's air bases for some time. The airbases were only targeted intermittently, more as a token show of force than with any serious intent of inflicting damage. This strategy was, however, reviewed later during the war when both sides again started targeting each other's airfields.

On 8 September, India opened a new front as it launched its 1

Corps in the Sialkot sector. Simultaneously, a limited offensive by the Indian 11 Infantry Division was undertaken in the Gadra sector of Rajasthan. With the need of supporting these, the IAF got down to engaging interdiction targets and providing limited support to the field formations.

As the two air forces were carrying out CAS (close air support) missions, PAF lost an F-86 Sabre to friendly fire when Flight Lieutenant Sadruddin's aircraft was hit by Pak AA fire in the Sialkot sector.[25] In an unverified claim, the Indian 3rd Cavalry claimed to have destroyed a PAF F-86 Sabre, using a tank mounted .50 AA MG on 8 September.[26] In other sectors, ADA claimed to have shot down an F-86 over 230 SU at Amritsar.[27] During the night of 8/9 September, SA-2 Pechora SAM were reportedly fired by the IAF for the first time as it claimed to have engaged and destroyed a PAF C-130 on a bombing run over Delhi. As per the reports, a loud explosion was heard over Delhi but no debris was found.[28]

By the morning of 9 September, the battle of Khem Karan had started and the IAF was tasked to provide close support to the Army. During one of these missions, Wing Commander Zacharia's Hunter was hit by severe AA fire that damaged the electrical resulting in the controls being jammed. Zacharia switched over to manual control and just about managed to pull out of the dive in time but not before his aircraft hit the ground tearing off the airbrake. Though Zacharia reached base with his damaged Hunter, another pilot, Flying Officer M.V. Singh, in the same mission was not so lucky. His Hunter was hit by AA fire and damaged seriously, forcing him to eject. He was taken prisoner and he had to spend the rest of the war as a POW.[29]

Two more IAF Hunters were severely damaged while carrying out interdiction missions during the day. Though they managed to return, one of the aircraft was damaged beyond repair and was a write-off while a second plunged to the ground as the pilot tried landing. It was, however, listed as a 'technical loss' only.[30] A PAF Sabre and a B-57 were claimed to have been shot down by AA fire at Wagah and Halwara, respectively, during the day.[31]

IAF continued to suffer losses to Pak AAA while carrying out CAS missions in the Khem Karan sector, losing two aircraft in two days. In a rare admission, PAF acknowledged the loss of an F-86 at

Amritsar as the F-86 piloted by Squadron Leader Munir-ud-Din Ahmed was shot down by ADA. PAF, in its accounts, refers to the raid as the final mission against the Amritsar radar, claiming that the radar was destroyed though the radar was not damaged and remained operational.[32] On the other side, at another radar, PAF suffered a greater loss as its RB-57 was shot down by Pak AAA at Rahwali in a case of fratricide. The RB-57 was carrying out a practice run, but as the information of the same was not passed on to the AAA, it was taken as hostile and shot down.

On 12 September, a Pakistani helicopter was shot down by a tank of 17 HORSE, using its main gun during the battle of Philaura. Quoting the regimental history:[33]

> C Squadron continued to be in a location at Phillaurah, while the rest of the regiment was deployed between Kotli Bagga and Libbe. While C Squadron was at Phillaurah, a Pak helicopter landed just South of Kalewali. This was immediately engaged and destroyed by Naib Risaldar Harbhajan Singh and his gunner, Sowar Harbans Singh. The rotor blades of this helicopter are on display in the regimental quarter guard-good shooting indeed!

Adampur faced its worst air raid of the war on 13 September as the PAF B-57 bombers carried out three raids during the night. The first raid was at 2200 hours, by a lone B-57 which had come to be admiringly referred to as the '8 Pass Charlie'. It got its name from its bombing run as it flew at a leisurely pace in a circuit, dropping just one bomb in each run. On this night '8-Pass Charlie' is believed to have shown up again.[34] Even as '8-Pass Charlie' flew along at almost a leisurely pace, the AD guns opened up but did not get any hit. This was all the more surprising as the newer radar-controlled L-70 AA guns were deployed at Adampur. It was suspected that the tracking radars were being tampered with, making them ineffective. All the radars were re-calibrated and rechecked after the raid.[35]

As the war entered its third week, there was a marginal increase in air activity by both the air force. PAF returned on the night of 14/15 September to raid the Indian airbases and at Adampur it suffered a major setback as a B-57 was shot down by the ADA. The raid was by two PAF B-57s and as the bombers were on their second run, the fire of AD guns hit one of the B-57s. The stricken B-57 dropped its bomb load and managed to fly a short distance before plunging into the ground nearby. The B-57 No. 33-891 (Call sign SG-261) of No. 7 Squadron/31 Bomber Wing PAF had taken off from Peshawar and was on its 13th mission of the war. Both the crew members, the pilot, Flt Lt Altaf Sheikh, and the navigator, Flying Officer B.A. Chaudhary ejected safely. They could evade capture only till morning when the villagers rounded them up.[36] The shooting down of the B-57 was greeted by all the personnel at the airbase. Flying Officer Rajkumar recollects[37]

> The roar which came up from all personnel as they leapt out of the trenches must have been heard as far as Amritsar and, if not there, at least in Jallandhar. There was undisguised glee and drinking near the trenches in the moonlight was indeed a sight to behold.

The next day another PAF pilot was taken prisoner as Mohd Shaukat-ul-Islam's Sabre was shot down by the ADA at Amritsar forcing him to eject. He was rounded up and taken POW.[38]

During the ongoing battle in Khem Karan, AA fire claimed to have shot down three PAF Sabres on 20 September while a B-57 was claimed to have been shot down at Ambala and the wreckage was reported to have fallen near Shambu railway station.[39] These claims were, however, not verified as no wreckage of the claimed kills was found.

IAF revisited Sargodha as four Canberras of No. 5 Squadron IAF raided the premier PAF airbase on the night of 20/21 September. The Canberras reached the airfield without an interception and as one of the Canberras, piloted by Flight Lieutenant Manmohan Lowe, turned away after delivering the ordnance, it was hit by AAA fire. The damaged Canberra started losing fuel due to the hit. It was at about 1,000 ft at that time. Lowe decided to gain height to 13,000 ft to save fuel, but as it was gaining height, an F-104 Starfighter piloted by Wing Commander Jamal Ahmad Khan picked it up. Locking on to the target, Khan fired an AIM-9B Sidewinder missile that hit the Starboard Avon engine of Canberra and exploded. This was the first confirmed kill by an F-104 using the Sidewinder missile.[40]

On the other end, Canberras of No. 16 Squadron were raiding the PAF radar at Badin. The radar consisted of two domes mounted on towers, about 80 ft tall, with several dummy domes constructed nearby. The closest PAF airbase was PAF Mauripur. A reconnaissance of the radar had earlier been done and it was recognized that the more important azimuth antenna was housed in the eastern tower. It was decided that one Canberra would be equipped with rockets while the remaining three would be carrying bombs only. The plan was for the rockets to be fired first, to mark the target for the follow-on Canberras. The raid succeeded in destroying the eastern dome but it was later confirmed that it contained the height and GCI antenna and not the azimuth unit. However, the effective bombing ensured that the whole set-up was neutralized for the rest of the war.[41]

IAF suffered its first, and only, fratricide casualty on the last day of the war as Flt Lt C.S. Doraiswami's Mystére was shot down by own ground fire. No. 3 Squadron, IAF, had been tasked with a close support mission to take out Pakistani targets around Dogri. Four Mystéres led by Flt Lt Doraiswami took off from Ambala and by the time they arrived over the target, the ground position had changed. The 'target' was now in Indian hands but this information could not be communicated to the strike leader in time. As the Mystéres attacked, now held by Indian troops, they came under effective ground fire that hit Flying Officer Prem Ramchandani's Mystére. As the aircraft caught fire and flames engulfed the Mystére, Ramchandani ejected. He was critically injured and even as the Jat troops evacuated him to the nearest military hospital, Ramchandani succumbed to his injuries.[42] In another incident, IAF lost a Hunter to AA fire as Flt Lt K.C. Cariappa's aircraft was shot down by ground fire over Kasur. He managed to eject but was taken prisoner.[43]

The ceasefire was declared at 0330 hours on the morning of 23 September. After the declaration of ceasefire, PAF B-57s, escorted by two F-86 Sabres, attacked Amritsar at 1615 hours. Though PAF claimed to have dropped the bombs on an Indian Army concentration near Attari, they fell on a civilian locality, causing a large number of casualties. AAA brought down both the Sabres. One of the aircraft reportedly fell near Thima and the second near a gun position. One of the B-57s was also hit and was seen emitting smoke as it went back.[44]

Almost a month later, PAF used its RB-57, on loan from USAF (United States Air Force), for a post-war reconnaissance mission over India. 'Droopy', as the aircraft was nicknamed due to its enormous 122 ft wingspan, could cruise comfortably at 80,000 ft out of the reach of any fighter of the IAF. When the RB-57 was detected, three

SA-2 Guideline missiles were fired from Ambala which exploded in close proximity of the aircraft damaging one of its engines. The RB-57 was nursed back to its base Peshawar by its pilot, Squadron Leader Rasheed Meer, but the aircraft suffered more damage when the nosewheel did not function and the aircraft skidded along the runway. PAF claims that the aircraft was repaired and returned to the US. But the damage was so extensive that the aircraft could not be repaired and was a write-off.[45]

Thus ended the war of September 1965. Pakistan had failed to achieve its goals and had lost the war. Participating in a war for the first time, ADA performed creditably against all odds. Equipped with Second World War weapons that had no integral radars, hopelessly inadequate in numbers, taking on modern jets for which the guns were not designed, both the Indian and Pakistan ADA did well. PAF lost a total of 43 aircraft of which 25 were to ground fire. Though it includes the losses to small arms and the one loss to a tank main gun, the majority of these 25 losses were to ADA. Another factor to consider is that a large number of PAF aircraft may not have been shot down but were hit by ADA, and damaged. As per one source, as many as 58 F-86 Sabres were hit by ADA and damaged.[46] Also, all the four B-57 lost by PAF during the war were to ADA. Given the fact that IAF could not shoot down a single B-57 during the war and the 40 mm L/60 guns had serious limitations, this performance is indeed creditable.[47] The exact losses are hard to ascertain in absence of any corroboration by PAF through one source lists the total PAF losses as per official figures at nineteen, of which five were shot down by Indian AAA.[48]

The IAF losses are listed as 59 of which 24 were in the air and 35 on the ground due to enemy action. Of the 24, Pakistan AAA claimed 10, though IAF (like the PAF) has always been hesitant in giving credit to AAA and covers up some of its losses as 'technical loss' even if they are attributable to AAA fire. There were a couple of fratricide incidents involving PAF as it lost two aircraft to a 'friendly' fire. IAF lost one aircraft to AA fire by its own troops but the aircraft was fired at when attacking its own troops. The incident did not involve the ADA.

If there was one important takeaway from the war it was the importance of better coordination and control of ground air defences. Even a cursory look at IAF losses is enough to show that it lost a large number of aircraft 'on the ground'. Clearly, the coordination of air defences was lacking in 1965 and this was one aspect that needed to be improved urgently. During the next few years, it was duly addressed and the drills and procedures refined. How effective these had been can only be assessed by looking at the performance of air defences and in this, the IAF and ADA did not disappoint.

## NOTES

1. R.D. Pradhan, *1965 War, The Inside Story: Defence Minister Y.B. Chavan's Diary of India-Pakistan War*, Atlantic Publishers and Distributors, New Delhi, 2007.
2. Ibid., pp. 22-4.
3. B.C. Chakravorty, *History of the Indo-Pak War 1965*, History Division, Ministry of Defence, Government of India, New Delhi, 1992, p. 117.
4. P.V.S. Jagan Mohan and Samir Chopra, *The India-Pakistan Air War of 1965*, Manohar Books, Delhi, 2005, p. 74.
5. Shekhar Gupta, The War Pakistan Lost and India Didn't Win, NDTV, 15 September 2015 accessed on 20 April 2020 at https://www.ndtv.com/opinion/the-war-pakistan-lost-and-india-didnt-win-1217407
6. Chakravorty, op. cit., p. 217.
7. Martin W. Bowman, *Cold War Jet Combat: Air to Air Jet operation 1950-1972*, Pen and Sword Books, Barnsley, 2016.
8. Havildar Perumal was awarded the Vir Chakra. This claim is based on the regimental history of Indian ADA but is not included in any other record/document. The official history of the India Pakistan War 1965 also does not mention this incident.
9. Most accounts and histories consider this to be the first kill by the Indian ADA though this kill is also not included in the official history. 'A War Hero Remembers', *The Hindu*, 3 September 2015, accessed on 11 March 2019 at http://www.thehindu.com/todays-paper/tp-national/tp-andhrapradesh/a-war-hero-remembers/article7610482.ece
10. Chakravarty, op. cit., pp. 141-2.
11. Jagan Mohan and Chopra, op. cit., pp. 68-9.
12. Ibid.
13. Squadron Leader V.C. Goodwin, 'Combat Diary of a Tusker', *Bharat Rakshak*, accessed on 11 March 2019 at http://www.bharat-rakshak.com/IAF/History/1965War/1149-Goodwin.html
14. Chakravorty, op. cit., p. 247.
15. Ibid., p. 251.
16. The warning of the incoming air raid was given to Pathankot and Adampur. While a CAP was launched from Adampur, Pathankot did not take any action. (Jagan and Chopra, pp. 103-5 and Chakarvorty, p. 251.)
17. Most Indian accounts including the one by Jagan and Chopra mention that

four F-86 Sabres carried out the raid at Halwara though the Pakistani accounts mention only the Sabres. [Kaiser Tufail, 'Theirs but to Do and Die', *Aeronaut,* 20 November 2008 accessed on 18 March 2019 at http://kaiser-aeronaut.blogspot.com/2008/11/theirs-but-to-do-and-die.html ]

18. Lon O. Nordeen, *Air Warfare in Missile Age,* Smithsonian Books, 2010 and p. 141, Chakarvorty, op. cit., p. 251. See also, 'Unsung Heroes: Fate of Lost PAF Aviators', The Tribune, Islamabad, accessed on 18 March 2019 at http://tribune.com.pk/story/248981/unsung-heroes-fate-of-lost-paf-aviators-uncovered/
19. Shaukat Riza, *Izzat-o-Iqbal, History of Pakistani Artillery 1947-1971,* School of Artillery, Nowshera, 1980, pp. 289-91.
20. Ibid.
21. Corporal Sher Mohammad who was manning the LAA gun was awarded the Tamgha-i-Juraat, the only instance of PAF Regiment personnel being awarded a gallantry medal. His citation reads:
During the War, Corporal Sher Mohammad was manning a Light Ack. gun at P.A.F. Station, Sargodha. On 6th September 1965, while the Indian aircraft were strafing and rocketing the base, Corporal Sher Mohammad courageously performed his duty by keeping up an accurate fire against the invaders and damaged one enemy aircraft. This was the first engagement of P.A.F. guns against the enemy and the determined fire by Corporal Sher Mohammad greatly enhanced the morale and fighting spirit of the P.A.F. gun-crew.
22. Jagan and Chopra, op. cit., pp. 135-6.
23. As with other cases, Jasbeer's loss is shown as due to 'technical failure/accident' and is not attributed to AAA. However, the citation for Jasbeer's Vir Chakra mentions that his aircraft was hit by AA fire. (Gazette Notification: 15 Pres. 66, 1-1-66.)
24. Naik Madlaai Muthu was awarded the Vir Chakra, the last ADA recipient of the war. https://www.gallantryawards.gov.in/Awardee/madalai-muthu, accessed on 14 September 2020.
25. Jagan and Chopra, op. cit., p. 212.
26. This claim is not supported by any other source and it was more likely that the AAMG hit the Sabre but did not shoot it down. [Kutub Hai, *The Patton Wreckers,* Times Group Books, New Delhi, 2015, p. 41.]
27. Chakarvorty, op. cit., p. 259.
28. Jagan and Chopra, op. cit., pp. 208-20.
29. Ibid., p. 212 and Chakravarty, op. cit., p. 260.
30. Ibid., pp. 213-15.
31. The claim of shooting down of a B-57 on 8 September and the wreckage found near Sidhwan Khas is not mentioned in any other account (Chakravarty, op. cit., pp. 259-60).
32. The PAF version is given at http://paf-eagles.blogspot.in/2010/09/air-war-of-1965-revisited-missions.html, accessed on 18 March 2019. Also see PAF Museum: Historic Events 1965 War http://www.pafmuseum.com.pk/historic-events/war-1965. The citation for Squadron Leader Munir-ud-Din Ahmed can

be found at http://www.paf.gov.pk/paf_shaheeds.html, accessed on 18 March 2019.

33. History of POONA HORSE available at http://www.bharat-rakshak.com/ARMY/images/Poona%20Horse.pdf, accessed on 16 June 2019.
34. Chakarvorty, op. cit., p. 262 and Jagan and Chopra, op. cit., pp. 241-3.
35. Ibid.
36. Flt Lt Altaf Shaikh was nominated for SJ as gallantry award, but it was delayed during captivity and later forgotten by authorities. Incidentally, the pilot's only son Wg Cdr Numan Altaf died in a bizarre 'blue on blue' caused by a trainee pilot's error during a training sortie in Jordan while he was on deputation as an instructor with the Royal Jordanian Air Force in 2005.
Chakarvorty, op. cit., p. 263. See also Jagan and Chopra, op. cit., pp. 248-50. Details are also given at http://www.pafmuseum.com.pk/historic-events/war-1965, accessed on 18 March 2019.
37. Jagan and Chopra, op. cit., p. 248.
38. Chakravarty, op. cit., p. 264.
39. Ibid., p. 266.
40. Jagan and Chopra, op. cit., pp. 275-76 and Davies Peter, *F-104 Starfighter Units in Combat*, Osprey Publications, Oxford, 2014, pp. 79-80 and Usman Shabbir & Yawar A Mazhar, *F-104 Starfighter in Pakistan Air Force Service* accessed on 21 March 2019 at http://pakdef.org/f-104-starfighter-in-pakistan-air-force-service/
41. Jagan and Chopra, op. cit., pp. 278-81 and Air Commodore Prashant Dikshit, '16 Squadron and Badin Radar Raid', *The Salute*, 3 October 2018, accessed on 13 October 2019 at https://salute.co.in/strike-on-the-badin-radar-by-no-16-cobra-squadron/
42. Jagan and Chopra op. cit., p. 288.
43. Jagan and Chopra, op. cit., p. 282. See also Cariappa, 'My Reminiscences as A Prisoner of War', *Bharat Rakshak,* accessed on 9 November 2019 at http://www.bharat-rakshak.com/IAF/history/1965war/1152-cariappa.html 43
44. Chakravarty, op. cit., p. 267. See also Sultan M. Hali, 'B-57 The Intrepid Bomber of PAF', accessed on 4 October 2019 at http://www.defencejournal.com/may99/b-57.htm
45. Jagan and Chopra, p. 287. See also Martin RB-57F at www.spyflight.co.uk, accessed on 3 August 2020 and Arshad Hussain, 'PAF s' No 24 Elint Squadron A stealth unit of the PAF', accessed on 3 August 2020 at http://paf-eagles.blogspot.in/2010/09/air-war-of-1965-revisited-paf-b-57rb-57.html
46. Kenneth Werrell, *Archie to SAM: A Short Operational History of Ground-Based Air Defense*, Air University Press, 2005.
47. Pakistan acknowledges the loss of three B-57s during the war of which the only one is attributed to 'enemy action'. However, if the loss of B-57 at Jamnagar on 6 September and of the RB-57 at Rahwali is also included, the total loss comes to four.
48. Jagan and Chopra, op. cit., pp. 349-50.

CHAPTER 2

# Taking Stock: The Opposing Forces

The war of 1965 between India and Pakistan had been a baptism by fire of the Indian air defence artillery. While both Indian and Pakistani AA artilleries were deployed during the 1948 war, the Indian ADA was never really tested with PAF staying away. During the Sino-India War of 1962, the Indian AD regiments had been deployed in the north-east but they were not tested with the two sides refraining from using their air forces in offensive role. The September War in that context is important as it was the first test of air defence artillery for both sides and the experience gained was to shape its employment in subsequent operations.

## INDIAN AIR DEFENCE ARTILLERY

In the years preceding the 1965 war with Pakistan, there had been a marked though gradual, expansion of the Indian air defence artillery as it grew from just two regiments at Independence to eighteen regiments by 1962 to include ten regular and eight Territorial Army (TA) regiments. The more important change was the decision to go in for radar-controlled air defence guns to replace the vintage 40 mm L/60 AA guns. For this, 40 mm L/70 guns were selected. For the fire control radar, the Superfladermaus radar made by Oerlikon Contraves was selected after comparative evaluation with the radars made by Arenco of Sweden, Aldebaran of Italy and Compagnie Générale de Télégraphie Sans Fil (CSF).[1]

While the L/70 guns were to be made by the gun carriage factory at Jabalpur, Bharat Electronics entered into an agreement with Contraves in 1961 for the licenced production of the same. As the production was scheduled to commence in 1963, it was decided to place an order for 20 radars with Contraves.[2] It was required to match the induction of L/70 guns, but even so only a battery worth of equipment had been inducted by the time India went to war in 1965; with a battery of 19 AD Regiment having shifted to the new radar-controlled guns. During the war, the regiment continued to collect the radars and L/70 guns and converted three more troops but these L/70 troops could be deployed only after the war had ended and did not take part in the operations.[3]

The expansion and conversion of AD regiments continued after the 1965 war with four AD regiments raised in 1966. Two regular units, viz., 151 AD Regiment and 152 AD Regiment, were raised at Secunderabad on 1 July 1966 while two TA regiments, i.e. 140 Medium Regiment (TA) and 144 Field Regiment (TA) converted to AD Regiments (TA) on 1 February 1966 and 18 January 1966, respectively. All four were equipped with L/60 guns.

The only other regiments to be raised before the 1971 war were 130 AD Regiment (TA) and 131 AD Regiment (TA) that were raised in 1967 and 1968 respectively, bringing the total TA regiments to twelve. With fourteen regular AD regiments, the total number of AD regiments at the time of going to war was twenty-six, an increase of five regiments, but what was important was the conversion of eight more regiments to radar-controlled L/70 guns.

The efforts to expand the ADA had included the proposal to induct SAM as well, but all efforts had failed to fructify till 1969. ADA had taken up the proposal of inducting SAMs as early as 1962 and a demonstration of the Bloodhound missile system was also carried out, but unfortunately, the Indian Air Force objected to the proposal and the idea was effectively scuttled. The proposal was revived again in 1969 and a study was ordered for the same. This time around, the proposal was agreed to with the Tigercat Air Defence Missile being selected for induction. The raising of the first missile battery started in 1971 at Deolali, but the battery could not participate in the war as the raising was not completed on the eve of the war.[4]

Other than the AD units, one more formation headquarter was raised after the 1965 war making a total of four AD brigade headquarters in all. Headquarters 211 (Independent) Artillery Brigade had been raised in 1967 at Bangalore and was re-designated as Headquarters 211 (Independent) AA Brigade in 1969 before being re-numbered as Headquarters 342 (Independent) AD Brigade on 20 December 1969. The brigade headquarters moved to Panagarh and took over the responsibility of the West Bengal sector from Headquarters 312 (Independent) AD Brigade. With this, there were two brigade headquarters each in both the east and the west.

The main responsibility of ADA remained the air defence of strategic installations and Air Force assets, with the majority of the twenty-six regiments deployed on such static tasks.

## PAKISTANI AIR DEFENCE ARTILLERY

Pakistani Air Defence Artillery had given a good account of itself during the war of 1965, shooting down ten IAF aircraft but, as with all arms and services, it was seriously affected by the United States arms embargo imposed thereafter. The motley collection of AA guns that Pakistan had in its inventory had been built over the years and was a mix of Second World War vintage British AA guns, US guns left over from the Vietnam war and Chinese copies of ex-Soviet guns. It was more of a desperate collection of weapons from whatever source they could tap.

In the years following the September War, Pakistan raised the following AA regiments[5]:

| | |
|---|---|
| LAA regiments | Seven (incl. 43, 58, 74 and 75 LAA Regiments) |
| HAA regiments | Two (41 and 52 HAA Regiments) |
| Independent LAA batteries | Two |

Continuing with the newly-established relationship with China, Pakistan Army Air Defence received the Type 65 37 mm AA guns and the 14.5 mm Quads to equip its newly-raised regiments and batteries. It resulted in a mix of AA weapon systems with the US, British and Chinese gun systems but, with the traditional Western sources for arms drying up, there was no other option but to have such a mix of an inventory. The Quads were also used to equip the AA Mujahid companies formed to augment the regular regiments and were used to provide air defence to static installations in the rear under command logistic areas. In all, Pakistan AD artillery comprised of the 3rd AA Brigade, twelve light AA regiments, two light AA regiments (self-propelled), three heavy AA regiments and two independent light AA batteries.[6] The exact details of the order of battle and the designation of units are not very clear with different sources giving varying details. The report of the Hamoodur Rehman Commission of Inquiry into the 1971 War mentions that Pakistan had a total of 99 AA batteries, including the Mujahid batteries raised before the war using ex-servicemen.[7]

One of the AA regiments, viz., 75 LAA Regiment, was stationed in Jordon in the 1960s and was recalled in time for the war of 1971. The regiment served with the Jordanian army during the Arab-Israel war of 1967 and helped establish Jordanian air defences for which it was honoured by Jordan with 'Kokab i Ula', its highest military award.[8]

The AA brigade was responsible for the air defence of Pakistan Air Force installations and naval dockyard at Karachi while the AA regiments allotted to the field formations were directly controlled by them. In the east, 6 LAA Regiment was deployed at Tezgaon with a Battery at Chittagong. Some AA guns were distributed to the field formations and were deployed in ones and twos.[9]

## INDIAN AIR FORCE

The Indian Air Force was far better equipped, trained and prepared than what it was just six years ago. It had inducted newer aircraft, established a reasonably efficient radar network, build up the infrastructure to include hardened shelters and learnt the tactical lessons well. It was the fifth largest air force in the world with six hundred and twenty-five combat aircraft organized into thirty-four fighter squadrons and five bomber squadrons. Twenty-eight squadrons were deployed against West Pakistan and eleven squadrons against East Pakistan. Fifteen squadrons were equipped with supersonic aircraft. In addition to the Gnats, Hunters and MiG-21s, IAF had two new aircraft – the Su-7 and the indigenous HF-24 Maruts – while the older Canberras, Mystéres and Vampires remained in service.

In the mid-1960s, even as the MiG-21 was being received in

increasing numbers, the IAF had sought a high performance offensive air support aircraft to replace the Mystére IVA and enhance its strike force that was made up solely of Hunter F Mk.56s. One of the options was the first Indian-developed jet aircraft HF-24. It was developed by Hindustan Aircraft Limited (HAL), with Kurt Tank as lead designer, and the first Asian jet fighter to enter active service. Its maiden flight took place on 17 June 1961 and the first production Marut officially delivered to the IAF on 1 April 1967. The status of HF-24 Marut remained uncertain as it lacked a suitable power plant, leading to delays in its production programme.[10] Owing to this, India decided to evaluate the Sukhoi Su-7 tactical fighter in the summer of 1966. Within a year, a contract was finalized for some 90 Su-7BM fighters, and Su-7U two-seat conversion trainers in 1967, and 26 Squadron became the first squadron to convert to Su-7B by March 1968. It was followed by No. 101 Sqn (ex-Vampire FR Mk 55) in July 1968, with No. 221 Sqn (ex-Vampire FB Mk-52) converting to the Sukhoi in August. Two more batches of Su-7s were contracted for, taking total procurement to 140 aircraft, and enabling formation of 3 more squadrons (No. 32s Mystéres, No. 108s Vampires, and the newly-raised No. 222, the last-mentioned being formed in September 1969). The Su-7 force was earmarked for the roles of offensive air support, counter-air, short-term interdiction and tactical reconnaissance.[11]

For the IAF, Su-7 had two 'firsts' to its credit. It was the services first combat aircraft with a full-fledged autopilot and also the first with a Jet Assisted Take Off (JATO) facility. Although fifteen air forces were operating the Su-7 as standard tactical fighter-bomber by the early 1970s, it was to be the Indian Air Force that conducted this type's baptism in combat in December 1971.

Notwithstanding the production delays, IAF started inducting HF-24s as well and the first HF-24 entered service in November 1969 with 10 Squadron (Daggers). Marut was initially envisioned as an interceptor aircraft but was primarily used for ground attack missions. A total of 147 Maruts were manufactured and they finally equipped three squadrons (10, 220 and 31) with an additional AD flight to train radar intercept officers. A total of 18 trainers designated Mk-ITs were also received by the IAF. By 1971, only two squadrons (220 and 10) operated the type from Jodhpur and Uttarlai, with No. 31 Squadron yet to convert from Mystéres. The only other squadron flying the older Mystéres was No. 3 Squadron, IAF. The solitary squadron of Vampires was at Jodhpur and a detachment each at Srinagar and Halwara. The four Canberra squadrons operated from the depth air bases of Agra and Poona.[12]

The transport aircraft included fifty-five C-47 Dakotas, sixty C-119 Packets, twenty Il-14, thirty An-12, twenty-five Otters, twelve HS-748 and fifteen Caribous. There was one maritime reconnaissance squadron equipped with L-1049 Super Constellations. The detailed deployment of IAF in the west, prior to the onset of hostilities, was as follows[13]:

| *Air Base* | *Squadron* | *Aircraft* | *Remarks* |
|---|---|---|---|
| Srinagar | No. 18 Sqn | Gnat | |
| | Detachment | Vampire | |
| Rajouri | | Harvard | |
| Pathankot | No. 20 & 27 Sqn | Hunter | |
| | No. 23 Sqn | Gnat | |
| | Detachment | Mystére | |
| Amritsar | No. 2 Sqn | Gnat | |
| | TACDE (One Flt) | MiG-21 | |
| Adampur | No. 1 Sqn | MiG-21 | |
| | Nos. 26 & 101 Sqn | Su-7 | |
| Halwara | No. 9 Sqn | Gnat | |
| | Nos. 108 & 222 Sqn | Su-7 | |
| | Detachment | MiG-21 | |
| | Detachment | Vampire | |
| Chandigarh | No. 45 Sqn | MiG-21 | |
| Sirsa | No. 3 Sqn | Mystére | |
| Ambala | No. 32 | Su-7 | |
| | Deatchment | Gnat | |
| | TACDE (One Flt) | Su-7 | |
| Hindon | No. 29 Sqn | MiG-21 | Moved to Jodhpur/ Uttarlai on 14 December |
| Nal | No. 7 Sqn | Hunter | |
| | No. 31 Sqn | Mystére | |
| Uttarlai | Nos. 10 & 220 | HF-24 | |
| | No. 21 | Gnat | |

| | | |
|---|---|---|
| Jamnagar | No. 47 Sqn | MiG-21 |
| | OCU | Hunter |
| Agra | Nos. 5 & 106 Sqn | Canberra |
| | JBCU | Canberra |
| Poona | No. 35 Sqn | Canberra |

There was greater emphasis on air defence with ten squadrons of MiG-21 and Gnats meant exclusively for the air defence role. In this, four squadrons were tied down for the air defence of Delhi-Chandigarh and other VAs.

IAF had deployed ten fighter squadrons in the east with one Canberra squadron from Central Air Command also allotted for operations in the east. With only one PAF squadron in East Pakistan, it was more than an adequate force level to cater support to the army which would be the primary responsibility of the IAF. The detailed deployment of the squadrons was as follows:[14]

| *Air Base* | *Squadron* | *Aircraft* | *Remarks* |
|---|---|---|---|
| Kalaikunda | No. 30 Sqn | MiG-21 | |
| | No. 14 Sqn | Hunter | |
| | No. 22 Sqn | Gnat | |
| Panagrah | No. 221 Sqn | Su-7 | |
| Bagdogra | No. 7 Sqn | Hunter | |
| | No. 15 Sqn | Gnat | |
| Hashimara | Nos. 17 & 37 Sqn | Hunter | |
| Tezpur | Nos. 4 & 28 Sqn | MiG-21 | |
| | No. 24 Sqn | Gnat | |

Agartala airfield was activated on 8 December for No. 24 Sqn, IAF (Gnats), to provide close support to IV Corps. Similarly, Dum Dum, Barrackpore, Guwahati, Jorhat and Kumbhigram airfields were used by different squadrons/detachments, including transport squadrons, as the operations progressed.

## PAKISTAN AIR FORCE

There are varying accounts about the strength of Pakistan Air Force in 1971 though the difference is marginal. According to *The India-*

*Pakistan War 1971: A History*, Pakistan had thirteen combat squadrons with 273 combat aircraft, though it includes the RT-33 squadron (No. 20 Sqn, PAF) in its list of combat squadrons.[15] Kaiser Tufail, a former commander of a fighter squadron of the Pakistan Air Force and director of operations of the Pakistan Air Force (PAF) during the Kargil conflict, in his book *In the Ring and on Its Feet* gives the figure of 290 aircraft on the eve of the war of which, according to Tufail, only 215 could be fielded.[16]

In September 1965, Pakistan had 260 odd total aircraft of which 157 were combat aircraft, to include 112 F-86 Sabres, 12 F-104 Starfighters and 29 B-57s. The other aircraft with PAF included 3 RB-57s, 22 T-33A/ RT-33s, 25 T-6Gs and 21 T-37Bs. These were organized into eight squadrons of F-86s, one of Starfighters, two of B-57s and two of T-6G, T-33, RT-33 and T-37. The three RB-57s formed the No. 24 Squadron.

Pakistan reportedly lost 43 aircraft during the September War, including operational losses and accidents but it has never admitted to these numbers and maintained that the total losses were only 19 though it did admit that over 50 of its F-86s were hit by ground fire and damaged to varying degrees. The inventory would have been down to 120 odd combat aircraft following the war with a large number damaged, requiring repairs. The situation was made grim for the PAF as the United States imposed an arms embargo following the war. With all its combat aircraft of US origin, the embargo hit PAF hard. Not only was the supply of new aircraft halted, but even the spares for the existing inventory were not provided by the US. The only option was to look at other sources, to try and beat the embargo.

A new ally for Pakistan, albeit an unlikely one, was the Soviet Union, which supplied its Mi-8 medium lift helicopters to equip one squadron of army aviation.[17] The proposal to provide Mi-6 heavy lift helicopters fizzled out after the lone helicopter supplied to Pakistan crashed in the Karakoram mountains.[18] What the PAF did get was two P-35 radars of which one each was deployed in the West and East Pakistans. The reported offer of MiG-21s and Sukhois was not taken up by Pakistan though Tufail contends that the Soviet Union never offered these as India was seen as a socialist ideologue and hence the prospect of a Soviet-Pakistan relationship was a non-starter.[19]

Pakistan found a new ally in China who was all too willing to supply Pakistan with its locally produced F-6s, which were copies of the Soviet MiG-19.[20] China supplied the initial batch of 60 F-6 free of cost and even the later batches were supplied at very affordable prices. Pakistan had 90 F-6s in its inventory when the war broke out in 1971 with the Chinese fighters being assigned the primary role of day interceptors. The aircraft was modified to carry two AIM-9B Sidewinder missiles in addition to the 30 mm cannon, greatly enhancing its capabilities. The major upgrading and innovative modifications include the provision of western avionics, Martin and Baker ejection seats, the AIM-9 Sidewinder air-to-air missile, S-5 57 mm rockets, additional under-wing tanks and under-belly 'Gondola' fuel tanks and a special ground-power unit for instantly starting its twin engines to shorten 'scramble' time. The F-6 was to prove itself in close support role, also using the 30 mm cannon armed with armour-piercing bullets, along with two rocket launchers having 8 × 57-mm rockets each to a deadly effect.[21] During the war, F-6 served with Nos. 11, 23 and 25 Squadron, PAF, each with 16 aircraft. No. 11 Squadron was based at Sargodha while No. 23 Squadron, the first unit to be equipped with the F-6 in early 1966, moved from its parent base Sargodha to the forward base at Risalewala. No. 25 Squadron was split into two detachments of eight aircraft each, based at Sargodha and Mianwali.[22]

Though the PAF inventory was boosted by the induction of F-6s, the main worry for Pakistan was the upkeep of its F-86 Sabre fleet. Given its experience with the Sabres in the September War, Pakistan was keen to tap a new source for procuring the replacement Sabres to make up for the losses and also to build up its inventory. Coincidentally, West Germany was planning to dispose of its surplus Canadair CL-13 Sabres Mk.6 but the US embargo ruled out a direct procurement by Pakistan. A way out was found as Iran acted as front, purchasing the Sabres from West Germany and then sending them to Pakistan for 'overhaul'.[23] These Sabres were better endowed than the 'F' model in service with PAF in terms of thrust-weight ratio, due to a more powerful engine and a total of 90 CL-13 Sabres Mk.6 (called the F-86E in Pakistan Air Force) were procured in 1966 going on to equip four of the eight Sabre squadrons.[24]

In 1967, Pakistan decided to buy the Dassault Mirage III from

France and successfully entered into a contract for twenty-four of these aircraft to include 18 Mirage IIIEP, 3 Mirage IIIDPs and 3 Mirage IIIRPs.[25] With their arrival in 1968, they were the newest and most advanced combat aircraft in the PAF inventory, which enabled them to generate a higher daily sortie rate as compared to the other combat aircraft with PAF. Added advantages was their capability to navigate accurately to relatively deeper targets, and after the attack, egress at high speed though it still used the vintage Mk-117 (750 lbs) high explosive bombs while air-to-air weapons included first generation AIM-9B Sidewinder heat-seeking missiles. With one aircraft lost in a flying accident, Pakistan went to war with 23 Mirages, equipping its No. 5 Squadron based out of Sargodha with a detachment at Mianwali.[26]

The other aircraft in PAF inventory were the 65 F-96F Sabres, 8 F-104s and 17 B-57s. Pakistan had modified 12 T-33 Trainer aircraft for bomb carriage as were the T-6G and a few of the C-130 transport aircraft. The total number of aircraft with the Pakistan Air Force was 290 as per details shared shortly, but, with some aircraft undergoing routine maintenance and overhaul, including 33 F-86s, under repair, only 215 aircraft were available for operations.[27]

## DEPLOYMENT

Sargodha was the main air base and was expected to be the hub of most air activity with its central location in the northen sector of Pakistan. It had three-and-a-half squadrons including one each of the newly acquired Mirage IIIs, F-86E and F-6, along with a half-squadron detachment of F-6.[28] The Mirages were earmarked for day-and-night air defence, photo-reconnaissance and strikes against airfields, mainly Amritsar and Pathankot, while the F-86E and F-6 were tasked with day air defence and tactical air support. A half-sqaudron detachment of B-57s was positioned at Mianwali along with 4-5 Mirage IIIEs. As these were tasked with deep strikes, a half-squadron of F-6 was also deployed at Mianwali for their safety.[29]

Masroor was the main PAF base in the southern sector and had a heavy deployment including a beefed-up squadron of F-86E/F for air defence and tactical air support, a half-strength squadron of F-104 for day-and-night air defence, a half sqaudron detachmnet of B-57s and a half-squadron of T-33s.[30]

The other bases where PAF deployment was carried on included Peshawar with No. 26 Squadron of F-86F, Murid with No. 15 Squadron (F-86F), Riaslewala with No. 23 Squadron (F-6), Rafiqui with No. 17 Squadron (F-86E) and Talhar with a detachment of four F-86Es of No. 19 Squadron.[31]

The Pakistan Air Force had only one squadron in the east – No. 14 Squadron with 16 F-86E, of which only four were modified to carry GAR-8 Sidewinder missiles. The other aircraft included a dual-seat T-33 for pilots' check-outs, a photo reconnaissance RT-33. The rescue squadron was made up of all of two Alouette-III helicopters.[32] The deployment of PAF in West Pakistan is shown in Map 1.

## INDIAN CONTROL AND REPORTING SYSTEM

One of the weaknesses observed during the September war of 1965 was the Indian radar network and the control and reporting system. There were large gaps in the radar coverage with just one high-level coverage radar on the western border at Amritsar. In addition, there

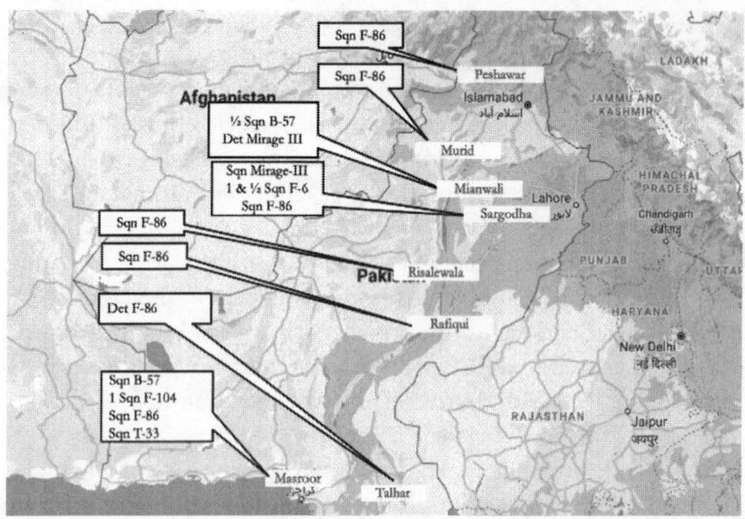


Map 1: PAF Deployment – West. *Source:* Author's Collection.

were a number of low power radars all along the border, mainly the low power radar at Ferozepur, but they were rendered almost useless by the very limited reaction time and coverage they provided. The control and coordination of all air defence operations was the responsibility of No. 1 ADDC (then called the Air Defence Area Headquarters) located at Delhi.

The situation in the east was worse as there was no high-power radar in the entire sector. 411 SU at Rampurhat provided some rudimentary GCI capability while 55 SU at Kalaikunda with a Second World War vintage radar was the only other early warning radar. No. 2 Air Defence Area Headquarters located at Jaffarpore, about 4 km from Barrackpore, was responsible for the air defence support of the eastern sector.

Having realized the seriousness of this shortcoming, India went about upgrading the radar network after the 1965 war. In addition to the P-35 radar already deployed at Amritsar, a P-30 radar was moved from Adampur to Amritsar to cater to a contingency of the signal unit at Amritsar being damaged. Similarly, a P-30 radar was moved from Jodhpur to Uttarlai, while a radar was moved from the east to Ahmedabad, in order to cover the gap between Jamnagar and Jodhpur.[33] A more important change that the IAF did was to initiate the Base Air Defence Centre (BADC) concept wherein nominated air bases were given autonomous control over the deployed aircraft and AD weapons.[34] This was to mitigate the inadequacy of low-level cover and dedicated communications available to the IAF. The concept did prove to be of much advantage during the war though it had its limitations which were exposed by the first strike by PAF on 3 December. Still, it was a far better radar and early warning network than what the PAF had.

In the east too, the radar network had been upgraded with deployments at Shillong, Dinjan in Assam and Bagdogra in Bengal. There were a total six radar units in the east on the eve of operations that provided adequate radar cover.[35]

The air defence system had improved considerably with radar-controlled guns and SAM-2 surface-to-air missiles added to the inventory. These had been integrated with the radar network creating an air defence zone along the western border though some gaps remained. The inadequate radar cover and lack of dedicated air defence communications resulted in adoption of the Base Air Defence (BAD) concept wherein important air bases were given local autonomy for control over both aircraft and ground-based air defence weapons. The dedicated air defence squadrons of MiG-21s and Gnats were placed under the Air Defence Direction Centres (ADDC), each of which was responsible for the air defence operations within its sector of responsibility. The SA-2 surface-to-air missile squadrons, initially located at Delhi and Ambala, were re-deployed to cover four major areas, viz., Delhi, Adampur (Jallandhar), Halwara (Ludhiana) and Chandigarh-Ambala areas.[36]

The radar cover was augmented by the visual observation posts and flights (later called the MOPs and MOUs) that were formed and deployed along the border. The HF radio sets with the detachments enabled them to be integrated in the overall air defence network as also in the BAD organization. The thinly spread detachments with not-so-reliable communications left much to be desired but they served a useful purpose during the operations and often provided much-needed early warning.

There were gaps in the Indian air defence network but it was a much-improved version of what existed just six years back and effective enough not only to deter the PAF but also inflict serious attrition.

## PAKISTANI CONTROL AND REPORTING SYSTEM

During the 1965 war, one of the advantages that the Pakistan Air Force had over the Indian Air Force was its well-integrated control and reporting (C&R) and radar system which was far better and efficient than what India had at that time. Pakistan had installed the first AD radar in mid-1950s. The main surveillance radar in the north was at Sakesar. Located on the outer fringes of (Pakistani) Punjab's Soan valley, Sakesar is a 4,992 ft peak which used to be the summer headquarters of three districts – Campbellpur (now Attock), Mianwali and Sargodha. In view of Sakesar's ideal location and height, it was selected by PAF in the late-1950s as the site for a high-powered radar which would provide air defence cover for the north-eastern part of the western wing. In 1960, a radar installation was commissioned at Sakesar for its role as a master ground controlled interception (GCI) station. The base comprised a sector operations centre (SOC) commanded by Group Captain Rehmat Khan, and a GCI element. The radar at Sakesar was the Bendix AN/FPS-20, a L-Band surveillance radar that had an effective range of 300 km.[37]

A Cold War era radar, FPS-20 used to the backbone of US early warning network and underwent a number of upgrades since entering service in 1950. The radar being a 2D radar, however, did not have the height finding capability and was used with AN/FPS-6, a height finder radar manufactured by General Electric.

The medium-level cover was provided by four Condor radars sited at Chuhr Kana, Muridke and Tatepur near Multan. In addition, the four AR-1 radars located at Rafiqui, Cherat, Kallar Kahar and Kirana provided low-level coverage. The radars at the latter three locations were able to extend their range by as much as 50 per cent due to their siting on elevated ground but their siting in depth rather than along the international border meant that the air bases had only three minutes of warning in case of a low-level ingress. Also, major towns remained outside the low-level radar cover as the PAF believed that the low-level radars were better utilized for providing cover to its bases. In the end, they served no useful purpose. The three minutes warning was insufficient to vector in the nearby CAPs for the defence of the air bases *and* the major town remained outside their coverage.[38]

Sector Operations Centre (South) under Group Captain Anwar Shamim operated from its war-time location at Korangi and was dependent on the FPS-20 radar at Badin for high-level radar surveillance which had been commissioned in 1962. Located close to the Indian border, the radar was capable of keeping a watch on Indian airfields in Rajasthan and track all aircraft movement towards the lower Sindh region between Sukkur and Karachi.

Keeping in mind the importance of Karachi, PAF had moved a P-35 radar from Dacca just before the start of hostilities. Malir had another P-35 radar but it was moved to Jacobabad mid-way in the war. It, however, did not become operational at its new location before the end of hostilities. A Type 21 radar was located at Khanpur but it was not reliable due to its vintage. Due to the paucity of air force low-level radars in south Pakistan, a Civil Aviation ASR-4 approach

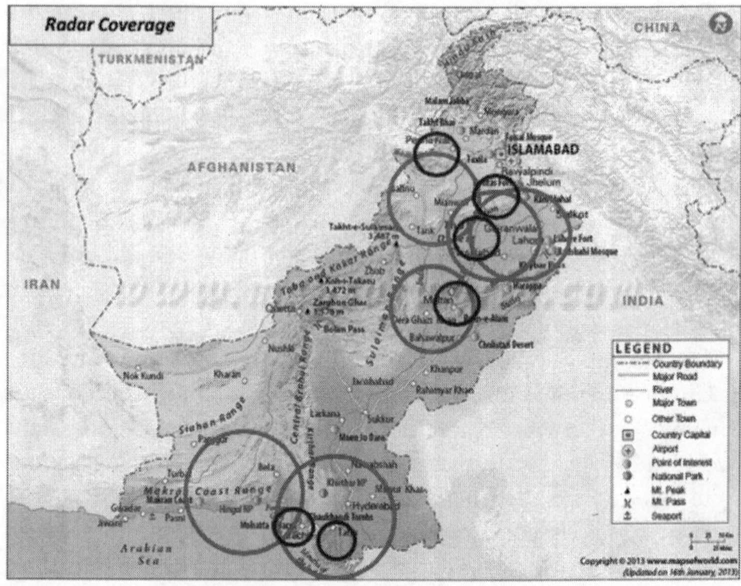


Map 2: Radar Coverage. *Source:* Author's Collection.

radar at Karachi Airport, a vintage Type-21 radar located near Khanpur and an AR-1 radar at Pir Patho had been integrated in the PAF radar network but, even so, the low-level radar coverage remained woefully inadequate with the low-level early warning in the southern sector resting on the reports by mobile observer units (MOUs).[39] The radar coverage in West Pakistan is shown in Map 2.

The radar coverage in East Pakistan was provided by a single AR-1 low-level radar at Mirpur, about 15 km north-west of Dacca. The P-35 high-level radar that was available at Dacca, as mentioned earlier, had been moved to Malir near Karachi in October 1971. Making the situation more difficult for PAF was the withdrawal of MOUs by PAF in March due to local actions against them by the Mukti Bahini. This meant that the sole source of warning was the AR-1 radar at Mirpur.[40]

The PAF control and reporting system and radar network may have proved to be adequate during the previous war of September 1965 but faced with a far better-equipped and trained IAF in 1971 was not up to the challenge and it was to fail, time and again.

## NOTES

1. S. Prabhala, K.V. Koshy and S. Krsihnan, *Inside the Solid State: The Story of Bharat Electronics Westland*, Chennai, 2014, pp. 32-4.
2. Ibid.
3. Interview with Colonel M.R. Pimpalkhute.
4. Interview with Brigadier Deepak Sharma and Captain Arvind Nautiyal. Interestingly, Col H.S. Shankar, an EME officer was awarded the Vishisht Seva Medal for providing Night-Firing capabilities to Tigercat Missiles.The information available in public domain is that Colonel Shankar 'was awarded the Vishishta Seva Medal (VSM) by President of India for providing Night-Firing capabilities to Tigercat Missiles during 1971 Operations with Pakistan' whereas the missile system was not used during the war. (Excerpt from an interview with Colonel Shankar 'Alpha Design Technologies Made Its Small Step A Giant Leap' accessed on 16 May 2020 at https://www.aviation-defence-universe.com/alpha-design-technologies-made-small-step-giant-leap/
5. Maj Gen Shaukat Riza, *Izzat-o-Iqbal History of Regiment of Artillery 1947-1971*, School of Artillery, Nawshera, 1980, pp. 294-5.
6. Ibid., pp. 452-4.
7. The Report of the Hamoodur Rehman Commission of Inquiry into the 1971 War, University of Michigan Press, 2000, pp. 248-54.
8. Dana Adams Schmidt, 'Pakistani Troops Reported Serving With Jordanians', *The New York Times*, 11 February 1970 accessed on 13 May 2020 at https://www.nytimes.com/1970/02/11/archives/pakistani-troops-reported-serving-with-jordanians-infantry-regiment.html
9. Maj Gen Shaukat Riza, op. cit., p. 453.
10. Sebastien Roblin, 'India's Disappointing Marut Jet Fighter Proved Itself in Combat', *National Interest*, 13 August 2017 accessed on 8 June 2019 at https://nationalinterest.org/blog/indias-disappointing-marut-jet-fighter-proved-itself-combat-21875
11. R. Chattopadhyay, 'Su-7 BMK: A Whale of a Fighter', *Bharat Rakshak*, 26 July 2015 accessed on 11 June 2019 at http://www.bharat-rakshak.com/IAF/aircraft/past/1306-sukhoi-7.html#gsc.tab=0
12. S.N. Prasad and U.P. Thapliyal, *The India-Pakistan War of 1971: A History*, Natraj Publishers, New Delhi, 2014, pp. 206-8.
13. Ibid. See also, Air Marshal A.K. Tiwary, *Indian Air Forces in the Wars*, Lancer, New Delhi, 2012, pp. 144-5.
14. Jagan Mohan and Samir Chopra, *Eagles Over Bangladesh: The Indian Air Force in the 1971 Liberation War*, Harper Collins, 2013, pp. 59-60.
15. Prasad and Thapliyal, op. cit., pp. 208-9.
16. Kaiser Tufail, *In the Ring and on its Feet: Pakistan Air Force in India-Pakistan War 1971*, Ferozsons, Lahore, 2018, pp. 53-5.
17. Zubeida Hasan, 'Soviet Arms Aid to Pakistan and India', *Pakistan Horizon* 21,

no. 4, 1968, pp. 344-55. Accessed on 22 January 2021, http://www.jstor.org/stable/41392937

18. Shaheen Foundation, *Story of the Pakistan Air Force 1947-1988: A Saga of Courage and Honour*, Shaheen Foundation, Islamabad, 1988.
19. Tufail, op. cit., p. 43.
20. M.D. Upadayay, *Sino-Pak Nexus and Implications for India*, Vij Publications, New Delhi, 2016.
21. Tufail, op. cit., p. 43
22. Ibid., pp. 45-7.
23. Asad Durrani, *Pakistan Adrift: Navigating Troubled Waters*, Oxford University Press, 2018, p. 57.
24. According to Tufail, only 74 of these F-86Fs were in service at the time of the war.
25. *Arms Transfer Register*, Stockholm International Peace Research Institute, accessed on 20 July 2019 at https://web.archive.org/web/20100414022558/http://armstrade.sipri.org/armstrade/page/trade_register.php
26. Tufail, op. cit., pp. 45-7.
27. It was not only the F-86s under repair and/or maintenance that brought down the number of serviceable aircraft. 42 F-6s were also under overhaul in China.
28. Tufail, op. cit., p. 46. Prasad and Thapliyal in *The India-Pakistan War of 1971: A History* mention three squadrons (one of Mirage III and two of F-6) to be deployed at Sargodha on the eve of hostilities.
29. Tufail, op. cit., p. 46. There are variations with the details of deployment at Mianwali as given by Prasad and Thapliyal as they do not include the Mirages.
30. Tufail, op. cit., pp. 46-7.
31. Ibid.
32. Jagan Mohan and Samir Chopra, op. cit., pp. 32-3 and Tufail, op. cit., p. 47.
33. Prasad and Thapliyal, op. cit., p. 212.
34. Air Chief Marshal P.C. Lal, *My Years with the IAF*, Lancer, New Delhi, 1986, pp. 247-8 and C.V. Gole, 'The Air Operations of December 1971: Reflections of an Air War', *Vayu*, vol. VI/1991.
35. Jagan and Chopra, op. cit., p. 62.
36. Prasad and Thapliyal, op. cit., p. 212.
37. 'PAF Sakesar', Global Security accessed on 28 July 2019 at https://www.globalsecurity.org/military/world/pakistan/paf-sakesar.htm
38. Kaiser Tufail, *Air Defence in the Northern Sector,* accessed on 29 July 2019 at http://kaiser-aeronaut.blogspot.com/2011/02/air-defence-in-northern-sector-1971-war.html
39. Kaiser Tufail, *Air Defence in the Southern Sector,* accessed on 29 July 2019 at http://kaiser-aeronaut.blogspot.com/2010/12/air-defence-in-southern-sector-1971-war.html
40. Tufail, op. cit, pp. 137-8.

# CHAPTER 3

# Setting the Stage

The previous two wars between India and Pakistan had been sparked by the Pakistani designs over Kashmir with the last conflict in 1965 ending with the ceasefire on 23 September 1965, followed by the Tashkent Agreement of 4 January 1966. For five years the situation between the two neighbours remained relatively peaceful but tensions simmered under the surface in the east largely due to the long-standing political and cultural tension/conflict between the traditionally dominant West Pakistanis and the majority of East Pakistanis.

This tension between East Bengal and West Pakistan had its origin in the creation of Pakistan itself when the two were carved out of India as a separate nation on religious lines but the geographical distance between the two wings of Pakistan and the cultural/linguistic differences could not be glazed over for long with the popular language movement in 1950 breaking out after just three years of Independence. Mass riots broke out in East Pakistan in 1964 and even after the war with India in 1965, the two wings never co-existed in peace for long. By 1969, the differences were rapidly growing.

The year 1969 saw mass protests leading to the resignation of President Ayub Khan, who invited army chief General Yahya Khan to take over the central government. To overcome the Bengali domination and prevent formation of the central government in Islamabad, the controversial 'One Unit' programme established the two wings of East and West Pakistan. West Pakistanis' opposition to these efforts made it difficult to effectively govern both wings. In 1969, President Yahya Khan announced the first general elections. Before the elections were held in December 1970, Khan disestablished of the status of West Pakistan as a single province and restored the four provinces of West Pakistan to their status as originally defined in 1947.

The general elections held in 1970 resulted in East Pakistan's Awami League gaining 167 out of 169 seats for the East Pakistan Legislative Assembly, and a near-absolute majority in the 313-seat National Assembly while the seats in West Pakistan was mostly won by the socialist Pakistan People's Party. The Awami League leader Sheikh Mujibur Rahman stressed his political position by presenting his Six Points and endorsing the Bengalis' right to govern. The League's electoral success caused many West Pakistanis to fear that it would allow the Bengalis to draft the constitution based on the six points and liberalism.

To resolve the crisis, the Admiral Ahsan Mission was formed to provide recommendations. Its findings were met with favourable reviews from the political leaders of West Pakistan, but the mission's proposals were vetoed by the military brass and, to add to the conundrum, Zulfikar Ali Bhutto endorsed the veto. He also refused to yield the premiership of Pakistan to Sheikh Mujibur Rahman. The situation deteriorated and the inauguration of the National Assembly was postponed by Yahya Khan. Disillusioned, the Awami League was forced to call for general strikes in the country leading eventually a shutdown of the government. The targeting of the ethnic Bihari community, which had supported West Pakistan, made it worse with one of the worst incidents being the massacre of 300 Biharis in Chittagong in March 1971.[1]

This incident was used by the Government of Pakistan to justify its deployment of the military in East Pakistan on 25 March and a crackdown on the dissidents, followed by operations, Searchlight and Barisal.[2] Sheikh Mujibur Rahman was taken prisoner and taken to West Pakistan. On 26 March 1971, Major Ziaur Rahman of Pakistan Army declared the independence of Bangladesh on behalf of Sheikh Mujibur Rahman and a government-in-exile was formed in April. Escaping the tyranny, almost 10 million people sought refuge in India. Refugee camps were set-up all along the border, in the Indian states of West Bengal, Bihar, Assam, Meghalaya and Tripura. Appeals by the Government of India for help from the international community failed to elicit any response.

While Prime Minister Indira Gandhi expressed full support of her government for the independence struggle of the people of East Pakistan, she decided to act to resolve the crisis rather than look for assistance that was not forthcoming in any case. On 28 April 1971, the Gandhi cabinet ordered the Chief of the Army Staff General Sam Manekshaw to 'go into East Pakistan'.[3] But citing the onset of monsoon, General Sam Manekshaw refused. He asked for more time – at least till November – when the snows closed the passes from Tibet, preventing any Chinese intervention.[4] This set the stage for the preparations for the impending operations in the East but the situation was no less serious in the West.

As the situation in East Pakistan worsened, the likelihood of Pakistan launching a pre-emptive attack on India in the west increased. Building up the force level in the west was with its own constraints. Not only the large distances involved in moving troops from their peace time locations to the borders but also the possibility that it could lead to an apprehension that India was preparing to launch an attack in the west – and it could force India into a situation not as per its plans. This resulted in India desisting from any large-scale movement of troops to the western sector in spite of clear indications of Pakistan's intentions.

In August 1971, Yahya Khan announced that 'war with India is very near and in case of war Pakistan would not be alone'.[5] As the situation worsened, a regrouping of forces was carried out by India and the boundaries of Western and Eastern Air Commands were realigned to make them compatible with Indian Army command boundaries. Eastern Air Command was now made responsible for air defence of Calcutta area and West Bengal as well, instead of the Central Air Command. Similar changes were done in the west with Central Air Command made responsible for looking after the bomber and transport squadrons as also the maritime support operations.[6]

Cactus Lily was ordered by India in August 1971 and the ADA regiments started deploying on major airfields, radar stations and other important installations. For the next few months, drills and procedures of the newly-formed BADC were practiced and refined.[7]

Passive AD (PAD) was given special attention during the preparatory stage with the adoption of the surrounding agricultural field pattern right up to the runways, merging them with the surrounding areas. Hardened shelters had been constructed and were available for most of the aircraft but the last-minute move and induction of new units resulted in paucity of such shelters and improvization had to be made.[8] At places, the aircraft were parked under trees. The call-up notices were issued for the Territorial Army personnel for the embodiment of TA units, including AD regiments (TA). The embodiment and mobilization of the regiments was completed by October 1971 except for one battery of 103 AD Regiment (TA) that was deployed as late as 1 December 1971.

By September, Pakistan had started moving troops to the likely battle areas and the Pakistan army was put on a 12-hour alert on 5 October 1971.[9] Two days later, Gen A.A.K. Niazi, the Pakistani commander in East Pakistan, declared that the war will be fought on Indian soil.

By the middle of October, the entire military might of Pakistan had been deployed along the borders and it was clear from various reports that a pre-emptive attack by Pakistan was imminent.[10] It was only after this that certain covering forces were deployed and formations were moved forward to their concentration areas closer to the border in the western theatre in a graduated and progressive manner.

Amongst the first of the deployments was in Chhamb and Jammu sectors, followed by the deployment of covering troops in J&K and Punjab on 8 October. By 18 October, 7 and 15 Infantry Divisions were fully deployed and units of 14 Infantry Division moved to their operational localities. Orders were also issued for 1 Corps and 1 Armoured Division to move to their operational locations. Concurrently, the air defence regiments were also moving to their operational tasks and the air defence plan was put into place with all deployments completed by 20 October 1971.[11] In addition, the reservists were recalled on 22 October 1971.[12]

In the last week of October, Pakistani troops shelled Agartala airport continuously for more than three days while a heavy exchange of firing took place in Uri Sector in the west and north Tripura in the east on 29 October.[13]

## THE PLAN

With the situation fast deteriorating, India prepared a detailed contingency plan for military operations with the following objectives:[14]

(a) To assist Mukti Bahini in liberating a part of East Pakistan, where the refugees could return and live under their own government,
(b) To prevent Pakistan from capturing any Indian territory of consequence in Jammu & Kashmir, Punjab, Rajasthan or Gujarat. This was to be done by following a policy of offensive-defence, and
(c) To defend the country if an attack developed in the north.

The western front was divided into two sectors. In the northern sector, Pakistan was likely to launch a concerted attack in Poonch and also an attack to disrupt the line of communication between Jammu and Patahnkot. To foil this, India planned two thrust lines, one from the north between the rivers Basantar and Beas, and the other from the River Ravi at Thakurpur. Limited attacks were planned in Shyok Valley, Kargil, Chicken's Neck and the area west of Dera Baba Nanak bridge to improve the defensive posture. Another thrust was planned in Chhamb but was subsequently cancelled.[15]

In the southern sector, stretching from Ganganagar to the Arabian Sea, a thrust was planned in the Barmer area along the rail line towards Naya Chor. A thrust towards Rahimyar Khan from Jaisalmer was also planned.[16]

## ALLOCATION OF FORCES

The Western Command had three corps deployed from north to south as follows:[17]

(a) 15 Corps comprising 3, 10, 19, 25 and 26 Infantry Divisions, HQ 'V' Sector, HQ 121 (Independent) Infantry Brigade, HQ 3 (Independent) Armoured Brigade,
(b) 1 Corps comprising 54, 36 and 39 Infantry Divisions with HQ 16 (Independent) Armoured Brigade and HQ 2 (Independent) Armoured Brigade, and
(c) 11 Corps comprising 7, 14 and 15 infantry Divisions, 1 Armoured Division, 14 (Independent) Armoured Brigade and 'F' Sector.

The Southern Command had 11 and 12 Infantry Divisions plus an infantry brigade.

## PAKISTANI FORCE LEVEL AND PLANS

As per available intelligence reports, the following force level was deployed by Pakistan in the west:[18]

- 12 and 23 Infantry Divisions in Pakistan occupied Kashmir (PoK),
- 8 and 15 Infantry Divisions with 8 Independent Armoured Brigade between Chenab and Ravi rivers,
- 10 and 11 Infantry Divisions, 3 (Independent) Armoured Brigade and 105 (Independent) Brigade Group in Lahore-Bhawalpur sector, and
- 18 Infantry Division in Sindh.

The strike force was made up of two armoured divisions and three infantry divisions. Pakistani 1 Corps was made up of 6 Armoured Division and 2 Corps had 1 Armoured Division and 33 Infantry Division. The third infantry division, viz., 7 Infantry Division could act independently or be allotted to either of the corps. The location of these formations could not be ascertained through the intelligence agencies and it led to the Indian commanders unnecessarily holding back reserves in many areas.

As per Pakistani strategic thinking, the 'defence of East Pakistan lay in its western wing'. In pursuance of this policy, Pakistan planned to go on the offensive in the west and its plan had two ingredients. First, formations other than those in reserve were to launch limited offensives. Second, a major counter-offensive was to be launched concurrently into India. The latter part of the plan was altered by General Yahya Khan with respect to its timings. As per the revised plan, the main offensive would take place only after local operations had secured ground. This change ostensibly was made due to shortage of equipment and also due to operational voids caused by move of forces to its east wing. The detailed plans of the preliminary/fixing operations were as follows:[19]

(a) 12 Infantry Division opposite Poonch with the result of compelling India to reinforce Poonch and thereby weaken its defences in the other sectors of Indian 15 Corps.
(b) 23 Infantry Division in Chhamb Sector to pre-empt any Indian designs in the sector and to secure the Pakistani north-south line of communications.
(c) 18 Division opposite Jaisalmer-Longewala with the aim of pulling Indian armour to facilitate Pakistan's 1st Armoured Divisions task in Ganganagar area. Another aim was to protect the vulnerable Pakistani north-south road link which was just about 65 km from the border in this area.
(d) 105 Independent Infantry Brigade Group opposite Fazilka to ensure the safety of the Sulaimanke Headworks.

Depending on the success of the aforementioned operations, Pakistani 2 Corps, with 1 Armoured Division and two infantry divisions (7 and 33), was to be launched opposite Ganganagar-Anupnagar. As operations progressed, all plans underwent changes and the actual conduct was quite different from the operations envisaged before the commencement of hostilities.

With the deployments completed by both sides by November and an increasing number of border incidents, an Indian-Pakistani war seemed inevitable. Things came to the head at Boyra with Indian Army destroying tanks and the IAF shooting down two F-86 Sabres on 22 November 1971.[20] The next day, President Yahya Khan declared a state of Emergency. Operation Chengiz Khan, the pre-emptive strikes by Pakistan Air Force on 3 December 1971, were only the formal declaration of hostilities; the third round between India and Pakistan that lasted all of fourteen days.

## NOTES

1. Bina D'Costa, *Nationbuilding, Gender and War Crimes in South Asia*, Routledge, New York, 2010, p. 103.
2. Abu Md. Delwar Hossain, 'Operation Searchlight', in Sirajul Islam and Ahmed A. Jamal (eds.), *Banglapedia: National Encyclopedia of Bangladesh* (2nd edn.), 2012, accessed on 7 April 2020 at http://en.banglapedia.org/index.php?title=Operation_Searchlight

3. K.C. Pravel, *Indian Army After Independence*, Lancer Publishers, New Delhi, 2009, p. 415.
4. 'Sam Manekshaw: Sam Manekshaw, soldier, died on 27 June, aged 94', *The Economist*, 3 July 2008, p. 107. Retrieved 21 Januaray 2021.
5. General K.V. Krishna Rao, *Prepare or Perish: A Study of National Security*, Lancer, New Delhi, 1991, p. 207.
6. Lt Gen J.F.R. Jacob, the Chief of Staff of Army's Eastern Command, in his book *An Odyssey in War and Peace* mentions that he had discussed the problem of dealing with two Air Command Headquarters (Central and Eastern) and had requested for an advance Headquarters to be located at Calcutta. A.C.M. Lal agreed to look into the matter and after a few days of the discussion, the boundaries of Air Command Headquarters were aligned with those of Army's Commands and an Advance Headquarters was approved to be set up at Fort William, Calcutta. (Lt Gen J.F.R. Jacob, *An Odyssey in War and Peace*, Roli Books, New Delhi, 2011, pp 84-6) and Air Chief Marshal P.C. Lal, *My Years with the IAF*, Lancer, New Delhi, 1986, pp. 47-8.
7. C.V. Gole, 'The Air Operations of December 1971: Reflections of an Air War', *Vayu*, vol. VI/1991.
8. S.N. Prasad and U.P. Thapliyal, op. cit., p. 107.
9. K.K. Thomas, *Asian Recorder*, Recorder Press, New Delhi, 1972, p. 10536 and *The Statesman*, New Delhi, 4 December 1971.
10. S.N. Prasad and U.P. Thapliyal, op. cit., pp. 104-5.
11. Lt Gen K.P. Candeth, *The Western Front: The Indo-Pakistan War 1971*, The English Book Depot, Dehradun, 1997, p. 28.
12. Prasad and Thapliyal, op. cit., p. 104.
13. Ibid.
14. Ibid., pp. 105-6.
15. Ibid., p. 106.
16. Ibid.
17. Ibid., pp. 108-9.
18. Ibid., p. 112
19. A.H. Amin, 'The Western Theatre in 1971: A Strategic and Operational Analysis', *Defence Journal*, Karachi, February 2002.
20. Lal, op. cit., p. 154.

CHAPTER 4

# The Pre-emptive Strike that Wasn't

In 1965, the Pakistan Air Force had carried out a rather successful strike against Indian airbases on 6 September 1965. It was not a pre-emptive strike as the war had been raging on for six days – Operation Grand Slam was launched on 1 September by the Pakistani 12 Infantry Division in Akhnoor sector held by Indian 191 Infantry Brigade – but it was still a good example of using an air force in an offensive manner and inflicting some serious damage on the adversary. The technique of the pre-emptive strike had since then been mastered by the Israeli Air Force who had employed it very successfully in the 1967 war and any air force with an initiative would be expected to carry out a similar strike to deliver a crippling blow to its enemy.

The PAF did carry out strikes on 3 December 1971 but this time around there were no bold plans like the Air War Plan No. 6 of the previous war but it was more of a cautious approach with limited strike packages aiming to hit select targets. As Kaiser Tufail says:[1]

> Contrary to the general perception, PAF's dusk strikes of 3 December against some of the forward Indian airfields were not pre-emptory at all, as the Indian invasion of East Pakistan had already taken place in earnest, on 21 November. While these strikes were, of course, aimed at cratering runways and destroying radars, they also had an intrinsic 'provocative' element that the PAF planned to cleverly exploit through its well-prepared air defences, when IAF retaliated the following morning. Mirages got a small share of 8 airfield strike sorties in the opening round of the counter-air operations campaign that also included 24 airfield strikes by F-86s and 4 radar strikes by F-104s.

Tufail goes on to comment that PAF's plan was different from the previous campaign of 1965 as this time around it had a lesser number of combat aircraft and these meagre resources 'could not be frittered away too early in the war'. A similar rationale is given by

Air Commodore Mansoor Shah, who was the Assistant Chief of Air Staff (Operations) during the war and who claims that the strikes were meant to provoke IAF into retaliating against PAF bases, which were the only well-defended target sets in the country. Shah goes on to claim that it was important to keep the IAF's attention focused on the bases, or else, it might have switched to countrywide interdiction of lines of communications.[2] Whatever the reasons for the scaled-down strikes may have been, they failed to have any impact and did not achieve even their purported aim.

The decision to finally set the D-Day as 3 December and to go ahead with a pre-emptive strike by the PAF was taken during a meeting on 30 November between the President, the Air C-in-C, the army chief of staff, General Abdul Hammed Khan, and the chief of general staff, General Gul Hassan. It was reportedly agreed by the Pakistan GHQ that the army's opening actions would be coordinated with the PAF's first strikes and the airstrikes were said to have been planned accordingly. PAF planned a total of seven strikes, as per the following details:[3]

| *Mission Serial* | *Target* | *Strike & Escort Aircraft* | *Munitions* | *Mission Leaders* |
|---|---|---|---|---|
| 1. | Srinagar Airfield | 8 F-86F | Bombs – Some with delay fusing | Wing Commander S.A. Changezi |
| 2. | Avantipur Airfield | 8 F-86F | Bombs as above | Wing Commander Abdul Aziz |
| 3. | Pathankot Airfield | 8 F-86F | Bombs as above | Wing Commander S.A. Jilani |
| 4. | Amritsar Airfield | 4 Mirage | Bombs as above | Wing Commander Hakimullah |
| 5. | Pathankot Airfield | 4 Mirage | Bombs as above | Squadron Leader Aftab A. Khan |
| 6. | Amritsar Airfield | 2 F-104 | Gun attack with special aiming | Wing Commander Amjad H. Khan |
| 7. | Faridkot Radar | 2 F-104 | Gun attack with special aiming | Wing Commander Arif Iqbal |

The first strike was against Srinagar airfield. The go-ahead for the strikes was given by General Yahya Khan, President and chief martial law administrator of Pakistan, at the PAF's Command Operations Centre (COC) on 3 December 1971 at 1630 hours (PST). The strike aircraft, four F-86Fs armed with 2x500-lb general-purpose bombs and two escorts with guns only, of No. 26 Squadron, PAF, took off 20 minutes later with TOT of 1709 hours (PST).[4]

Srinagar was defended by 1511 AD Battery of 151 AD Regiment. The regimental headquarters was also deployed at the airfield, responsible for providing early warning to the AD battery at the airfield and AD troop ex-1513 AD Battery at Ammunition Depot, Khundru, and to organize ground defence of the airfield. The squadron deployed for air defence was No. 18 Squadron, IAF. The terrain did not allow for any worthwhile radar coverage and the only early warning was provided by the IAF's observer posts that had been deployed every 30 to 35 km apart. The warning received from these posts was of just about two minutes and it suffered from a serious handicap as their 'aircraft recognition was generally poor'.[5]

With no early warning available from the radars, the PAF strike aircraft were picked up at about 1732 hours (IST) by the AD Artillery's observation posts (OPs) when they were almost overhead. Even with this limited warning, the AD gunners were able to take on the PAF aircraft as they dived in for the attack. Though no aircraft was hit or claimed, the AD guns were able to compel the PAF pilots to take evasive action, resulting in the bombs falling away from the targets. No damage was caused to the airfield though PAF claimed that 'all bombs fell on operating surfaces and the escort aircraft made strafing runs'.[6]

Brigadier (then 2nd Lieutenant) Deepak Sharma, who was one of the troop commanders of the 151 AD Regiment at Srinagar, recalls:[7]

> I was the 'A' Troop Commander at Srinagar with just over a year-and-half service. The battery had been deployed at the airfield in August 1971 and we had enough time to familiarize ourselves with the drills and procedures before the hostilities started. Incidentally, my troop JCO was Naib Subedar Abdul Razak and my troop havildar major was Abraham. It was all very normal and we never felt that we were from a different religion(s).
>
> I remember the first raid that came in on 3 December. When the PAF aircraft came and strafed the airfield, the guns had opened up and tried to engage the Sabres but we could not achieve any kill.

After the raid was over, I was not very clear as to what I should do. After all, this was my first experience of an enemy air raid and I had just about a year's service. It was then that my troop leader and havildar major, both veterans of the 1965 war, guided me and gave a very piece of valuable advice. They asked me to go around the troop and meet the boys. 'Just talk to them', they told me. 'Most of them are also new gunners. Your presence and pep-talk will do a world of good.'

It was then that I realized that experience of a soldier in battle is priceless. Rank is not always important and we need each other in war. We need to learn from each other and even as officers, there is much to learn from JCOs and NCOs.

The strike on Avantipur airfield was carried out by F-86 Sabres led by Wing Commander Abdul Aziz but with no deployment of either the air force or AD artillery, it was more of a symbolic nature. 151 AD Regiment moved some AD guns from Srinagar to Avantipur at a later stage to cover for any PAF raid in the future. Brigadier (then 2nd Lieutenant) Deepak Sharma recalls the initial deployment of the ADA elements at Avantipur.[8]

The airfield at Avantipur was a disused airfield with drums placed on the runway to prevent any aircraft landing there, especially by PAF, to try and seize that airfield.

After the raid, the 'C' Troop of 1511 AD Battery was moved to Avantipur. A BSF company under Assistant Commandant Sharma was deployed to provide a ground defence. The troop was later relieved by an AD troop from 46 AD Regiment and my troop moved back to Srinagar.

The second strikes were launched against the radars at Amritsar and Faridkot to help the follow-up strikes against Amritsar and Pathankot airfields ingress without detection. The strikes were carried out by a pair of F-104s each and only strafing was done. The Starfighters could not cause any serious damage to the radar at Amritsar that was defended by a troop of 27 AD Regiment. Pakistan claimed to have damaged it with 'both pilots claiming to have hit the antenna' while the official history of war acknowledges that 'minor damage' was caused to the communication equipment of the signal unit.[9] The radar had been one of the prime targets during the previous war of 1965 war as well and its exact location was always a challenge for PAF to find. As the RB-57s were not available for PAF to lead and guide the strike aircraft, it was relying on a locally developed radar homing device mounted on an F-104.[10]

The Amritsar radar was also attacked, with both pilots claiming to have hit the antenna; some damage to the communication equipment is acknowledged by the IAF. The lead F-104 (tail no 56-804) was equipped with a locally developed radar homing device, which was the only one of its type in the PAF. Trials had shown it to be a promising gadget and, as expected, it had been instrumental in locating the well-camouflaged Amritsar radar. Damage to the radar was, however, short-lived as it became fully operational sometime during the night, which warranted a repeat mission the next morning.

The damage caused to the radar was soon repaired and it was operational within that very night. The antenna of the radar at Faridkot was also claimed by PAF to have been hit. In addition, a Krishak light aircraft of the Air Observation Post (AOP) at the adjacent landing ground was damaged, though Wing Commander Arif Iqbal, the PAF pilot, claimed to have set it on fire.[11]

The next target was Amritsar airfield for which the Mirages had been earmarked with a TOT of 1716 hours (PST). The strike on the radars had had some intended effect as the Mirages reached Amritsar without being detected. The AD guns were on 'guns tight' as an AN-12 had just taken off. The four-ship Mirage formation was led by Wing Commander Hakimullah who recalls:[12]

I detailed the two strike missions and asked the boys to update the maps and logs and prepare the aircraft inappropriate configuration (2 × 1,000 lbs HE bombs and 2 × 1,300-litre external fuel tanks). I led the mission to Amritsar at dusk on 3 December 1971. The mission was flown as planned except another formation (two F-104s on a mission against a radar unit) which had entered the runway ahead of us, occupied it unusually long and thus delayed our take-off by a few minutes. The ingress to the target was as low as 100 ft AGL with an initial speed of 480 knots. We had planned a dive-bombing attack using the north-south axis. The pull-up for the attack was at 540 knots, at 2 miles north of the airfield to about 6,000 ft and was uneventful except as we pulled up, we were surprised to see that the runway lights were on. Whether someone was landing or taking off, one thing is sure that we caught them by complete surprise. We saw no interceptors and the anti-aircraft guns started intense firing only after we had delivered the attack.

Three of the attackers were able to deliver their bombs while the fourth had hung bombs and had had to call them off. The Mirages were able to exit without any damage, leaving behind in their wake 'four to five craters from the beginning of the runway to about 600 metres'. This left only one serviceable runway for the IAF Sukhois to use as they took off for strikes against Pakistani airfields as a 'return gesture'. As soon as the Sukhois had taken off, PAF B-57 bombers came over but failed to cause any damage.

The raid on Pathankot led by Wing Commander S.A. Jilani was to be the biggest disappointment of all, though even PAF would have known that repeating the success of 1965 when PAF managed to destroy ten aircraft was not possible in changed circumstances. The raid on Pathankot on 3 December was a series of two strikes executed in quick succession with four unescorted Mirage IIIs in the lead followed by four F-86s in the second raid. The Mirages had a TOT of 1717 hours (PST). With dusk setting in, visibility was poor and the pilots could not identify the designated targets. The task was made more difficult with the AD guns of 27 AD Regiment and 128 AD Regiment (TA) taking on the Mirages. The regimental history records that the Mirages broke formation and turned away. Even the PAF admitted that 'nobody could execute a proper attack' and the bombs fell in the general vicinity of the airfield.[13] The following strike was at 1723 hours (PST) by four F-86F along with four similar escorts, all from the No. 15 Squadron based at Murid. Three of the attackers were able to deliver their bombs while the fourth was unable to release his load. But the bombs were off their targets and caused no damage.[14]

This brought an end to the first wave of PAF strikes and they had failed to cause any serious damage. Tufail concedes that a quarter of the 32 planned bombing and strafing sorties were unsuccessful. He also mentions that 'shallow dive dictated by the AAA avoidance tactics' reduced the possibility of deeper runway penetration and the damage was repaired overnight.[15]

Most of the attacking PAF aircraft were taken on by the AD artillery deployed at the airbases and the PAF aircraft did not get a free pass. The alert ack-ack gunners opened up against the Mirages and F-86s and, even though they did not shoot down any aircraft, they were successful in preventing the PAF from causing any damage.

The official history of the India-Pakistan War, 1971, notes that 'IAF claimed one B-57 and one F-104 over Amritsar' though there is no corroborating record for this nor is it claimed by any ADA regiment. What was claimed was that an F-86 had been hit over Pathankot, but even the regimental records note that the Sabre managed to get away.[16]

As had been planned, the Pakistan Army launched its offensive in the Chhamb sector to coincide with the PAF strikes. Minutes after the Mirages and F-86s struck the IAF airfields at sunset on 3 December, Pak 8 Division's artillery opened fire over the Dharam enclave on the Ravi River while Pak 12 Division launched its offensive in the north towards Poonch and Pak 23 Division started its offensive across Tawi River in Chhamb. Pak 10 and 11 Divisions commenced their operations across the border to try and gain tactical ground, while in Husainiwala and Sulemanki sub-sectors, the limited attacks were launched by the Pak 106 Brigade and 105 Brigade Group. However, the offensive by Pak 18 Division to capture Ramgarh was postponed for 24 hours.[17]

One of the AD regiments deployed with the field army was 45 AD Regiment. 2nd Lieutenant Anil Thapliyal of the regiment recalls:[18]

> It was on 3 Dec. evening, around 8 p.m., that I, along with Maj Khanna, were in a makeshift bunker planning to have our dinner and he asked me to pick up his transistor radio from his bunker to listen to the latest news. Radio Pakistan was giving news that Indian forces have attacked Pakistan resulting in their strong retaliation all over our western border. Radio mentioned they have bombed many of our airfields in Punjab and Rajasthan, and Pakistani forces have launched a massive attack on us in the Chhamb-Jaurian sector and their troops are advancing towards Akhnoor after crossing River Munnavar Tawi. This news surprised us and we took this news as propaganda of Pakistan. At 8.30 p.m., when the news was over, Maj Khanna asked me to examine the progress of work about digging trenches around the command post and come back quickly for dinner. While I was hardly 100 yards away from the bunker, Pakistani shelling started and one of our JCOs present in that area confirmed to me that war has broken out.

The war had officially started.

While the air war was more intense and AD artillery tested more in the western sector, it was the eastern sector that was the focus of operations; liberation of East Pakistan being the primary aim of the war.

## NOTES

1. Kaiser Tufail, *In the Ring and on its Feet: Pakistan Air Force in India-Pakistan War 1971*, Ferozsons, Lahore, 2018, pp. 50-2.

2. Mansoor Shah, *The Gold Bird*, Oxford University Press, Karachi, Oxford University Press, Karachi, 2002.
3. Sayed Sajad Haider, *Flight of the Falcon*, Vanguard Books, 2009 and Tom Cooper, with Syed Shaiz Ali, 'India-Pakistan War, 1971; Western Front, pt. I', Air Combat Information Group.
4. Kaiser Tufail, 'PAF on the Offensive 1971 War', *Aeronaut*, 6 August 2011 accessed on 6 Decemebr 2019 at http://kaiser-aeronaut.blogspot.com/2011/08/paf-on-offensive-1971-war.html
5. P.C. Lal, *My Years with the IAF*, Lancer Publications, New Delhi, 1986, p. 227.
6. Kaiser Tufail, *In the Ring and on its Feet: Pakistan Air Force in India-Pakistan War 1971*, Ferozesons, Lahore, 2018, p. 53.
7. Interview with Brigadier Deepak Sharma.
8. Ibid.
9. Prasad and Thapliyal, op. cit., p. 205.
10. Kaiser Tufail, op. cit., p. 54.
11. Prasad and Thapliyal, op. cit., p. 213.
12. Kaiser Tufail, op. cit., pp. 53-4.
13. Ibid. See also, Kaiser Tufail, *Mirages in the 1971 War,* accessed on 6 December 2019 at http://urbanpk.com/pakdef/pakmilitary/airforce/1971war/mirages_in_1971_air_war.html
14. Lal, op. cit., p. 256.
15. Tufail, op. cit., pp. 54-5.
16. Prasad and Thapliyal, op. cit., 214. Lon O. Nordeen in his book *Air Warfare in the Missile Age* claims that 'four PAF aircraft during these raids' but no source is mentioned nor are any corroborating details provided to support the claim.
17. A.H. Amin, 'The Western Theatre in 1971: A Strategic and Operational Analysis', *Defence Journal*, Karachi, February 2002.
18. Interview with Captain Arvind Nautiyal.

## CHAPTER 5

# An Endless Wait: War in the East

India had nine air defence regiments in the east grouped under two independent brigade headquarters. Of these, only four regiments were equipped with radar-controlled 40 mm L/70 guns while the remaining five regiments were still equipped with the older L/60 guns. Headquarters 312 (independent) AD Brigade was located at Panagarh, responsible for West Bengal, while Headquarters 312 (Independent) AD Brigade at Shillong looked after the Assam sector. This division of responsibility was not fixed as there was a lot of cross attachment of batteries and troops.

The initial location of the regiments was as follows (see Map 3):

| | |
|---|---|
| 19 AD Regiment | Shillong |
| 25 AD Regiment | Kanchrapara |
| 28 AD Regiment | Tezpur |
| 46 AD Regiment | Oodlabari |
| 47 AD Regiment | Panagarh |
| 48 AD Regiment | Guwahati |
| 107 AD Regiment (TA) | Calcutta |
| 130 AD Regiment (TA) | Guwahati |
| 131 AD Regiment (TA) | Siliguri |

During that year, some of the units had been converting to the new weapon system, the L/70 radar-controlled AD guns, and were busy with conversion training and field firings, while the units in West Bengal had been tasked with internal security (IS) duties against the Naxals. As the situation became clearer, with indications of war, the AD batteries began to be deployed by April 1971. One of the first to be deployed was an AD battery of 48 AD Regiment that was

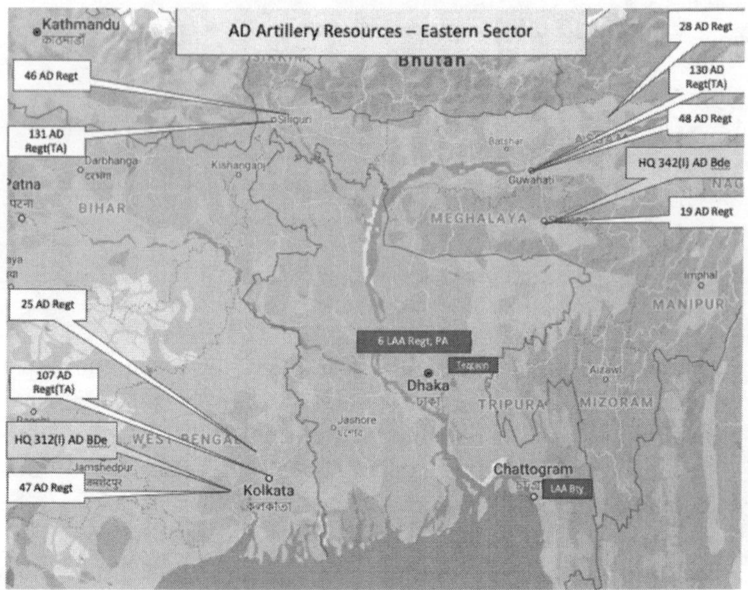


Map 3: AD Artillery Resources: Eastern Sector. *Source:* Author's Collection.

deployed to defend the signal unit (SU) at Sighora near Shillong on 20 April 1971. This was followed by the deployment of an AD troop at Bagdogra airfield. As the situation progressed, some AD units and sub-units were placed under field formations though the deployment was overwhelmingly on air force assets, primarily because of the anticipated pre-emptive airstrike by the Pakistan Air Force.

One of the units deployed for IS duties was 25 AD Regiment, located at Kanchrapara under Headquarters 342 (Independent) AD Brigade. Colonel (then Lieutenant) M.C. Appanna recollects[1]:

> The unit was located at Kanchrapara and had just converted to the L/70 gun system in June 1971. We used to remain busy with training. The old airfield was our training ground where we went about the training religiously. Meanwhile, we received orders to be deployed for IS duties under HQ AD Brigade. It was anti-Naxal operations that we were tasked to undertake.
>
> One day, a lungi-clad civilian came to our unit and handed over a letter written in blood. I remember it said, 'Help us, Indian brothers'. It was obviously sent from across the border. We sent the letter post-haste to Headquarters Eastern Command at Calcutta and, though I do not know what happened to the letter

or what action was taken thereafter, soon enough the unit was visited by the top brass from Calcutta. It was obvious that things were getting heated up.

It was about the same time that the 28 AD Regiment located at Tezpur finished its conversion to the L/70 gun system. Having been deployed in the east during the previous war and having acquitted itself honourably, notably at Kalaikunda, it was awaiting its orders for deployment. But it was to wait for a couple of months more for the same. Meanwhile, the Indian Air Force was preparing for the impending operations and was putting its plans for the defence of its bases and installations in action. The entire Eastern Air Command theatre was sub-divided into three sectors:

(a) Bengal/Bihar sector,
(b) The Assam Valley sector, and
(c) Kumbhigram/Tripura sector.

The area west of the Siliguri corridor comprising West Bengal and Bihar were the responsibility of Advance HQ Eastern Air Command (EAC), with the AOC Advance HQ responsible for all air operations in the sector and the area west of River Brahmaputra in East Pakistan. The air defence of the Assam Valley sector and Kumbhigram sector was entrusted to Commander No. 3 Air Defence Direction Centre (ADDC).[2] To coordinate the deployment and employment of AD artillery units, Headquarters 342 (Independent) AD Brigade was co-located with 253 SU Barrackpore and Headquarters 312 (Independent) AD Brigade with 3 ADDC. IAF, learning from the experience of the 1965 war, had built up a well-coordinated radar network and had three surface-to-air missile squadrons to cover its more important bases.[3] The radar units deployed in the east were 253 SU, Barrackpore, 507 SU, Singharsi, 257 SU, Bagdogra, 511 SU, Dinjan and 509 SU, Latikor Peak, Shillong. The SAM squadrons were 68 Sqn at Kalaikunda, 69 Sqn at Barrackpore and 70 Sqn.[4] Pakistan Air Force was going to find the going tough this time around.

As the ADA units were getting deployed, one SAM squadron was deployed around Calcutta and regular/TA troops were deputed at major airfields and signal units for protection against possible para-commando raids.[5] It was a different matter that the Pakistan Army in East Pakistan was in no way capable of mounting such raids but the experience of paratroopers' raids during the 1965 War had made IAF overtly cautious.[6]

Pakistan had a functional air defence network in name only, relying on a single AR-1 radar located at Mirpur, about 10 miles north-west of Dacca. As the prevailing situation was not favourable for the deployment of mobile observation units or posts (MOU), the radar with its line of sight range of about 40 km, which gave a reaction time of barely three minutes once the intruders were detected, was the only asset providing some semblance of early warning. Pakistan had another radar at Dacca, a P-35, but it had been withdrawn in October 1971 and re-deployed at Malir in West Pakistan.[7] Tezgaon had been left to fend for itself with just about enough resources to put up a decent fight.

The lone Pakistani AD regiment in East Pakistan was 6th LAA Regiment that had started moving into East Pakistan in September 1971, to replace 43rd LAA Regiment. The latter had been involved with Operations Searchlight when it had been tasked to secure the Tezgaon airfield as part of its plan of action for Dacca. The changeover was a slow process and, by the time the war started, only the regimental headquarters and two LAA batteries had interchanged with 50th LAA Battery of 43 LAA Regiment, the now joining as the third battery of 6th LAA Regiment. The final line-up of the regiment commanded by Lt Colonel Mohammad Afzal during the war would be:

| | |
|---|---|
| 21 LAA Battery | Major Durrani |
| 34 LAA Battery | Major Tehzib |
| 161 LAA Battery | Major Ghulam Mustafa |

In mid-November, one LAA troop under Captain Mohammad Anwar was sent to Chittagong where it was beefed up with some Razakars and Mujahids to make it an ad hoc LAA battery.[8]

## THE PREPARATORY STAGE

As the plans were being firmed up at Army Headquarters and HQ Eastern Command, one thing was getting clear and that was that there was a need to keep the border alive through continuous and vigorous skirmishes in all sectors under cover of Mukti Bahini action.[9]

Sectors 8 and 9 comprising the south-west of erstwhile East Pakistan were amongst the most active sectors. This formed the area of responsibility of 2 Corps which had 4 Mountain Division and 9 Infantry Division orbatted to it.[10]

It was in this sector that some of the AD batteries saw early action, well before the formal declaration of war. The south-west sector had been witnessing a frequent heated exchange of fire, developing into local skirmishes. 9 Infantry Division, in the thick of this action, asked for a few AD guns to be used in direct firing role, and possible deployment in its primary role of air defence, as there had been a few border violations by the PAF, too. The responsibility of providing these guns came to 25 AD Regiment which sent three L/70 guns to 9 Infantry Division in early June 1971, to be deployed with the forward localities. Two of these were deployed in Boyra from 9 June onwards, while the third was placed with the headquarter company of 13 Dogra on 11 July 1971 and stayed with the unit till 8 December. The other AD regiment to deploy at this stage was 46 AD Regiment that moved from Chhabua to Oodlabari in June 1971 and sent a battery each at Kumbhigram and Bagdogra airfields.

One of the hotspots in the sector was Shamsher Nagar where Border Security Force (BSF) had a border outpost (BOP) (see Map 4). This was a riverine sector with no road communications and was the site of literally the last Indian BOP. Shamsher Nagar is located on the River Kalindi, at the confluence of the Harinbhanga and Raimongola rivers, where they join to merge with the Bay of Bengal. A Mukti Bahini camp was established there and was a frequent target of a Pakistani gunboat that was operating from its harbour in a mangrove island.

In July, a detachment from 107 AD Regiment (TA) under Havildar S.C. Goswami was attached to BSF and deployed at the BOP, Shamsher Nagar. As the BOP was not connected by road, the L/60 guns were dismantled, taken across the river in BSF boats and then re-assembled. The guns were placed along the embankment of River Kalindi, camouflaged by the fallen trunk of a palm tree.

On 23 August, the Mukti Bahini was asked to fire some blanks and lure the Pakistani gunboat. At 0400 hours, the Mukti Jodha's started firing and soon enough the Pakistani gunboat emerged from the mangrove hide. It was about 0430 hours when the gunboat came

Map 4: Shamsher Nagar. *Source:* Auhtor's Collection.

out in the open, silhouetted against the rising sun and presenting a clear target. Havildar Goswami loaded the guns with HE and AP shells and as the gunboat came within 500-600 yards, ordered one AP round to be fired. It hit the gunboat, blowing off the top glass cabin. Before the gunboat could turn away, Goswami fired one HE round hitting the boat right in the centre, followed by another HE round. The gunboat was now burning, emitting smoke. It was soon deserted by the Pakistani crew as it sank.

The Shamsher Nagar camp was never targeted again by the Pakistanis.

August saw more AD regiments get deployed on their operational tasks as 19 AD Regiment at Shillong deployed two AD batteries at Hashimara airfield and the third battery at SU, Shillong. Meanwhile, 28 AD Regiment finally got its deployment orders and moved its 104 AD Battery to Borjhar airfield near Guwahati, 105 AD Battery and a troop ex-106 AD Battery to Tezpur and 106 AD Battery-less one troop to Jorhat airfield. The other deployments during August were of an AD battery of 25 AD Regiment for protection of SU Barrackpore near Calcutta. During the following months, additional AD batteries were deployed as 25 AD Regiment deployed a battery and two sections at Kalaikunda, a troop and a section at Panagarh and a battery at Dumdum airfield.

As part of the Mukti Bahini, a naval wing of the Mukti Bahini had been formed with 400 naval commandos and frogmen. The nucleus of the naval wing was built around the Bengali sailors who had deserted from the new Pakistani Daphne class submarine Mangro.[11] It had a modest start but, as they were required to step up their activities in case of full-scale hostilities, the West Bengal government was approached for assistance. The state government was very helpful and gave two motorboats, MV *Palash* and MV *Padma*, on loan.[12] As the fitment and training of the crew of the boats was to be done by the Indian Navy, four L/60 guns were provided by 107 AD Regiment (TA) on loan to the Navy.

The boats were fitted with a pair of L/60 guns each at the Garden Reach ship-building workshop and the initial training on handling and operating the guns was given by 107 AD Regiment (TA). The boats were regularly operating in Sunderbans area of the South 24

BNS PADMA

BNS PALASH

Fig. 5.1: The Converted Gunboats that took part in Liberation War.
*Source: History of Army Air Defence*, AAD Directorate, IHQ of MoD(Army), New Delhi, 2008.

Parganas thereafter and were successful in harassing the Pakistani Navy.[13] Unfortunately, both the ships were sunk in a fratricidal incident involving the India Air Force on 10 December 1971.[14]

October saw the next round of deployments with 47 AD Regiment deploying a battery each at Kalaikunda, Dumdum and Pangarh airfields. A battery each of 107 AD Regiment (TA) was deployed for protection of the Howrah Bridge at Calcutta and SU Singharsi, Bihar, while a troop was deployed at Ammunition Point, Krishnanagar, which had been established for 2 Corps. The other troop had already distributed its detachments with the BSF and the naval wing of Mukti Bahini. 130 AD Regiment (TA) was deployed with a battery each at Narangi near Guwahati, two troops at Pandu Bridge over the Brahmaputra and two troops at Tiger Bridge over Teesta. Two troops of the regiment had been sent to the Southern Command where a troop each was deployed for the protection of Tarapur atomic power station and the Baroda oil refinery. The third TA regiment, 131 AD Regiment (TA), had deployed a battery each at Field Ammunition Depot, Shahabad, and the rail bridge at Jalpaiguri.

These allotments were all for static tasks and mainly for AF bases and installations. The Eastern Army, too, had its share of assets to be defended and there was a need to allot AD batteries and troops for the corps and divisions in the command. At that time, the Eastern Command had three corps under it, viz. the newly raised 2 Corps, 4 Corps and 33 Corps, in addition to 101 Communication Zone (Comn Z) with its headquarters at Shillong. The latter, a logistics and administrative formation, had an infantry brigade under it and was also given operational responsibilities.

The allotment of AD troops to the field formations was done by November and the batteries/troops had joined up with respective formations and units. The allotment was done in a piecemeal manner with an apparent lack of any considered application of 'threat to task'. As events unfolded and *formations asked for AD resources*, batteries and troops seem to have been pulled out and given to the formations.[15]

2 Corps was provided with a battery of 48 AD Regiment, two sections of 25 AD Regiment for the medium artillery, a troop of 107 AD Regiment for AP, Krishnanagar, and the three guns with 9 Infantry Division. Similarly, 33 Corps had three troops of L/60

protecting several VA/VPs including the signal centre at the Corps HQ, however, the deployment of AD guns was largely in ones and twos. The AD troops of 46 AD Regiment were distributed for the defence of, amongst other assets, 63 Cavalry, 69 Armoured Regiment and the medium regiments of the 6 and 20 Mountain Artillery Brigades. A battery of 131 AD Regiment (TA) had earlier been deployed at the field ammunition depot, Shahabad which was to support the Corps.

4 Corps was allotted a battery from 48 AD Regiment which was further sub-allotted to the 23 Mountain Artillery Brigade for operations in Belonia. Another battery of the same regiment was allotted for protection of the divisional headquarters and forward defended localities. Two troops of 28 AD Regiment joined up with the corps on 1 December, i.e. just before the formal commencement of hostilities and were deployed for protection of the corps headquarters and the corps maintenance area.[16]

By November, the deployment of AD regiments had been completed with the majority of ADA resources deployed on IAF bases and installations. The airfields that had been provided with AD batteries were Hashimara, Kalaikunda, Dum Dum and Panagarh, with two AD batteries each, while Kumbhigram, Bagdogra, Borjhar and Tezpur were allocated with an AD Battery each. Jorhat had been allotted with one AD troop only.

| *Airfields* | *ADA Allotment* | *Regiment* | *Gun System* |
|---|---|---|---|
| Kalaikunda | Battery + Two Sections | 25 AD Regiment | L/70 |
| | Battery | 47 AD Regiment | L/70 |
| Dumdum | Battery | 25 AD Regiment | L/70 |
| | Battery | 47 AD Regiment | L/70 |
| Panagarh | Troop + Two Sections | 25 AD Regiment | L/70 |
| | Battery | 47 AD Regiment | L/70 |
| Bagdogra | Battery | 46 AD Regiment | L/60 |
| | Troop | 48 AD regiment | L/60 |
| Hashimara | Two Batteries | 19 AD Regiment | L/70 |
| Borjhar | Battery | 28 AD Regiment | L/70 |
| Tezpur | Battery + Troop | 28 AD Regiment | L/70 |
| Jorhat | Troop | 28 AD Regiment | L/70 |
| Kumbhigram | Battery | 46 AD Regiment | L/60 |

The allocation of ADA resources to the airfields was largely of radar-controlled L/70 guns with all the four L/70 regiments being deployed on airfield defence and only Bagdogra and Kumbhigram allotted L/60 guns. The quantum of allocation was a marked change from the previous war as most of the airfields had more than an AD battery allocated to them. The signal units at Barrackpore and Singharsi were defended by an AD battery each while 509 SU, Shillong, had two AD batteries for its protection.

| *Signal Unit* | *ADA Allotment* | *Regiment* | *Gun System* |
|---|---|---|---|
| 509 SU, Shillong | AD Battery | 19 AD Regiment | L/70 |
| | AD Battery | 48 AD Regiment | L/60 |
| 253 SU, Barrackpore | AD Battery | 25 AD Regiment | L/70 |
| 507 SU, Singharsi | AD Battery | 107 AD Regiment (TA) | L/60 |

257 SU, Bagdogra, and 511 SU, Dinjan, were not provided with any ADA cover.

The deployment of ADA continued even as the plans for operations in East Pakistan were being firmed up. The strategy that finally evolved from the war games at all levels was that the Pakistani Army in Bangladesh should be drawn out by keeping the border alive through continuous and vigorous skirmishes in all sectors under cover of Mukti Bahini action. At the same time, every effort was to be made to create the impression that India was interested only in the capture of a niche where the Bangladesh government could be installed, and no more. It was expected that this would induce Gen. Niazi to strengthen his border defences at the cost of the interior and, in the process, dissipate his reserves.

As the Indian Armed Forces were preparing for the impending operations, the situation was getting grim for Pakistan Army in the East, with the Mukti Bahini and sympathisers continuing to harass and inflict severe damage. Beyond the cities, the writ of Pakistani administration did not run, and by November, Pakistan had practically lost its hold over large areas of East Pakistan. Peter R. Kann, a US journalist who won the Pulitzer Prize for his coverage of the war reported:[17]

Dacca diplomats believe the Muktis are in outright control of about 25 per cent of the thanas (subdistricts) of East Pakistan, and much of the rest of the land would have to be considered 'contested'. There are gunfights and explosions in Dacca almost every night, and one diplomat tells of being halted by a Mukti unit on the main city street one night earlier this week. 'Where the army is not, Bangla Desh now is,' a Western diplomat says.

This had a direct impact on the PAF operations.

With only one Plessey AR-1 radar, operated by No. 4017 Radar Squadron, with a range of about 30 km for low-level ingress, PAF was largely blind to IAF raids. To augment the radar cover, 246 MOU Squadron, PAF, and other mobile observers were deployed around the country, armed with radios and telephones. These men were exposed to Mukti Bahini attacks which tended to reduce their effectiveness. By November, the control of Mukti Bahini over large tracts of areas meant that the MOUs could no longer be deployed and they were ultimately withdrawn, depriving No. 14 Squadron, PAF, of vital early warning about IAF missions. The only way to defend was to fly CAPs but, with limited resources and overriding IAF numerical superiority, it was a costly proposition.

## THE INDIAN PLAN

The primary focus of Indian strategy in 1971 was on the operations in East Pakistan. The war aimed to create conditions that would allow the refugees to return and would leave an Awami League government in power in Dacca. With diplomacy having limited success and the Mukti Bahini not in a position to carry out a political resolution to the crisis, it was clear that the only way forward was a military campaign against Pakistan.

Based on the assumption that there would be international pressure to bring an early halt to military operations and/or direct international intervention, the plans had to be for a swift, short campaign. Keeping in mind the need to ensure the security of the border with China, the operations were delayed until November or December to allow winter snow to close the passes leading from Tibet into India.

Adding to the challenges was the terrain in East Pakistan with its rivers, marshes, rice fields, and innumerable small lakes and watercourses that made movement difficult and effectively prohibited major military operations during the monsoon (approximately May to late September). The larger rivers broke the country into four principal zones: north-west, south-west, centre, and east. These sectors were connected by only two railroad bridges: the Hardinge Bridge across the Padma (Ganges) linking the south-west and the north-west, and a bridge at Ashuganj across the Meghna River to tie the eastern and central zones together. Except for these two bridges, neither of which was decked for vehicular traffic, movement across the Padma, Jamuna and Meghna could only be accomplished by water or by air (see Map 5).

Eastern Command, under Lt-Gen. Jagjit Singh Aurora, was issued orders to destroy the bulk of the Pakistani forces in the east and to

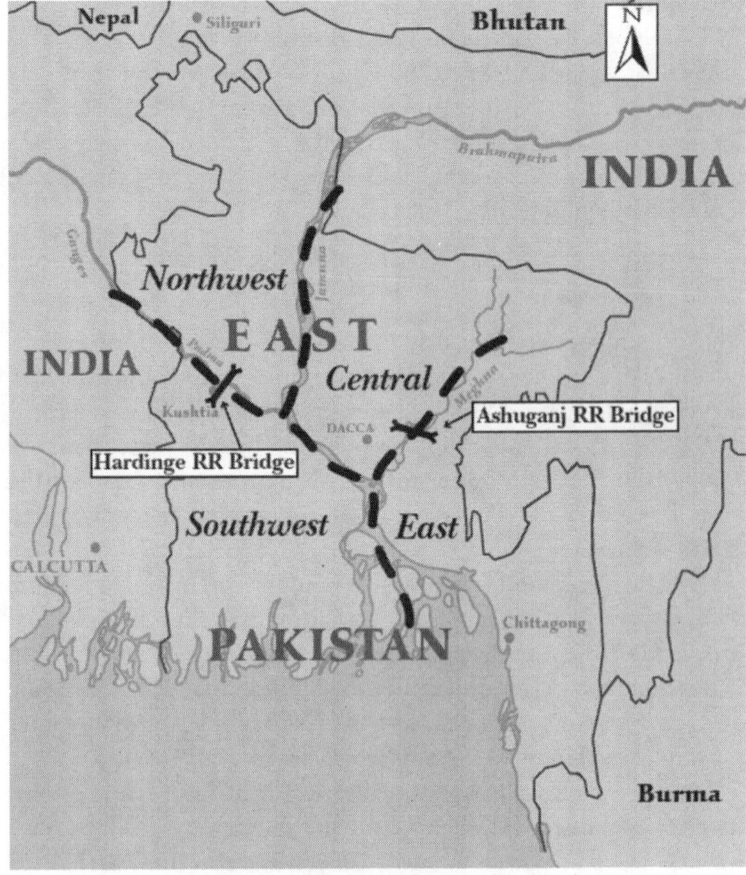


Map 5: East Pakistan Geographical Zone. *Source:* Author's Collection.

occupy most of East Pakistan.[18] These two objectives seem to have been allotted equal priority and plans were accordingly made with one corps allotted to each of the geographical sectors: II Corps in the south-west, XXXIII Corps in the north-west, and IV Corps in the east. There was no formal reference to Dacca in the orders. Apparently, it was thought to be impossible to secure the city within the time frame of a short war. Assigning the best approach to the East Pakistani capital, the central or northern sector to HQ 101 Communication Zone with only one regular brigade seems to stem from this assumption. But then things turned out differently once the operations commenced.

## THE PRELIMINARY OPERATIONS

On the south-western flank was the newly assembled 2 Corps which had been raised on 7 October 1971 by Lt Gen. T.N. Raina at Krishnanagar. It had 4 Mountain Division and 9 Infantry Division on its orbat and was tasked to take Khulna, Jessore, Goalundo Ghat, Faridpur, and the Hardinge Bridge. Before the main offensive commenced, this sector was to witness some intense preliminary operations including an aerial duel between Indian and Pakistani Air Forces.

The major objectives assigned to 2 Corps during the preliminary planning were Jessore and Khulna. Considering that Khulna had been identified as one of the keys to East Pakistan by Gen. Manekshaw, the special emphasis had been placed on its capture in the Indian Army plans. 2 Corps, on its part, planned to advance on two axis with 4th Mountain Division in the north towards Jhenida and 9th Infantry Division aiming for Jessore on the southern approach. The launchpad for this was the Boyra Salient.

The importance of the Boyra Salient can easily be understood by just a look at the map of East Pakistan. It affords a launchpad towards any operation towards Jessore and on to Khulna. It made for an ideal area to commence the offensive in its sector. Though Gen. Jacob mentions that 'from 22 November we ordered our troops to undertake offensive actions into East Pakistan to prepare to jump off areas for the planned operations', the actions by the formations had started earlier.[19]

350 Infantry Brigade of 9 Infantry Division, ordered to secure a lodgement area inside East Pakistan, launched operations on the

night of 11/12 November 1971 with 1 JAK RIF to capture Pakistan's Masli BOP – East of Boyra Salient in Jessore sector. The objective was later changed to only invest the BOP to avoid any prisoners of war being taken by Pakistan. On the night of 15 November 1971, 4 SIKH deployed north of Boyra Salient to provide flank security to 1 Jakrif and to invest Barni BOP in the north. It deployed in area Makapur to exploit and expand the lodgement area. By 19 November 1971, a squadron 63 CAV was deployed in the area held by 4 SIKH for subsequent offensive operations.[20]

These actions drew the immediate attention of the Pakistan army as it launched probing patrols against them but they failed to evict the Indian lodgements. To enable build-up across the River Kabadak and to induct armour and artillery, a Krupmann bridge was constructed over River Kabadak by 102 Engineer Regiment on the night of 18/19 November. Early on the morning of 19 November, the bridge was targeted by four F-86 Sabres of Pakistan Air Force, destroying one pontoon. Following this, it was decided to induct two AA guns for the protection of the bridge.

Describing the PAF actions during the day, Kaiser Tufail, writes:[21]

> On 19 November, the PAF swung into action against troops and gun positions that were part of the Indian 9 Division, which had brazenly violated the international border and penetrated several miles deep in Jessore sector. Several sorties were flown against them till the afternoon of the next day. Well-camouflaged tanks were spotted by an RT-33 on a recce sortie near Chaugacha, and action against them was again initiated by F-86s starting from the morning of 22 November.

Though none of the Indian accounts mentions the move forward and deployment of AD guns the salient *Mukti Bahini Wins Victory* by A.T.M. Abdul Wahab notes that:[22]

> The Allied forces initially tried to cross the Kabadak River under Bayra. But the crossing site was destroyed by the Pakistani Air Force. The allied force brought anti-aircraft gun near the crossing site.

Before the PAF, it was the Pakistan Army that launched a counter-attack with its 107 Infantry Brigade supported by 3rd Independent Armoured Squadron after dawn on 21 November. The counter-attack was not only beaten back, 11 Pakistani tanks were knocked out during the battle.[23]

The PAF returned on 22 November. The first PAF strike was carried out by four F-86 Sabres led by Sqn Ldr Dilawar Hussain and it managed to knock off a ferry across the river near Garibpur. They faced no opposition as the AD guns were not deployed near the site and the IAF was not able to react in time. The second strike by the Pakistanis, at noon, also went unchallenged. With both the missions coming back unscathed, No. 14 Squadron, PAF, decided to go for yet another strike. It was again to be by four Sabres with the squadron commander leading it, but with one change that Flt Lt Parvez Mehdi Qureshi replaced Sqn Ldr Dilawar Hussain. The PAF formation took off at 1420 hours. As one of the Sabres developed an R/T problem, it turned back leaving three Sabres to proceed to Boyra.[24]

When overhead the battle area, the Sabres loitered for some time trying to pick up targets. Wing Commander Chaudhary took on a tank formation and after that was carrying out a reconnaissance when he found himself being engaged by AD guns near Chaugacha. Apte recollects,[25]

> At 2.45 p.m. or so, I saw these Sabres climbing up to about 2,000 ft and then coming down to about 500 ft for the weapon release like those German Stuka bombers in the Second World War. Our LMGs on ack ack role and our air defence (AD) guns were not very effective but we could see their white puffs trying to deter the enemy aircraft. I very clearly saw a mission of three Sabre fighters from the east of my gun area swooping over us at a low level.

The Sabres had difficulty picking up targets due to the camouflage and concealment and the AA fire that kept them from getting them a closer look. Unknown to them, the Sabres had been picked up by the IAF radar and Gnats from No. 22 Squadron, IAF, at Dum Dum had been scrambled. As the Sabres were strafing the ground targets, the flight of Gnats appeared on their tail. In a matter of just three minutes, two of the Sabres were shot down with the aircraft crashing near village Bongaon.[26]

Flt Lt Parvez Qureshi Mehdi was one of the PAF pilots who was shot down. He managed to bail out and was captured by 4 SIKH. Lt Gen. H.S. Panag recollects the incident:[27]

> I told him that he was now a prisoner of war (PoW) and would be treated as per Geneva Convention. Interestingly, he had not seen the Gnats approaching and thought that he was hit by ground fire. His conduct, despite the shock of

being shot down and taken a PoW, was that of a very brave man – stoic and dignified.

The third Sabre was also hit but it managed to get back to Tezgaon.[28] Some accounts mention that three Sabres were shot down that day with the third Sabre crashing in East Pakistan. As the ADA was deployed and had engaged the Sabres, some accounts claim that the third Sabre was shot down by the ADA.[29]

The Pakistani account of the air battle that mentioned the AA guns trying to engage the PAF Sabres was used to support this claim. As Tufail mentioned in his book:[30]

> In the third mission of the day, around 1530 hrs (all times EPST), three F-86s led by the Squadron Commander, Wg Cdr Afzal Choudhry, with Flag Off. Khalil Ahmad as No. 2 and Flt Lt Parvaiz Mehdi Qureshi as No. 3, attacked a couple of tanks that had been reported in the area. After the attack, ground control asked the leader to look for more tanks that were suspected to be concealed around. Loitering in the battlefield amounted to inviting trouble, especially when flying without radar cover. Trouble came swiftly when four ground-scrambled Gnats, of the Dum Dum-based No. 22 Squadron, were able to sneak in and bounce the F-86 formation. At that time, the leader, Wg Cdr Choudhry, was attacking a AAA battery that was noticed to be firing at them.

The claim of the third Sabre having been shot down, leave aside by the ADA, was, however, found to be false and was just an exaggeration.[31]

## THE STAGE IS SET

While the formations were preparing for the offensive, the deployment of ADA troops was also getting completed. On the eastern flank, was 4 Corps under Lt Gen. Sagat Singh. It was the heaviest formation with 8, 57 and 23 Mountain Divisions but, as with other formations, the allotment of AD artillery troops was minimal. All it had was six troops – two of L/70 and four of L/60. One AD battery of 46 AD Regiment (L/60) was deployed at Kumbhigram airfield that was subjected to frequent enemy ground fire and shelling. To secure the sector, it was decided to carry out a preliminary operation on 29/30 November 1971 with troops crossing over in ferries with the 'C' Troop of 179

AD Battery of 48 AD Regiment deployed to protect the ferry sites. One of the guns was crossing over when four Sabres came in for a strike.

With the other guns lined up in their designated serial, waiting for the ferry to cross, it was only one gun on the home bank that engaged the Sabres. They were coming in at a right angle to the ferry sites, along the line of the river, when Naib Subedar Rattan Singh took the layer number's seat and engaged them. The guns fired 81 rounds in all and one Sabre was claimed to have been hit. Though the regimental accounts claim that one of the Sabres 'spiralled out of control and plunged into the river and the remaining three flew away', the Sabres returned without any loss. Rattan Singh was 'mentioned in despatches' for this action.[32]

PAF did not carry out any other operation thereafter and it was expected to be the lull before the storm with a pre-emptive strike expected as was in the past during the September war of 1965.

## DECLARATION OF WAR

The pre-emptive strike by PAF in the west on 3 December 1971 was the formal declaration of war but, unlike in the previous engagement, PAF did not carry out any offensive mission in the east. With only fourteen serviceable aircraft, No. 14 Squadron, PAF, was not in a state to risk losing any further aircraft during such strikes against a more powerful and better-prepared adversary. It is not surprising that PAF wanted to preserve them for the battles ahead. That the IAF had learnt its lessons well and was prepared for the operations had already been demonstrated during the Battle of Boyra and there was, in any case, no need for the PAF to provoke the IAF into carrying out any strikes. Even so, it was not long before the IAF obliged PAF with the first strikes taking place during the night of 3/4 December.

The honour of carrying out the first strikes after the formal declaration of war was that of the Kilo Flight of Mukti Bahini. Their lone Otter flown by Flt Lt Shamshul Alam and Captain Akram attacked the oil installations at Chittagong while the armed Alloutte III helicopter went on to target the oil installations at Narayanganj.

The raids managed to achieve a complete surprise and it was only in the second run over Chittagong that the Pakistani AA guns opened up but failed to hit the Otter. Both the strikes were successful.

Alam managed to target and hit a Pakistani ship on its way back, setting it on fire. In their wake came the Canberras of 16 Squadron, IAF, at Gorakhpur. Eight Canberra B(I)58s were tasked for operations in the east – four each against the airfields of Chittagong and Tezgaon. The Canberras were carrying eight 1,000 lb bombs each and, though the raid carried on for over an hour in face of a spirited defence by the AA guns of 6th LAA Regiment of the Pakistan AD artillery, the airfield and all its installations remained undamaged. No aircraft was hit or damaged either.[33]

On its part, the Pakistani 6th LAA Regiment failed to cause any damage though Pakistani sources claimed to have shot down two Canberras. Describing the action, Siddiq Salik writes,[34]

> A harmless-looking light aircraft approached from the direction of the sea and lazily droned over the city. The Razakars manning the coastal guns did not realize the danger until it blew up the Chittagong refinery. Next came a wave of five Canberras. The ad hoc anti-aircraft battery was able to shoot down two of them.

While no Canberra was lost, the first bombing mission against Chittagong, Kurmitola and Tezgaon airfields 'had not been very successful in rendering the airfields non-operational'.[35]

Early morning on 4 December, Pakistan launched two Combat Air Patrols (CAP), anticipating Indian air raids at dawn itself but it seemed that the Indian Air Force had other plans and the CAPs came back without any incident. Just as the second CAP landed back at Tezgaon, the radar at Mirpur picked up Indian aircraft coming in towards Tezgaon. This was the first offensive mission by Indian Air Force in the East.

Hawker Hunters of Nos. 17 and 37 Squadrons had taken off at 6:30 a.m. and were escorted by MiG-21s from Guwahati. As the Hunters vectored towards their target, they were picked up by the Pakistani radar and a CAP was launched to intercept the same but it failed to deter the intruding aircraft. The raid at Tezgaon, however, did not do much damage – either to the aircraft parked on the ground or to the runway. It was followed by a four-ship formation of No. 28 Squadron,

IAF, but this mission also failed to do any damage to the airfield. The Su-7s of 221 Squadron though managed to hit a Sabre parked on the tarmac near the ATC. In the first wave, IAF had launched thirty-four sorties and claimed two Sabres while losing one Hunter to a Sabre and suffering damage to two more Hunters.

The raids had however caused little damage on the ground.

## PAK AD DRAWS FIRST BLOOD

It was in the second wave that the Pakistani AD artillery drew first blood. The first to strike Tezgaon were two Sukhois of 221 Squadron. Both were hit by AA fire but they managed to reach Panagarh. The next mission of two Hunters of 37 Squadron, IAF, was not so lucky as the Paki AA guns claimed their first victim.

The two Hunters reached Tezgaon unopposed by the PAF but the AA fire was fierce. Both the pilots failed to identify any viable target as the airfield appeared desolate. As the Hunters pulled up for their first pass, the AA guns of 21 AA Battery, PA found their mark, hitting Flight Lieutenant S.G. Khonde's Hunter. The aircraft crashed east of the runway barely fifty yards from the gun that had claimed it. *History of Pakistan Artillery* also mentions the incident: [36]

> It was hit in the cockpit and crashed 50 yards from the gun position in the vicinity of the ammunition pit. The gun commander went around pulling and kicking the aircraft shouting, 'My gun, my gun'. Fortunately, a fire truck came up within minutes and saved the situation.

The second Hunter also received several hits but, as the aircraft was not severely damaged, Flying Officer V.K. Arora, in turn, attacked the AA gun position itself with his front guns and claimed to have destroyed it. This claim is, however, refuted by the Pakistan Army which maintains that the gun was targeted but not hit or damaged.[37]

The next strike by 37 Squadron saw a second Hunter, flown by Squadron Leader A.B. Samanta, getting hit by AA fire and crashing on the outskirts of Dacca. The third loss over Tezgaon of the day was during the next strike by Sukhois of 221 Squadron as the AA guns found their mark, hitting Squadron Leader S.V. Bhutani's Su-7. In all, the Indian Air Force launched 112 counter-air missions on the

Pakistani airbases of Tezgaon and Kurmitola during the day in which Pakistan Air Force lost three F-86 Sabres in aerial battles over Dacca and three civilian aircraft were destroyed on the ground, but the Indian Air Force was not been able to deliver a decisive blow to the Pakistan Air Force, and at the end of the day, Pakistan still had the majority of its aircraft safe, and ready for another round.

Even this limited success had come at a heavy cost as the Indian Air Force lost five aircraft of its own over Tezgaon, including three to the anti-aircraft fire of 6$^{th}$ LAA Regiment.[38]

While the Indian Air Force was busy striking Tezgaon and Chittagong, the ground operations were progressing well. The ADA elements with the field formations had had no role to play as the PAF was not able to mount any sorties against the Indian Army.

On the other hand, the IAF carried out 50 close air support and interdiction sorties on 4 December, almost 20 per cent of the total air effort during the day. These included twenty-three interdiction strikes against infrastructure and transportation nodes.

Even with limited AA resources, a large number of installations and bases were covered by the Pakistan Army that had co-opted the Razakar AA detachments and small arms in their overall air defence plan. As a result, almost all sorties were met by AA fire even if it was only from small arms. While most of the interdiction sorties faced small arms fire only and suffered minor damage, a strike by 7 Squadron, IAF, launched against the bridge on Teesta was not so fortunate.

The bridge had been targeted by four Hunters of 7 Squadron early in the morning but it had only been partially damaged and hence merited a revisit. The two remaining pillars that were still standing were destroyed by the Hunters of 7 Squadron, IAF, but as the Hunters were exiting, a call from the Forward Air Controller (FAC) with 20 Mountain Division was picked up, asking for immediate air support against a target near Lal Munir Hat railway station. Responding to the FAC's call, the Hunters went for a dive attack against the designated target using their front guns. It was during the dive that the AA guns found their mark, hitting both the aircraft. Flt Lt A.R. Da Costa's Hunter was badly damaged and was trailing smoke. Unable to pull out of the dive, it was soon to hit the ground and explode in a huge ball of fire. Da Costa's citation for Vir Chakra mentions that he fell unconscious as a result of which his aircraft crashed, leading to his death:[39] 'Flight Lieutenant Da Costa was also hit and although he tried to bring his aircraft back, he fell unconscious and his aircraft crashed because of which he died.'

Squadron Leader S.K. Gupta, piloting the other Hunter, was luckier as he managed to nurse his aircraft back and eject close to the Indian border where he was picked up by an IAF Alouette III.[40] There were no more losses during the remaining close support missions though quite a few aircraft got hits from the AA fire.

Throughout the day, Pakistani anti-aircraft artillery had been very active and took a heavy toll on the intruding Indian aircraft. In addition to the five aircraft shot down, at least four more aircraft – two Sukhoi Su-7 and MiG-21s were damaged. Luckily, these aircraft managed to reach back, otherwise, the Indian losses would have been higher.

During the day, the real attrition was caused by Pakistan AAA. No raid by IAF went uncontested as the AAA, put up a heavy barrage, unexpectedly so. As one IAF pilot recalled:[41]

> All those losses that we suffered were not from any enemy aircraft but just ground fire. We never expected such heavy ground fire.... It was like a barrage of ammunition dotting the sky and everyone who flew through that would have been lucky to get through.
>
> I, myself, had many narrow escapes too: many punctures in the wings and the sides, but fortunately not hitting any of the vitals to dismember the aircraft or destroy it. Some went through the cockpit as well. We decided we will not hit Dacca at a low level because we were going against heavy flak.

Adding to the woes was the disappointment of knowing that some of the F-86s claimed by IAF to have been destroyed on the ground at Tezgaon were dummies.[42] Another disappointment for the Indian Air Force was its failed attempt to try and locate an AR-1 radar suspected to be located near Kurmitola. The only consolation was that the IAF did not suffer any loss during this mission. It was not that the Pakistan anti-aircraft defence did not have their losses. The second Indian wave over Tezgaon comprising of Sukhois claimed to have damaged two AA guns. On balance, though, the Pakistani flak had held an upper hand during the day. As Jagan and Chopra write in their book *Eagles over Bangladesh*,[43] 'PAF sat tight and let its AA guns do the hard work when the IAF came calling in numbers.'

And the hard work of anti-aircraft guns had surely paid off on day one.

In addition to the three Indian aircraft shot down over Tezgaon, IAF lost two aircraft from its fifty-five close air support missions on day one, a rather heavy attrition rate of over 3.6 per cent. Overall, the loss of seven aircraft, with two more severely damaged and two flameout incidents, painted a not too rosy picture for IAF. Coupled with its failure to locate the AR-1 radar, the Indian Air Force would have wished for a better way to end the day.

Though the counter-air missions were only partly successful on day one, there was no serious threat to Indian airbases and maintaining such heavy deployment of ADA troops was not deemed necessary. Accordingly, a battery of 19 AD Regiment deployed at Hashimara was airlifted to Agra on 4 December. Agra had been raided thrice during the night of 3-4 December.[44] While the need to strengthen the defences at Agra cannot be disputed, the lack of deliberate planning in the allocation of ADA resources was exposed on the very first day itself. Von Moltke the Elder was right after all when he had said – 'No plan survives contact'. Whatever had been the plan for allocation of ADA, it was not so well thought out after all.

The counter-air operations by the IAF continued in the night with a raid on the night of 4/5 December against Tezgaon and Kurmitola by four Canberras with each delivering 8,000-lb bombs on its hi-lo-hi mission but they again failed to cause any damage to the runway.[45]

The MiGs had been using rockets to target the parked Sabres at Tezgaon, but, owing to the use of effective camouflage by the PAF, the IAF had failed to pick up the Sabres and not much had been achieved till now except for harassing the Pakistanis. It was then suggested that bombs be used against the runways and thereby not only keep the PAF grounded but also prevent any reinforcements from moving in. The IAF already had just the weapon in its inventory as most of the MiG and Sukhoi squadrons had the Soviet FAB-500 M-62.[46]

The go-ahead to use the M-62 was given by Headquarters Eastern Command but it was an untried weapon that had not been used to date. It could be delivered in two methods – in near-level flight which was a recommended method to ensure the safety of one's aircraft against the anti-aircraft fire, but it was not very accurate, while the other method was a steep glide bombing attack along the length of the runway.

To 'test' the bomb and the delivery method, it was decided to first use it against Kurmitola where the risk to the aircraft would be less, but, before that, a raid was planned against the AR-1 radar at Tezgaon. A pair of MiG-21s armed with M-62 took off from Guwahati, escorted by a pair of MiGs, and reached Tezgaon at about 1:30 p.m. The MiGs failed to locate the radar and dropped their bombs at what they believed to be the radar and returned to base without any untoward incident. The AR-1 radar which was located at nearby Mirpur Zoo was not damaged and continued to operate unharmed.[47]

The bombing trial against Kurmitola was successful and the runway was badly damaged. This paved the way for use of the M-62s against Tezgaon but it was to wait one more day. Meanwhile, 221 Squadron, providing close air support to the 9 Infantry Division, had a near-fatal incident. A Sukhoi piloted by Flt Lt V.K. Chawla was hit by light machine gunfire while targeting a Pakistani gun position near Jessore. The LMG burst hit the cockpit with one bullet hitting Chawla in the leg. Chawla managed to reach back but had to be hospitalized, putting him out of action for the rest of the war through the Sukhoi was patched up and put back in service.[48]

The IAF close support and interdiction strikes continued to meet stiff opposition. Wg Cdr Kulbir Singh Harnal of 7 Squadron, IAF, based at Bagdogra, recounts a mission against a train at Lal Munir Hat:[49]

> The firepower of the Hunter's 30 mm × 4 Aden guns using HE ammo (not used before in practice firing on the range) was deadly. When I fired a 3 to 4-second burst on the train nothing happened for a sec and then the bogie just blew off the rails. Why was this train moving about in the day? By the time we swung around for the second pass, we drew heavy small arms fire. Some bullet holes underwing but not in any critical area.
>
> … I recalled the many flashes from the ground near the target on which I was firing in a dive, I said to myself, that they were trying to get me, too, for those flashes were real anti-aircraft fire.

On 6 December, PAF, for the first time, ventured out of Dacca airspace to provide close support to Pak Army, albeit just about 20 miles away, though the Sabres were reported to have been seen over Comilla, too. They were reportedly recovered back from an airstrip at Barisal, about 80 km from Dacca. While the confirmation of the use of the airstrip at Barisal was not available, it did add a target for the IAF to neutralize and to be tasked for counter-air missions. Though the reports of the use of Barisal later proved to be false, the IAF carried out counter-air missions against Barisal the next day.

The main strike planned for the day was against Tezgaon by MiGs using M-62s, though the heavy AA presence meant that the MiGs could not use the regular tactics of releasing the bombs at a low level at about 900 m above ground level (AGL) and pulling up from 600 m. The MiGs perforce had to change tactics and release the bombs at about 1,400 to 1,500 m, keeping well outside the effective ceiling of the AA guns. Another change in the delivery method planned was for the MiGs to come in at a steep dive angle of 35 degrees. Group Captain S.V. Ratnaparki of 4 Squadron, IAF, recollects:[50]

> The AA fire was fierce, that's why we dropped them from high. Normally, we dropped them at 900 m ... by the time we did a pull-up, we were more than a km high. The AA could not hit us even though there was a heavy umbrella of AA.

The changed tactics, though, paid off and the MiGs were able to place the bombs right where they wanted, on the runway, putting it out of use.[51]

After two days of relentless strikes by IAF, the Pakistan AA gunners had also changed their tactics and had now placed the guns at both sides of either end of the runway. These were four-barrelled 14.5 mm Quads with a higher rate of fire than the 37 mm guns. As the MiGs had streaked in, the AA guns opened up, but as the IAF aircraft were well above the effective ceiling, the AA fire proved ineffective. The MiGs were followed by Hunters of No. 14 Squadron, escorted by Gnats providing top cover, with Napalm to try and neutralize the AA guns. Luckily for Pakistani gunners, most of the Napalm failed to ignite. Throughout this, the AA fire remained as fierce as before, making one of the Hunter pilots 'duck in his cockpit' as the AA shells burst all around him.[52]

The other raid by the Indian Air Force on Kurmitola, was uneventful in comparison as the AA fire was ineffective and no opposition was faced by the Indian aircraft. The only loss of the day, the first MiG-21 lost in the east, was during the close air support. The Indian Air Force provided forty CAS missions to the Indian Army's 4 corps during the day. The first fourteen sorties had gone in without any loss, with the only damage being the small arms hits on the MiGs, but the mission flown by No. 4 Squadron was not to have the same fate. At Brahmanbaria, as two MiGs went in against a Pakistani position, one of the MiGs got hit by a small arms fire. The damage was serious and even as the pilot, Squadron Leader D.P. Rao, tried to head back to the base at Guwahati, the engine flamed out, forcing Rao to eject.[53]

This incident, and the fact that a large number of aircraft were being hit by small arms fire, forced the IAF to advise the pilots not to fly at excessively low level and avoid taking risks.[54]

Tezgaon was again raided the next day, this time by a solitary MiG armed with M-62 bombs in the early morning, and was followed by Hunters later in the day. As the runway was damaged beyond repair, the Sabres were effectively grounded and the opposition was limited to AAA but it was serious enough to hit one of the Hunters of No. 14 Squadron. The damaged Hunter tried to touch base but the engine flamed out forcing Dasgupta, the pilot of the ill-fated Hunter, to eject.[55]

This was not the end of action at Tezgaon. The Hunters were followed by MIGs of No. 28 Squadron and it was during the second attack that AAA found its mark as the AA fire hit Wing Commander Bishnoi's MiG:[56]

> I once again led another bombing mission to Tezgaon the next morning, December 7.
>
> The runway had not been repaired during the night and we added to their plight by adding another eight craters to the previous eight. During these attacks, we had also given enough practice to their anti-aircraft gunners and so at last they scored a hit on the left wing of my aircraft. I felt a big thud and the aircraft shook violently.
>
> By then I was nearing my firing range, pressed on and released the bombs and pulled out of the dive. I looked inside the cockpit – all instruments read normal, aircraft responded to controls and throttle. All was well. The gunner would have

been delighted had he known that he had scored a pinpoint hit, but there was no way that I could have told him. The damage was a 9-inch hole.

Thankfully, Wing Commander Bishnoi was able to recover his aircraft back to base. The runway at Tezgaon was not so lucky – it was so badly damaged that it could not be repaired to be in action by morning.

On 8 December, the counter-air missions by MiGs continued against Tezgaon while Gnats and Hunters were used against Barisal and Ishurdi. Photo-reconnaissance missions were carried out over Tezgaon and Kurmitola that revealed the extent of damage to the runways. With the runways put out of use and No. 14 Squadron, PAF, grounded for good, IAF had complete control over the skies and the air threat to Indian bases and installations was as good as over. Most of the ADA troops deployed in the east, except for those protecting radar stations, were accordingly released for use in the west.[57]

To prevent PAF from repairing its runway at Tezgaon and to continue to maintain its air supremacy, the IAF carried on with its counter-air missions. The fact that all PAF Sabres were not destroyed was an important factor in the decision to continue these strikes.[58] This relentless air campaign by the IAF put a strain on 6th LAA Regiment, PA, stretching its resources thin. Logistically, too, the Pakistani AD troops were under tremendous pressure with the ammunition availability reaching critical levels. Faced with a severe shortage of ammunition after a relentless IAF campaign against its bases and installations, Lt Col Afzal, the commanding officer of 6 LAA Regiment, was forced to restrict ammunition expenditure to 3 rounds per gun per sorties for 37 mm guns while the 14.5 Quads were restricted to engagement with two barrels firing short bursts of twelve rounds per barrel.[59]

The strict control over ammunition would have a direct consequence as it limited the efficacy of the AD guns in countering any hostile raid in future. The change in bombing tactics by the IAF to keep out of the range of AA guns also reduced the efficacy of Pak air defences. It was evident for the next few days as the Pakistani AA defences failed to score any kills against the attacking Indian aircraft.

The ground fire by small arms at a low level, however, remained effective. This was found out the hard away by the IAF as the pilots were getting again complacent and were carrying out 'leisurely' attacks. On 10 December, Flt Lt P.K. Tayal was attacking a target suspected to be a Pakistani brigade headquarters when his aircraft was hit by ground fire:[60]

> At Kushtia, we commenced rocket attacks and during the attack, we had done one pass and came around. When we did the second pass, I was in a dive and pulling out. Then ground fire. People seemed to be sitting around in trenches and firing blindly and my aircraft was hit.
>
> One of the bullets had punctured my main tank. I was contemplating ejecting but decided to at least go to the Indian side and then eject.

Luckily for Tayal, he was able to nurse his Gnat back to base. He led another mission over Khulna the same day and in the face of heavy ground fire positively destroyed one enemy tank and damaged another tank. Tayal was awarded, Vayu Sena Medal (Gallantry).[61]

In another close support mission, Fl Lt L.H. Dixon was lucky in a different manner. While carrying out a strike mission against a Pakistani Army headquarters in the Hilli sector, Dixon took his time identifying various ground targets. This gave enough time for the Pakistani troops to engage the Hunter:[62]

> There was some AA fire which did not bother the pilots. By now the close support sorties had turned into range practice: the pilots were taking their own time, making multiple passes from predictable directions and loitering over the targets. The Pakistani ground defences soon caught on to this.
>
> As Dixon came into an attack on one of the passes he felt his aircraft hit. Faced with the loss of hydraulic control and fire in the cockpit, Dixon turned the aircraft away into the Indian troop lines and ejected.

Dixon was picked up by a search team of a Grenadiers' battalion and was later heli-lifted to Hashimara.

Lady Luck continued to hold out for IAF as a Caribou of 33 Squadron was hit by ground fire during a supply drop at Sylhet. Flying Officer Rudra Bishnoi managed to bring back his stricken aircraft with a damaged engine to Kumbhigram. Though the Caribou had been hit at several places, the ground crew at Kumbhigram were able to patch it up for a flight back to Guwahati where it underwent major repairs. All in all, 10 December was lucky for the IAF in that a number of aircraft, though hit and damaged by ground fire, were brought back due to excellent pilot skills.[63]

The intensity and effectiveness of the AA fire varied at places with ad hoc subunits and detachments not being as effective as regular units. Unsurprisingly, the ad hoc light AA battery at Chittagong was able to put up only a weak challenge to the Canberras as they revisited it on 11 December. It was 'furious but lacking the same intensity as at Tezgaon'. The naval accounts, though, classify the AA fire as 'medium to heavy' when describing the Alize's raids at Chittagong.[64] Notwithstanding the differing classification, the AAA at Chittagong remained largely ineffective.

By now the Pakistani AA defences were losing their sting and were largely ineffective but only if the aircraft remained outside their range. Any aircraft that ventured within the range of AA guns still ran the risk of being hit as Sqn Leader K.J.S. Gill found out on 12 December. As the counter-air campaign continued, MiGs of 28 Squadron, IAF, were back to bomb Tezgaon. During the raid, the MiG-21 piloted by Sqn Leader Gill was hit by AA fire and sustained severe damage. Gill tried to head back to Agartala but as he neared the base, the fire had spread to the cockpit, forcing Gill to eject. Fortunately, he was picked up by the Mukti Bahini and did not end up being taken prisoner.[65]

As part of the continuing thinning of ground-based air defences, No. 69 Squadron, IAF, was moved from Barrackpore to Baroda.[66]

On 15 December, IAF was 'roaming the skies at will' over East Pakistan. To maintain the pressure on Kurmitola cantonment, a three-ship mission of Canberras of No. 16 Squadron, IAF, was sent as the Cobras' last mission of the war. Black 3, the third aircraft, was piloted by Fl Lt B.R.E. Wilson, with Flying Officer R.B. Mehta as navigator. In his exuberance, Wilson decided to carry out a shallow glide bombing attack on Tezgaon airfield though the orders were to avoid the airfields and not descend below 5,700 ft altitude. As Wilson's Canberra came within their range, the Paki AA gunners did not miss out on the opportunity and the Canberra was 'torn apart by the deadly Chinese AA guns'.[67]

It was an avoidable loss just an hour before the ceasefire. But the incident only reinforced the maxim that it is naive to assume that domination of the skies translates to the domination of ground-based air defences.

## WITH THE FIELD ARMY

In the absence of any air threat, the Indian AD artillery batteries with the field army were not tested during the entire war. Allotted to the field formations, the batteries and troops continued to remain with the respective formation/units till such time they were moved out for deployment in the west.

With the allocation of resources being done in a piecemeal manner, there was the cross deployment of units. The ADA batteries were further sub-divided into troops and sections while being deployed which was to cater to 'the increased demand by field forces for AD artillery protection'.

It was to meet such demands that a battery of 48 AD Regiment was initially allotted to 2 Corps and was followed by allotment of two sections of 25 AD Regiment that were pulled out from the battery deployed at Panagarh and allotted to 9 Infantry Division in November 1971. Two more sections of 25 AD Regiment were subsequently provided for protection of 78 Medium Regiment. It is difficult to understand the rationale of such allocation – both the quantum of ADA resources and also the piecemeal allotment 'on demand' for it was against all established norms of employment of ADA resources.

One of the troops with 2 Corps was the 'G' Troop of 48 AD Regiment with 4 Mountain Division which was further sub-allotted to 4 Mountain Artillery Brigade. 2$^{nd}$ Lt Bhupendra Singh Chhetri, the troop commander, in his book *Meandering into Memories* notes:[68]

> Meanwhile, my troop was further divided into three by the BM Artillery Brigade. Two guns with detachment were allotted to a field regiment. Two guns were allotted to a mountain regiment and the remaining two guns with the troop headquarters were allotted to a medium regiment. Now my command and control of the troop got smashed.
>
> Each regiment had been allotted two guns and these guns moved with their first and second lien ammunition: I was carrying the remaining ammunition which I was supposed to supply on a need basis. Two of my guns were commanded by my troop JCO and the remaining two by the troop havildar major. They were both miles away and I could only communicate with them through 4 Arty Bde radio and line communication system.

This practice seems to have been followed in all field formations and there was no means of exercising control over the ADA detachments

Map 6, 33 Corps conducted operations between the Jamuna and Padma rivers in the north-western sector of East Pakistan. The sector was defended by 16 Pak Div. While 71 Mtn Bde advanced on the Pachagarh-Thakurgaon axis, 20 Mtn Div attacked the waistline of the sector, i.e. Hilli area. It was finally reduced on 11

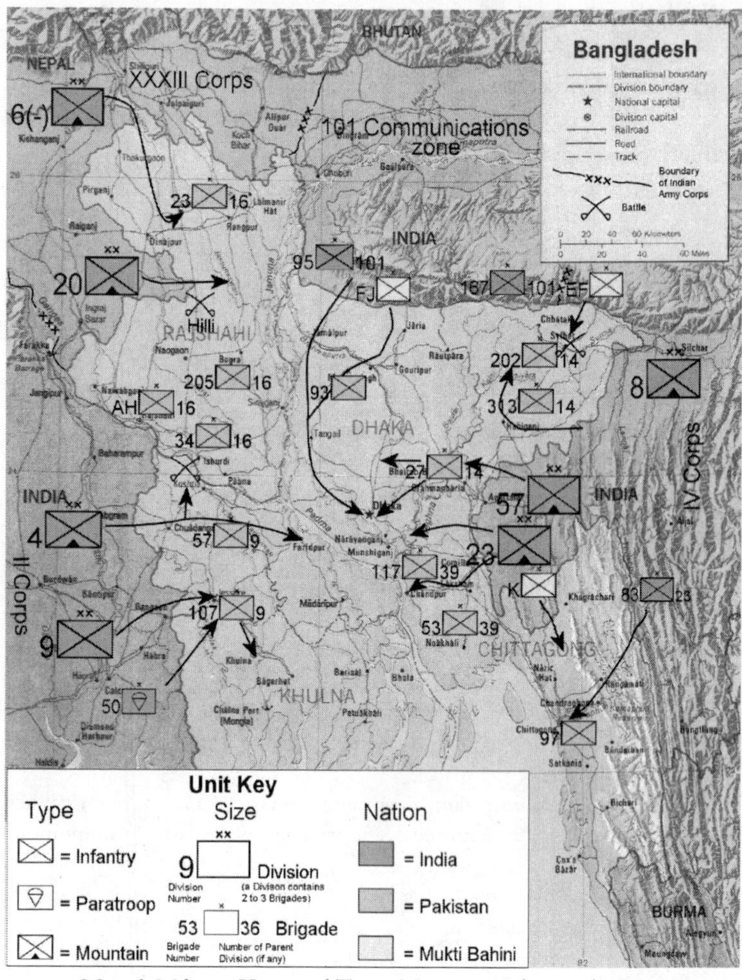


Map 6: Military Units and Troop Movements during the War.
*Source:* Wikipedia (open source).

December 1971. The Corps also captured enemy strongholds of Rangpur and Bogra on the 16th.

2 Corps carried out operations in the southwestern sector of East Pakistan. The sector was bounded by the Padma River in the north, Jamuna River in the east and the Bay of Bengal in the south. One Pak inf div was defending this sector. 4 Mtn Div carried out operations in the northern part of this sector. It fought its way through Jibannagar, Kotchandpur, Suadih, Jhenida and Magura. It also overcame tough enemy resistance at Kushtia. The Division fought a crucial battle on 15 December on the western banks of the Madhumati. 9 Inf Div carried out operations in the southern part of the Corps sector on the Garibpur-Jessore-Khulna axis. It captured Burinda and Jessore and then moved on to Khulna. The Pak Bde commander surrendered here on the 17th.

101 Communication Zone Area (CZA) carried out the operations from the north. It covered the area bounded by the Meghna in the east, Jamuna in the west and Padma in the south-west. The Zone launched its attack on two axis and encountered tough opposition at Kamalpur and Jamalpur. Heavy use of air and artillery power finally broke the enemy resistance at these strongholds. The enemy broke out from Jamalpur on the 10th night. Meanwhile, the FJ Force of 101 CZA made rapid progress on Haluaghat-Mymensingh axes. The Pak position at Haluaghat was outflanked and the defending battalion destroyed. The Force captured Mymensingh on the 11th and Madhupur on the 12th. The Pak Commander panicked and withdrew the small force, which was defending this sector, to meet the threat from IV Corps, from the east. This enabled 101 CZA to advance unchallenged. 2 PARA landing at Tangail and its securing the Poongli bridge also facilitated the advance of the CZA Force. It was the FJ Sector of 101 CZA which made it first to Dacca on the 16th.

The important thrust into East Pakistan was carried by 4 Corps. It covered the area stretching from Sylhet in the north to Chittagong in the south. The sector was defended by two Pak divs. 8 Mtn Div operated in Sylhet area. It encountered the major part of the

Pak 14 Div in this sector. It fought its way to Sylhet destroying all opposition en route. On 7 December a battalion was airlifted to Sylhet and the Div captured Sylhet on 14 December.

57 Mtn Div operated on Agartala-Akhaura-Ashuganj-Dacca axis. Lance Naik Albert Ekka of 14 GUARDS was awarded the Param Vir Chakra for his gallantry during one of the initial attacks on Gangasagar near Akhaura on 3 December. On 5 December, the Division attacked Akhaura with two Brigades and inflicted a crushing defeat on the defending 27 Pak Bde. It then advanced on to Ashuganj and beat a sharp counter-attack from the Pak Bde. Meanwhile, 61 Bde of the Div advancing on Comilla-Mynamati-Daudkandi axis in a wide outflanking move captured Daudkandi on 10 December. This move by 61 Bde forced 117 Pak Bde to vacate well-prepared defences at Lalmai and Comilla and fall back on Mynamati. This in turn facilitated the advance of Indian 23 Div.

The southern thrust in 4 Corps sector was carried by 23 Div on the Himatnagar-Laksham-Chandpur axis. It completely encircled and emasculated 53 Pak Bde at Laksham. By 9 December the division had captured Chandpur. It crossed the Meghna on 14 December and then pressed on to Dacca, where it reached on the 16th, just after 101 CZA. Further south a two-pronged attack was made on Chittagong. The northern hook was led by 83 Bde and the southern hook by the Kilo Force. The enemy surrendered on the 16th after a feeble resistance.

On 16 December at 1630 hrs, Lt Gen Niazi surrendered to Lt Gen Aurora with 93,000 regular and paramilitary men. War on the Eastern front ended in a complete victory for India.

except visual recognition and control by the detachment commander. With the regimental and brigade headquarters out of the loop and no dedicated communications, it was nothing short of a miracle that there were no incidents of fratricide.

The ADA troops were with the field formations till 8 December when they were all withdrawn as the formations raced towards Dacca with 101 Communication Zone beating the three corps to become 'First into Dacca'.

## MOVE WEST

The total dominance by the Indian Air Force meant that there was almost no requirement of AD artillery in the east though some of the critical establishments continued to be protected by ground-based air defences to cover for a possible 'sneak attack'.

The first to move West was 54 AD Battery of 19 AD Regiment that was partly airlifted on 4 December with the heavier loads being moved by train. It was followed by the withdrawal of troops of 28 AD Regiment from their tasks with 4 Corps on 6 December and the move of the regiment to Amritsar. 48 AD Regiment, having moved out from its tasks in the east, reached Bharatpur on 9 December, and was ready for the new tasks in Southern Command. 2nd Lt Chhetri, writing about his troop's move, mentions:[69]

> By the evening of 6 December, I got a message from BM Arty Bde to pack up the Ad troops and move back to Krishnanagar railway station. My four guns with field and mountain regiments too got the same message and they were asked to join me at the medium gun location.
>
> The convoy started at about ten o'clock on the night of 6 December 1971. We had to cover approximately 100 km. By 4 o'clock morning on 7 December, we reached the Krishnanagar railway station where a military police detachment guided us to the gun loading area in the railway station yard. Having loaded our guns, vehicles and stores, we were ready to move by two o'clock in the afternoon. I asked the station master about the destination but he told me. 'I do not know. I have to despatch you to the next station and the next station master knows about the next destination.'
>
> We reached Kanpur on 8 December at about five in the morning and after a brief halt, continued on our journey reaching Bharatpur by the evening. From here, we were to move by road to Gadra Road in the Barmer sector.

The move of other ADA troops was also carried out in a similar manner except for a selected few who moved by air. 25 AD Regiment started withdrawing its troops from the combat zone and the AF installations on 8 December and had a relatively faster redeployment as its subunits started deploying in the west from 11 December onwards.

47 AD Regiment was the other regiment to be moved from the Eastern to Southern Command, but as it moved out on 13 December only, it was not effective at its new location before the war ended.

The last to move out was 19 AD Regiment with its remaining two batteries and 46 AD Regiment that was moved out just before the ceasefire.

The two brigade headquarters were also moved out from the east with HQ 342 (Independent) AD Brigade moving out as early as 9 December and being re-located at Ludhiana on 14 December. HQ 312 (Independent) AD Brigade moved from Shillong on 8 December and set up the headquarters at Bharatpur on 15 December, taking over the responsibility of ADA units in Southern Command. These moves may have been seen to be necessary for better utilization of ADA resources but the late move meant that they were not avaialble for a large part and remained underutilsed.

The PAF largely remained bound to missions around Dacca for the entire duration except for a handful of close support missions against Indian troops including one at Akhaura on 4 December. This meant that the Indian AD regiments and batteries in the east, bar none, did not fire any round during the entire war. There were consequently no claims and no heroes this time around unlike during the previous war of 1965. All the five PAF aircraft lost in the air were to IAF fighters.[70]

The story on the other side was just the opposite. The IAF had been restrained during 1965 from carrying out any offensive missions. In December 1971, IAF carried out 2,033 sorties in the east including 390 on counter-air and 1,384 in offensive support and interdiction role.[71] It lost 19 aircraft in all – only three in air-to-air combat, six to accidents and ten to ground fire.

The air campaign by IAF was a sustained, relentless one that did not give any respite to Pakistani ADA but every raid was opposed in all earnest by the Pakistani AD gunners who put up a spirited opposition. In the end, 6th LAA Regiment had only one day's ammunition left at the time of ceasefire[72] but the regiment had delivered, destroying eight aircraft during the fourteen-day war.[73] It may have been the enemy, but in its conduct, there are lessons to be learnt by all AD gunners. As far as the Indian ADA was concerned, there was no PAF to contend with and no enemy to fire at. There were no kills to claim and no glory to be attained. In the end, it was just an endless wait.

## NOTES

1. Interview with Col M.C. Appanna.
2. S.N. Prasad and U.P. Thapliyal, *The India-Pakistan War of 1971: A History*, Natraj Publishers, New Delhi, 2014, pp. 353-4.
3. Jagan Mohan and Samir Chopra, *Eagles Over Bangladesh: The Indian Air Force in the 1971 Liberation War*, Harper Collins, New Delhi, 2013, pp. 59-63.
4. Ibid.
5. Prasad and Thapliyal, op. cit., p. 352
6. Pakistan carried out 'pre-emptive' strikes against Indian airbases and radars as part of its War Plan No. 6 during the 1965 war. Coupled with this was a Para drop to target select Indian airbases. The plan failed as most of the paratroopers were rounded up before they could reach their targets but the threat of a repeat of such an operation had made Indians overly cautious.
7. Air Mshl Inam-ul-Haq Khan, 'Saga of PAF in East Pakistan', *Defence Journal*, May 2009 and Kaiser Tufail, 'The Last Stand', *Aeronaut* accessed on 10 December 2019 at http://kaiser-aeronaut.blogspot.com/2012/10/the-last-stand-air-war-1971.html
8. Shaukat Riza, *Izzat-o-Iqbal, History of Pakistan Artillery 1947-1971*, Published by School of Artillery, Naushera, 1980, pp. 363-4.
9. Major General Sukhwant Singh, *The Transformation of Military Plan* (Book Excerpt: India's Wars Since Independence), *Indian Defence Review*, 16 December 2018 accessed on 8 February 2020 at http://www.indiandefencereview.com/spotlights/1971-war-the-transformation-of-military-plan/2/
10. Bangladesh was geographically divided into eleven areas known as sectors. Each sector had a sector commander who coordinated the military operations through sub-sector commanders. Sector 8 comprised the districts of Kushtia, Jessore, Khulna, Barisal, Faridpur and Patuakhali while Sector 9 covered the districts of Barisal and Patuakhali and parts of the district of Khulna and Faridpur.
11. Vice Admiral G.M. Hiranandani, *Transition to triumph, Indian Navy 1965-1975*, Spantech & Lancer, New Delhi, 2009, p. 139
12. Scott Gates and Kaushik Roy, *Unconventional Warfare in South Asia: Shadow Warriors and Counterinsurgency*, Routledge, New York, 2016, p. 119.
12. Hiranandani, op. cit., pp. 215-16.
13. Lt Gen J.F.R. Jacob, *Surrender at Dacca: Birth of a Nation,* Manohar, New Delhi, 1997, p. 91 and *An Odyssey in War and Peace*, Roli Books, New Delhi, 201, p. 102.
14. Hiranandani, op. cit., p. 168.
15. *History of Army Air Defence*, published by Directorate General of Army Air Defence, New Delhi, 2008, pp. 111-13.
16. Ibid. Also, Interview with Col Shivaji Chakarvarty who was the Adjutant of the 28 AD Regiment during the war.
17. Peter R. Kann, 'From a Dacca Hotel, Indo-Pakistan Conflict Resembles War

Movie: Reporters Clustered by Radios For News Remain in Dark', 6 December 1971. https://www.pulitzer.org/winners/peter-r-kann, accessed on 17 January 2020.

18. Maj. Gen. Lachhman Singh Lehl, *Victory in Bangladesh*, Natraj, Dehradun, 1991, p. 61.
19. Lt Gen J.F.R. Jacob, *An Odyssey in War and Peace*, Roli Books, New Delhi, 2001, p. 84.
20. Col Bhaskar Sarkar, *Outstanding Victories of the Indian Army, 1947-1971*, Lancer Publications, New Delhi, 2016, pp. 131-3 and Gaurav Pardeshi, 'Recollecting the Moments of 1971 War', *Desh Doot*, 23 May 2020 accessed on 16 June 2020 at https://www.deshdoot.com/deshdoot-times/blog-brief-interlude-with-an-enemy-prisoner-of-war-destined-to-become-chief-of-pakistan
21. Kaiser Tufail, *In the Ring and on its Feet: Pakistan Air Force in India-Pakistan War 1971*, Ferozsons, Lahore, 2018, p. 140 and Kaiser Tufail, *The Last Stand*, accessed on 10 December 2019 at http://kaiser-aeronaut.blogspot.com/2012/10/the-last-stand-air-war-1971.html
22. Abdul A.T.M. Wahab, *Mukti Bahini Wins Victory: Pak Military Oligarchy Divides Pakistan in 1971*, Colombia Prokashani, Dacca, 2004, p. 266
23. Ajit Apte, 'The Battle of Boyra', *Seniors Today*, 13 December 2019 accessed at https://seniorstoday.in/history/the-battle-of-boyra and Amrit Pal Singh, 'Revisiting the Battle of Garibpur, a Precursor to the 1971 Bangladesh Liberation War', *The Wire*, 16 December 2020, accessed at https://thewire.in/history/revisiting-battle-garibpur-precursor-bangladesh-liberation-war
24. Tufail, op. cit., p. 140 and Jagan Mohan and Samir Chopra, op. cit., p. 84.
25. Ajit Apte, 'The Battle of Boyra', *Seniors Today*, 13 December 2019.
26. Most of the accounts including martin Bowman's 'Cold War Jet Combat' erroneously mention four Sabres whereas there were only three. Martin Bowman, *Cold War Jet Combat: Air-to-Air Jet Fighter Operations*, Pen & Sword, Barnsley, 2016, p. 105 and Jagan and Chopra, op. cit., pp. 83-5.
27. Parvez Qureshi Mehdi went on to serve as the PAF Chief of Air Staff from 1997 to 2000 - During the 1999 Kargil War. Lt Gen H.S. Panag, 'How I captured and saved India's first prisoner of war in 1971', *The Print*, 4 December 2018, accessed on 26 March 2020 at https://theprint.in/opinion/how-i-captured-and-saved-indias-first-prisoner-of-war-in-1971/158246/
28. Jagan Mohan and Samir Chopra, op. cit., pp. 90-1.
29. Jacob, *An Odyssey in War and Peace*, p. 88 and Interview with Lt Col B.S. Chhetri who was the Command Post Officer at Krishnanagar.
30. Tufail, op. cit., p. 140.
31. Bowman, op. cit., p. 105.
32. This account is as per the regimental history but is not supported by any other source. The award of Mention-in-Despatches is noted at the Army Air Defence's official website accessed on 26 March 2020 at https://indianarmy.nic.in/Site/FormTemplete/frmTempSimple.aspx?MnId=Mn6qzXKyg/9O0iTIDnvFsA==

&ParentID=vwDk8FwZmA+Lu++Qx2E76Q==&flag=8CKP966uzg96kLov0aWdfQ==

33. Jagan and Chopra, pp. 108-9.
34. Siddiq Salik, *Witness to Surrender*, Oxford University Press, Karachi, 1978, p. 134.
35. Prasad and Thapliyal, op. cit., p. 356
36. The aircraft is wrongly claimed to be a Sukhoi in 'History of History of Pakistan Artillery 1947-1971' (Shaukat Riza, p. 365). See also, Jagan and Chopra, op. cit., p. 139.
37. Jagan and Chopra, op. cit., p. 140 and Riza, op. cit., p. 365.
38. Prasad and Thapliyal, op. cit., pp. 356-7, Lon O Nordeen, *Air Warfare in the Missile Age*, Smithsonian Books, 1985 pp. 163-4, and Jagan and Chopra, op. cit., pp. 150-1.
39. Citation for Da Costa's Vir Chakra can be accessed at 'Gallantry Awards' accessed at https://www.gallantryawards.gov.in/Awardee/flight-lieutenant-andre-rudolph-da-costa
40. Jagan Mohan and Chopra, op. cit., pp. 166-7 and Prasad and Thapliyal, op. cit., p. 359.
41. Jagan and Chopra, op. cit., p. 151.
42. Ibid.
43. Jagan and Chopra, op. cit., pp. 151-2.
44. Prasad and Thapliyal, op. cit., p. 356.
45. Ibid.
46. Air Vice Marshal Bishnoi, 'Thunder over Dacca', *Vayu Aerospace Review*, January 1997, accessed on 9 April 2020 at https://www.bharat-rakshak.com/IAF/history/1971war/1271-thunder-over-dacca.html#gsc.tab=0
47. Jagan Mohan and Chopra, op. cit., pp. 171-2.
48. Ibid., pp. 175-6.
49. Kulbir Singh Harnal, 'December Diary', *Bharat Rakshak*, 13 June 2017, accessed on 18 April 2019 at http://www.bharat-rakshak.com/IAF/History/1971War/1087-December-Diary.html#gsc.tab=0
50. Jagan and Chopra, op. cit., pp. 190-2.
51. Prasad and Thapliyal, op. cit., p. 357 and Air Vice Marshal Bishnoi, 'Thunder Over Dacca', *Vayu Aerospace Review*, January 1997.
52. Jagan and Chopra, op. cit., p. 193.
53. Prasad and Thapliyal, op. cit., p. 357.
54. Jagan and Chopra, op. cit., p. 193.
55. Ibid., pp. 209-10.
56. Air Vice Marshal Bishnoi, op. cit.
57. Prasad and Thapliyal, op. cit., p. 357.
58. Tiwary, op. cit., p. 152.
59. Shaukat Riza, op. cit., p. 366 .
60. Jagan and Chopra, op. cit., pp. 267-9.

61. Tayal was a test pilot later at the Aircraft and Systems Testing Establishment, Bangalore was awarded the Shaurya Chakra in 1977.
62. Jagan and Chopra, op. cit., pp. 275-6.
63. Ibid., pp. 279-82.
64. Hiranandani, op. cit., pp. 140-5 and Jagan and Chopra, op. cit., p. 299.
65. Jagan and Chopra, op. cit., pp. 307-8.
66. The SA-2 Squadron was not deployed at Baroda before 16/17 December. Prasad and Thapliyal, op. cit., p. 358.
67. Wing Commander Anil Ghosh, 'The Night Intruder: A Personal Tribute to the Canberras', *Bharat Rakshak*, 13 June 2017, accessed on 18 August 2020 at https://www.bharat-rakshak.com/IAF/history/1971war/1268-anil-ghosh.html#gsc.tab=0
68. B.S. Chhetri, *Meandering into Memories*, Purbayon Publication, Guwahati, 2020, pp. 83-5.
69. Ibid.
70. Prasad and Thapliyal, op. cit., pp. 367-8, Jagan and Chopra, op. cit., p. 387 and 'Pakistan Air Force Losses 1971 War', *Bharat Rakshak*, accessed on 18 August 2020 at http://www.bharat-rakshak.com/IAF/history/1971war/1289-pakistani-air-losses-of-the-1971-war-official-list.html#gsc.tab=0
71. Prasad and Thapliyal, op. cit., p. 367.
72. Ibid., p. 369.
73. Shaukat Riza, *Izzat-o-Iqbal: History of Pakistan Artillery 1947-1971*, Published by School of Artillery, Naushera, 1980, pp. 363-4.

CHAPTER 6

# Case West: Defending the Air Forces

Protection of air force assets remained a high priority for Indian ADA with over twenty AD batteries deployed in the west by India for protection of airfields alone. The deployment of Indian ADA on IAF bases and installations amounted to over half of its resources, and considering the deployment on strategic assets, the quantum of resources available for the field formations was much less than their requirements.

A change from the previous war was the induction of SA-2 surface-to-air missiles (SAM) by the IAF and, as with other IAF assets, India deployed AD troops for the protection of SAM sites as well. This was one of the earliest instances of deployment of ADA troops for the close defence of surface-to-air missile sites.[1]

The deployment of ADA units for the defence of air force bases and other installations was as follows:

| *Air Base* | *ADA Troops* | *Regiment* | *Remarks* |
|---|---|---|---|
| Leh | Troop | 151 AD Regiment | L/60 |
| Srinagar | Battery | 151 AD Regiment | L/60 |
| Jammu | Batteryless Troop | 128 AD Regiment (TA) | L/60 |
| Pathankot | Battery | 128 AD Regiment (TA) | L/60 |
| | Battery plus Troop | 27 AD Regiment | L/70 |
| | Troop | 26 AD Regiment | L/70 |
| | Troop | 140 AD Regiment (TA) | L/60 |
| Amritsar | Battery | 27 AD Regiment | L/70 |
| | Battery plus Troop | 49 AD Regiment | L/70 |
| | Battery | 105 AD Regiment (TA) | L/60 |
| Halwara | Battery | 104 AD Regiment (TA) | L/60 |
| | Battery | 26 AD Regiment | L/70 |

| | | | |
|---|---|---|---|
| Adampur | Troop | 26 AD Regiment | L/70 |
| Chandigarh | Troop | 144 AD Regiment (TA) | L/60 |
| Ambala | Battery | 126 AD Regiment (TA) | L/60 |
| Sirsa | Battery | 126 AD Regiment | L/60 |
| Palam | Battery | 144 AD Regiment (TA) | L/60 |
| Hindon | Battery | 144 AD Regiment (TA) | L/60 |
| Jodhpur | Battery | 127 AD Regiment (TA) | L/60 |
| Nal | Battery | 127 AD Regiment (TA) | L/60 |
| Jaisalmer | Battery | 129 AD Regiment (TA) | L/60 |
| Uttarlai | Battery | 129 AD Regiment | L/60 |
| | Troop | 103 AD Regiment (TA) | L/60 |
| Jamnagar | Troop | 129 AD Regiment (TA) | L/60 |
| Bhuj | Troop | 129 AD Regiment (TA) | L/60 |
| Agra | Battery | 103 AD Regiment (TA) | L/60 |
| Bareilly | Troop | 103 AD Regiment (TA) | L/60 |

Though the deployment of ADA resources was spread from Leh in the North to Jamnagar and Agra in the depth areas, it was not an even distribution and was biased towards defending the frontline bases of Halwara, Pathankot and Amritsar, with the two latter air bases provided over a regiment worth of ADA troops defending them. The ghost of 1965 was yet to be exorcised, after all.

Amongst the other assets, 230 SU at Amritsar was allotted a troop of 27 AD Regiment and an L/60 battery of 105 AD Regiment (TA). Similarly, the ADDC and SU at Barnala were allotted an L/60 battery of 104 AD Regiment (TA) and two L/70 Troops of 27 AD Regiment. The other SUs to be allotted ADA included SU, Nagrota, which was provided with a troop from 151 AD Regiment.

The deployment at most of the places went through smoothly though the deployment at 230 SU, Amritsar, was not without hiccups. 2nd Lt H.S. Sandhu, the troop commander of 27 AD Regiment was carrying out the reconnaissance to look for suitable site(s) for his guns and radars and found what appeared to be an ideal location. The only problem was that one of the gun positions was in the adjacent golf course and the deployment of the gun was opposed by the golfers. With no other suitable location available, the gun needed to be deployed at the selected site only but the golfers refused to budge. It was only after a personal intervention by Lt Gen K.P. Candeth, GOC-in-C, who visited the gun site and was briefed by Sandhu, that the gun was deployed at the selected location. The decision turned out to be the right one as the same gun shot down a PAF aircraft early on in the war.[2]

The ADA batteries were soon to be tested as the PAF launched Operation Chengiz Khan on 3 December. The PAF raids by Sabres and Mirages at dusk were closely followed by the second wave of strikes executed later in the night of 3/4 December by the B-57 Martins which came to be the mainstay of the night airfield bombing campaign. For this, No. 7 Squadron, PAF, was split up between Mianwali and Masroor, with ten and eight aircraft deployed at the two bases respectively. T-33s of No. 2 Squadron, PAF, was also planned to be used for strike missions, as were the odd C-130 in a bomber role.[3]

The details of the planned strikes were as follows:

| *Mission Serial* | *Target* | *Strike Aircraft* | *Munitions* | *Mission Pilots/ Navigators (*)* |
|---|---|---|---|---|
| 8 – 9 | Ambala Airfield | 2 B-57s | Bombs – Some with delay fusing | Wg Cdr Rais Rafi<br>Flt Lt Wasif Bokhari*<br>Wg Cdr Feroze Khan<br>Sqn Ldr Iftikhar Malik* |
| 10 | Agra Airfield | 2 B-57s | Bombs as above | Wg Cdr M. Yunus<br>Sqn Ldr W.D. Harney*<br>Wg Cdr Mazhar Amin<br>Flt Lt Nasim Khan* |
| 11 – 12 | Halwara Airfield | 2 B-57s | Bombs as above | Sqn Ldr Abdul Basit<br>Sqn Ldr G.A. Khan*<br>Flt Lt Iqbal Javed<br>Flt Lt G. Malik* |
| 13 | Amritsar Airfield | 1 B-57 | Bombs as above | Flt Lt Majid Javed/<br>Flt Lt M. Sarwar* |
| 14 | Pathankot Airfield | 1 B-57 | Bombs as above | Flt Lt Sultan Arshad<br>Sqn Ldr Qayamuddin* |

| | | | | |
|---|---|---|---|---|
| 15 | Srinagar Airfield | 1 C-130 | Bombs as above | Gp Capt M.A. Qayyum<br>Wg Cdr Nisar Yunus<br>Sqn Ldr Chaudhry Rizwan* |
| 16 | Sirsa Airfield | 1 B-57 | Bombs as above | Sqn Ldr Y.H. Alvi<br>Flt Lt S.M. Ali Shah* |
| 17 | Jaisalmer Airfield | 1 B-57 | Bombs as above | Sqn Ldr Ishfaq Qureshi<br>Sqn Ldr S.A. Khan* |
| 18 | Bikaner Airfield | 1 B-57 | Bombs as above | Sqn Ldr Baharul Haq<br>Sqn Ldr Ansar Ahmed* |
| 19 – 20 | Jodhpur Airfield | 2 B-57s | Bombs as above | Sqn Ldr Sohail Mansur<br>Sqn Ldr Aurangzeb Khan*<br>Sqn Ldr Aftab Zia<br>Flt Lt Zulfiqar Ahmed* |
| 21 | Jamnagar Airfield | 1 B-57 | Bombs as above | Flt Lt Ejaz Azam<br>Wg Cdr Murtaza Malik* |
| 22 | Uttarlai Airfield | 1 B-57 | Bombs as above | Wg Cdr M Akhtar<br>Flt Lt A.B. Subhani* |
| 23-26 | Uttarlai Airfield | 4 T-33s | Guns | Sqn Ldr Qureshi<br>Sqn Ldr A. Choudhry<br>Sqn Ldr Akhtar<br>Flt Lt Bashir |

These strikes were spread wider and deeper than the first wave with airfields targeted from Pathankot in the north to Jamnagar in the south and Agra in the depths. A total of eleven IAF airfields: seven in the north, viz., Agra, Ambala, Amritsar, Bikaner, Halwara, Pathankot, and Sirsa, and four in the south, viz., Jaisalmer, Jamnagar, Jodhpur and Uttarlai, were raided by the B-57s, with the T-33s striking Uttarlai.[4] The result of the raids was mixed.

As Pathankot and Amritsar had already been attacked earlier on by the Mirages and Sabres, the AD artillery troops were on a high alert and did not allow any damage to be inflicted on the runways or other installations. Halwara was raided by a pair of B-57s, dropping four bombs each that caused some damage to the runway. ACM Lal mentions:[5] 'The B-57 dropped eight bombs, three of which landed on the runway making two major craters.'

One of the two SA-2 Squadrons deployed to defend the airbase fired two missiles but failed to score any kills. The ADA deployed included both radar-controlled L/70 and the manually operated L/60s. They had been given 'guns tight' as the air raid sirens sounded even though there were no friendlies in the air. The guns were permitted to open up much later and as they tried to engage the two B-57s that were already overhead, they failed to hit either of them. Wing Commander T.K. Sen, who was the COO, writes in his blog:[6]

> Barnala was giving me a running commentary about the possible threat. The two aircraft were approaching from the south-west. Flying low, it bypassed Halwara and headed for Ludhiana. By now, my Visual Observation Posts and Mobile Observation Posts had come alive. The first local call came from the civil defence control room Ludhiana.
>
> At 2338 hours, Barnala declared Halwara as threatened and I sounded the air raid siren.
>
> I ordered 'guns tight' for the AD Arty units. I was now under a threat. No friendly aircraft were airborne within my airspace. It should have been logical, therefore, to place the guns free. However, it is a well-known fact that under actual attack, the gunners tend to fire indiscriminately. This fire discloses the location of the defended area and an attacking aircraft is aided in making last-minute corrections to his bombing run. I did not incline disclosing the location of the airfield. The airfield was well camouflaged and concealed. Night visibility was not very high. Hence, 'guns tight' was a better option.
>
> Both the SAGW units had also been alerted and their search radar had picked up the hostile tracks. However, the aircraft was too low and were outside the kill zone of both the units. I placed the missiles under the state of 'sky is clear' which empowered them to engage any flying object within their kill zone.
>
> By 2342 hours, the hostile aircraft entered my defended zone. They obviously had not spotted the airfield. Soon they realized that they had missed the airfield. They turned around and went back to Ludhiana. All this drama was being picked up by all my sensors deployed.
>
> After reaching Ludhiana a second time, the aircraft turned around and

followed the canal once again and approached the airfield from the east. They continued circumnavigating the airfield and at one stage turned quite hard to align themselves with Runway 13. The first aircraft came overhead at about 20 degrees to the runway and dropped its bombs. He was so low that his bombs did not explode. The L-60 guns opened up and the L-70s followed. The aircraft remained very low, below the missile cover and made a getaway.

The second aircraft managed the turn a little better. He was more aligned with the runway, albeit still not quite along it. Just before reaching the circuit zone, he gained a little height to drop his bombs properly. He was successful in his attempt and his bombs dropped and exploded. He had however exposed himself to one of the SA-2 squadrons. Unfortunately for us, the units fumbled a little, and the aircraft exited the kill zone of this unit before the missiles could be launched. In the getaway, the intruder turned west and tried to dive low. In this manoeuvre, he exposed himself to the kill zone of the other unit for a very brief while. The unit launched a salvo of three missiles. The intruder was driving hard to get close to the ground, but one of the three missiles exploded on proximity warning. The aircraft disappeared from the missile's radar. The missile crew was exuberant and wanted to claim a kill. I was unable to accept the claim until the wreckage of the intruder was found and identified.

The B-57 that was claimed to have been engaged by the SA-2 of No. 64 Squadron, IAF, was being flown by Sqn Ldrs A. Basit and Ghulam Ahmed Khan of 7 Sqn PAF out of Mianwali. The SA-2 squadron was deployed right next to the canal near Jagraon village, a few miles from Halwara. Aircraftman George Abraham of the squadron recollects:[7]

On the day of the bombing, my flight sergeant, Sgt Murthy (the chief) was in the RMA cabin. Sgt Murthy was Mentioned in Despatch. We fired the salvo. No idea who made the Kill, but PAF never tried to bomb Halwara again. The ack ack firing and bomb explosion are still in my memory.

The raid on Sirsa was partly a success for the PAF as the B-57 flown by Sqn Ldr Yusuf Alvi with his navigator Flt Lt Muhammad Ali managed to hit the runway with at least two bombs hitting their mark.[8]

Part of the runway was hit. ... It was enough though to make the runway unserviceable for the night ... the bombs had time-delayed fuses and kept on exploding at intervals till dawn delaying clearance and repair work.

What is disappointing is that the airbase was defended by an ADA battery but the ADDC had ordered 'Guns Tight' even though it was known that B-57 was 'not ours'. It was only after the raid was over that the AD guns were asked to open up but by this time the B-57 was well outside the range of the guns and their fire proved to be ineffective. The PAF had succeeded in delaying the use of Sirsa airfield at least and had done so without any casualty or loss.[9] The failure to engage the PAF B-57 was mainly due to the confusion that prevailed at the base. An eyewitness account describes the confusion that prevailed at Sirsa:[10]

> It was the evening of 4 Dec. 1971 and I was on duty at the improvised makeshift 15 ft high Air Traffic Control Tower. Around 2030 hrs. I had only two MiG from the base airborne, which were expected to rejoin around 2100 hrs. I was admiring the crescent moon in an absolutely cloudless sky, when, in the background of the Moon I spotted the outline of an aircraft at quite a distance. Fixing my gaze, I reconfirmed within myself that what I saw was right. Sure enough, the aircraft kept closing in and, instinctively, I said that it had to be an enemy aircraft approaching from the 'West' as no other known traffic was expected from that direction.
>
> I promptly informed the base commander, late Air Cmde K.K. Malik, then Wg Cdr on the hotline. In utter disbelief, he uttered, 'Impossible!' (as no radar had informed us about any intruder). Keeping my gaze fixed at the aircraft I directed all the ATC personnel except the ops clerk, to take shelter in the respective trenches, and time and again kept reporting to the base cdr about the approaching aircraft urging him to act.
>
> Lo and behold at 2033-34 hrs. the intruder arrived overhead and very cunningly dropped delay fuse bombs during this inbound run, one of which fell a few yards away from my tower. Soon afterwards, the first bomb explosion was heard, and a few seconds later I saw the same aircraft going back in the same direction from where it had approached, dropping many more live bombs.
>
> As the first bomb exploded, the hotline buzzed and the voice in excitement asked, 'what is it', I said, 'the same aircraft on its way back after completing his mission' and he exclaimed 'Oh sh...'. And almost simultaneously, I saw the most beautiful sight. The entire airfield was covered with the tracer bullets fired by the ack-ack guns as if by a magic wand the day had dawned. The entire airfield was momentarily illuminated but in vain. The brave Pak pilot had managed to get away unharmed, and I watched helplessly. The MiGs meanwhile were contacted and were diverted to Hindon as at that point of time, the damage to the R/W was not known.
>
> To our utter relief and amazement, not a single of the 16 bombs had fallen on the R/W or the taxi track. the base cdr must have heaved a much bigger sigh of relief on hearing from me! The silence of the night was broken 3-4 times when the delay fuse bombs kept exploding.

At Uttarlai, the lone PAF B-57 came with its navigation lights on and was taken as 'friendly' and not engaged giving it a free pass during the first run. As the aircraft came in for the second circuit to deliver its bombs, it had switched off its lights. It was then that the ack-ack opened up. The bombs fell on one side of the runway leaving the rest of it intact but the debris did fall onto the runway. The PAF raided the airbase two more times during the night and the debris could be cleared only by the morning with the first Gnat taking off at 0630 hours.[11]

The PAF raid at Agra was another case of a near-miss as the bombs did not hit the runway and fell alongside. Wing Commander Anil Ghosh of No. 35 Squadron, IAF, was stationed at Agra and was slated to carry out a strike the same night. His Canberra was lined up for take-off when PAF B-57s came calling:[12]

> We got going as per plan and I taxied out at 1900 hrs. Three aircraft were behind me. All loaded up but with minimum fuel. We were to top up at our staging base at Ambala. I was about to line up when a PAF B-57 came calling. I give the PAF pilot full marks. He made a shallow-glide pass with his guns blazing while dropping six bombs on the runway. The full moon was behind him just on the horizon. Unfortunately, the runway was camouflaged. He planted his bombs like buttons on what he thought was the runway. The grass had just been cut on the shoulders and in the moonlight, it was more prominent than the runway. All his bombs missed by just 10 yards. Only one bomb landed at the intersection of 05/23 throwing up some debris on one lane.

No. 74 Squadron, IAF, was one of the SA-2 squadrons and was deployed near Agra. It picked up a track and, after it had been processed, the track was declared hostile at about 2030 hours. A single SA-2 was fired at the target but with no apparent results as the B-57 escaped unscathed. The same unit fired more missiles the next day morning, on 4 December, at targets that appeared to be balloons.[13]

The two B-57s managed to carry out the raid in Agra without any mishap, but one of them, flown by Flt Lt Mazhar Bukhari with Flt Lt Nasim Khan as navigator, was mistaken as 'hostile' by the Pakistani AA gunners at Rafiqui, and it was fortunate that it was not hit by the AA barrage.[14]

The PAF raids against Indian airbases had only partly succeeded as most of the runways remained undamaged, though they were covered with debris from the bombs that fell nearby. The main damage that these raids caused was a delay in the use of runways at some airfields. In that, PAF could take consolation that they managed to partly disrupt the IAF's operations for some time.

Having faced the PAF raids, it was now time for the IAF to strike back. The lead was taken by the IAF Canberras that mounted twenty-three attacks on Pakistani airfields at Murid, Mianwali, Sargodha, Chander, Risalwala, Shorkot and Masroor and claimed to have scored direct hits on runways and installations.[15]

The Canberras from Agra included those of No. 35 Squadron, IAF, who carried out retaliatory strikes that night. There were no losses but some of the Canberras had near-misses. Wing Commander Ghosh recalls:[16]

> Our TOT got revised and re-revised. I finally taxied out from a pen at 0200 hrs. in total blackout conditions. My target was 300 nm inside Pakistan. It was payback time -- at last.
>
> On the first night, our planning cell pundits simply forgot that there was a difference between IST and PST. We maintained our TOT but much to our discomfort we found that dawn was breaking when still 100 nm on the wrong side of the IB. Our best defence was darkness. When exposed to daylight, we could only descend to tree-top level and belt at 450 knots on the return leg. This planning error proved fatal for a B(I)66 and a B(I)58 that night. While it was not clear what really happened, chances are both aircraft (from Agra) went into sand dunes in Rajasthan, when chased by enemy fighters. A few others had close shaves. One pilot reported a brilliant flash behind him and his aircraft yawed viciously to the right. He thought he had been hit by an AA missile. He landed at Sirsa on asymmetric power. After checks on landing, he found a piece of metallic wire on his fin. He had inadvertently flown under a power line. That night we also lost one Canberra from JBCU. He was a confirmed kill downed near Sakesar by a PAF Mirage III.

No. 5 Squadron, IAF, was also stationed at Agra and was tasked with the raid at Sargodha. The *Tuskers* were among the first to receive orders to retaliate and were airborne ten minutes before midnight the same night. The Pakistani account of the Indian Canberras describes the raid as follows:[17]

> The first raid came at 2335 hours (PST) on 3 December.
>
> At 1900 hours, 2/Lt Abbas Bokhari of 12 Light Anti-Aircraft Battery (5 Light Anti-Aircraft Regiment) received orders, 'Guns high and tight'. The order implied that guns were to be loaded but not to be fired unless given the orders 'Guns Free'. Abbas's troop consisted of two 37 mm (twin) and two 14.5 mm

(quadruple) guns. The guns were not equipped with night firing devices but Lt Col Shuja Haider, the commanding officer of 5 LAA Regiment, had positioned the guns to fire over the main runway at an elevation of 30 degrees. Col Shuja, along with Lt Naveed Anwar, had positioned himself on top of a killer control tower. From this precarious vantage point, he controlled the firing.

At midnight 3 December, a warning of the hostile aircraft was received along with the order 'guns free'. Five minutes later the sound of approaching aircraft came over the airfield. The guns fired a barrage. The Indian aircraft ran the gauntlet and dropped their bombs. A thousand pounder bomb landed near the runway but not near enough the runway to cause any damage. Two aircraft were hit. There were three more raids that night. The first two were at a low level and the last was at a high level, which gave a chance to 52 Heavy AA regiment to fire its guns. One Su-7 was hit.

The next morning on 4 December, the aircraft strength at the forward airbases at Pathankot, Amritsar and Halwara was augmented by twenty-six fighter bombers. At dawn, Su-7s, Hunters, MiGs and HF-24s struck Pak airbases and radar stations. The first counter-air missions were carried out by Su-7s with MiG-21s as top cover. No. 26 Squadron struck at Chander, No. 32 on Shorkot, No. 101 on Pasrur and No. 222 on Risalewala airbases. Loaded with two M-62 bombs each, the Su-7s swept in at extremely low lever and, in face of intense anti-aircraft fire, managed to deposit bombs on the runways.[18]

No. 32 Squadron had been given two targets – Sargodha and Shorkot. Leading the raid on Sargodha was Wing Commander H.S. Mangat, the squadron's commanding officer, while the strike on Shorkot was led by Sqn Leader V.K. Bhatia. In the words of Bhatia,[19]

I could spot the IP (initial point) approaching dead ahead. A quick NATO turn for the final run-in to the target at the correct/exact location. It was a sheer delight to find the airfield sprawled below and ahead of us. I rolled into the attack over my No. 3 and No. 4 heading for the nearest ORP pen, where I spotted a Sabre parked just outside the pen.

Sathaye, my No. 2 who was flying 300 metres behind me, spotted two Canberras that were being refuelled. Closing in to the correct range, I fired the first salvo of rockets at the Sabre and the pens at the other ORP. We recovered in a perfect pre-planned formation, flew for a few kilometres clearing each other's tail and then turned around for the second attack.

The second attack was equally successful. It appeared that we had taken the enemy completely by surprise as not a single shell of ack-ack was fired at us. We made a getaway by engaging the afterburners and accelerating to 1100 kmph. The skies behind us were clear of enemy aircraft, and we headed for home. After an uneventful return flight, we landed at Amritsar at about 1200 hours. The strike turned out to be the most successful one with one Canberra with a bowser and three Sabres as confirmed kills.

But all strikes were not so lucky as the day's operations cost the IAF thirteen aircraft, including seven during counter-air operations. Of these seven, two Su-7s were lost to AAA. Flt Lt M.S. Grewal of No. 32 Squadron, IAF, was one of them and was part of the strike package led by Bhatia. He had carried out a sortie in the morning as a member of a four-aircraft strike mission over the PAF airfield at Shorkot Road and had destroyed one PAF aircraft on the ground. He was on another strike mission in the evening, against the same airfield, when his aircraft was hit by AA fire and crashed. In Bhatia's words:[20]

A suggested TOT of 1430 hours was thus turned down and we were now slotted in for simultaneous dusk strikes at Shorkot Road and Sargodha, respectively. As I lost height in the dive I could see the tracer shells approaching the closer till the entire cockpit was engulfed by the exploding HE. Ignoring the ack-ack, I trained the gun-sight on the mouth of a blast pen where I could see the outline of an aircraft.

However, it was difficult to clearly spot the target in the gathering dusk. I fired a salvo of rockets and pulled out. During the runout, I noticed that my No. 3 (Tambay) was without his wingman – Mally. Continuous R/T calls elicited no response from him. All the same, I turned around for the second attack. Once again, we were enveloped by the ack-ack; however, all three aircraft recovered from the attack without any damage. During recovery and getaway, the formation noticed a ball of fire close to the airfield fence.

In all probability (later confirmed) Mally's aircraft was downed by the enemy ack-ack during the first attack.

While we were happy with another successful strike having claimed three aircraft on the ground, (all probable as gun cameras were ineffective in the fading light at the time of the attack) we missed gallant Mally Grewal who was shot down during the raid. (Later it was revealed that Mally had ejected successfully and was taken prisoner of war by the PAF.)

The AA guns that had failed to score any hits during the first strike had managed to score a kill in the very next strike. Grewal recounts his experience:[21]

This was my second mission of the day. I was in the process of pitching up to get into a dive when I lost control because my hydraulics got hit. The Sukhoi

> seat, K-30, is marvellous. It worked flawlessly and I landed on the ground, with no injuries, but was thereafter beaten up by villagers. But fortunately, I was very close to an airfield. The (Pakistani) air force people came, they rescued me from the villagers. They handcuffed me, blindfolded me, marched me to the airfield. Within 10-15 minutes, I was put in a jeep and overnight driven to Rawalpindi.

The other losses of the day included three Hunters and one Su-7 shot down by Pak aircraft and one Su-7 of No. 101 Squadron destroyed in an accident at Adampur. The Su-7's tyre burst on take-off, as a result of which the aircraft veered off the runway and was destroyed when the ordnance exploded. Also, a Hunter was hit by AA fire but it managed to return to base. Wing Commander Cecil Parker of No. 20 Squadron, IAF, who led the raid at Peshawar, had his Hunter hit by sporadic ground fire as he was near the border on his way back. It was never confirmed whether the AA fire was from the Pakistani troops or their own forces. One of the IAF aircraft was reportedly fired at by its own AA guns, but luckily no damage was done.[22]

Pakistan, on its part, claimed to have destroyed or damaged 48 Indian aircraft on 4 December. It included the claim of a Hunter at Peshawar.[23]

The Peshawar airbase was defended by 300 LAA Battery, PA. Havildar Mohammad Hussain was one of the 40 mm AA gun detachment commanders who engaged the Hunters as they approached the airbase. Though wounded in the strafing by the Hunters, Hussain continued engaging the Hunter and claimed to have scored a direct hit. The stricken Hunter reportedly hit the ground near Bara.[24]

There were other acts of gallantry by the Pak AAA personnel during the day as well. One of them was at Masroor near Karachi which was one of the targets for the IAF. As the IAF aircraft came over the base, they were met by AA fire but, as PAF aircraft were already airborne and in the process of engaging the IAF aircraft, the Pak Sector Control ordered 'hold fire' to the AAA. However, some of the Pak AA guns continued to fire. With the line communications to the guns damaged in the raid, there was no way to pass the orders to the detachments still firing. Signalman Mohammad Aslam of 74 Composite LAA Regiment ran out of the command post to warn the guns. He was severely wounded in the air raid but managed to stop the fire. He was awarded the Sitara-e-Jur'at posthumously.[25]

Even as Pakistan claimed to have shot down one Indian aircraft by AA fire at Karachi, it had its share of snafus during the day. An F-6 of No. 23 Squadron, PAF, had a narrow escape over Risalewala from friendly fire. The incident occurred as Indian Su-7s were raiding Risalewala.[26]

> Around 0930 hrs., as F-6s for the day's sixth mission was taxiing out of their pens, an air raid warning was sounded. A mission abort was ordered and loudspeakers relayed instructions for everyone to take cover.
>
> Then the raid was over as suddenly as it had started, and the AAA died down too as if heralding an all-clear.
>
> Shortly thereafter, a scramble was ordered for the next pair but confusion reigned as the taxiway had been blocked by the F-6s of the previous aborted mission. Over-ruling the Air Traffic Control's somewhat confused recall message, Latif checked if his No. 2 was also taxiing out. Hearing no response, he decided to take off alone.
>
> As the attackers (Indian Su-7S) approached the airfield, Latif positioned behind one of them. Firing all three of his cannons, Latif waited for some fireworks. Noticing that the aircraft was still flying unharmed, he fired another long burst till all his ammunition was exhausted. Just as he was expecting his quarry to blow up, he felt a huge thud. Thinking that he had been hit by the other Su-7, he broke right and then reversed left but found no one in the rear quarters. Checking for damage, he found that the left missile was not there and the launcher was shattered. The AAA shells bursting in puffs all around the airfield confirmed his suspicion that he had taken a 'friendly' hit, but luckily the aircraft was fully under control.

Latif not only managed to shoot down a Su-7, piloted by Flt Lt Harvinder Singh of Halwara-based No. 222 Squadron, which went down near Rurala railway station, but was also able to get back without any further mishap.

Having used the B-57s in the night, PAF returned on 4 December morning with strikes by F-86s and Mirages. During these raids, Indian ADA did well as PAF came calling on Amritsar, Pathankot and Srinagar airfields. PAF struck Srinagar early morning at 0420 hours but the F-86s, faced with the intense AA fire, jettisoned their bombs close to Mirgund village to the south of the airfield and aborted the mission. The airfield was again raided by a lone Mirage III at 1400 hours that failed to cause any damage.[27]

The PAF had missed hitting Pathankot airfield on 3 December with

Sqn Ldr Aftab Alam's formation missing the target and dropping the bombs in the general vicinity of the airfield. Alam's formation returned the next day and claim to have found its mark on the runway and taxi tracks.[28] As per Indian records, four PAF aircraft made a low-level single pass attack and the ADA was able to hit one of them, ripping off its wingtip. The damaged Mirage, however, managed to get back.

The Amritsar SU was always high on the priority list and was given more than its fair share of attention by the PAF during the opening days of the war. After the failed attempt on 3 December, it was expected that PAF would return and try to put the radar off the air. The first raid came early morning at about 0715 hours IST by two F-104s, but the strike could not be carried out as Starfighters were bounced by two Gnats, making the Starfighters abandon the raid. Tufail mentions:[29]

> The radar at Amritsar, which had come back on a few hours after being attacked the previous evening, warranted a revisit. Sqn Ldr Rasheed Bhatti along with Flt Lt Amanullah Khan took off on the morning of 4 December (0650 hrs.) and was able to spot the radar antenna despite the winter haze. As Bhatti was diving for the attack, Amanullah yelled that there was a Gnat behind him and gave a call to exit. Bhatti jettisoned his drop tanks, lit up the afterburner and sped away.

The PAF made another attempt to raid the radar but again failed to carry out the strike as a pair of Su-7s were orbiting overhead. One of the Su-7s managed to get behind the Starfighter flown by Sqn Ldr Amjad Hussain. Sensing trouble, the Starfighters disengaged and sneaked away. Attempt two of the day had also failed PAF.[30]

A Pakistani Starfighter was claimed by Lance Naik Shreepati Singh of 26 AD Regiment who was commander of a Superfladermaus radar detachment. L/Nk Singh was awarded the ADA's first gallantry award, a Vir Chakra, for the same. His citation reads:[31]

> Lance Naik Shreepati Singh was the commander of a radar unit deployed for the protection of a radar installation in the western sector. On 4 December 1971, the enemy attacked this installation with F-104 Starfighters. Lance Naik Shreepati Singh showed grit and determination in laying the radar tracker visually on the enemy aircraft attacking his radar set. Though seriously wounded, he continued to track the aircraft till it was shot down.
>
> In this action, Lance Naik Shreepati Singh displayed gallantry, determination and devotion to duty of high order.

An unfortunate mishap occurred at the Halwara airbase on the morning of 4 December. Two B-57s had raided the airbase on the night of 3-4 December and offloaded four bombs each. The bombs dropped by one of the B-57 had turned out to be 'duds' and not exploded. But it was not clear if they were in fact duds or the bombs were fitted with delayed-action fuses. A search was made to locate the four 'duds'. Of these four, only the tail section of a fractured bomb complete with an unexploded fuse and a few lumps of explosives yet to fall off from the casing was found. It was kept under a tree in the open with the site marked to prevent anyone from stumbling over it.[32]

On the morning of 4 December, as Major V.D. Sharma, the battery commander of an AD battery, was going around his battery and was near the site when the bomb exploded injuring Major Sharma. Wing Commander T.K. Sen, who was the COO of the airbase, writes about the accident in his blog:[33]

> I was perhaps 20 rungs up the ladder when a big explosion took place below me. I got a hot blast. Dust billowed up to cut off my vision. My first impression was that the airfield has been struck. I continued climbing and reached the top. I took over the RT and confirmed that indeed there had been no strike over the airfield and no intruders had arrived. I handed the RT back to the kids and climbed down to the ground.
>
> On the ground there was a lot of confusion. Slowly I pieced the story together. Major Sharma and Major Surjit were still near the tail cone when the fuse blew. Major Sharma had his toe blown off. Major Surjit received a full blast of shrapnel into his legs. (Ultimately one of his legs had to be amputated). One fragment sliced through the Gopal's aorta. He died on the spot. One small fragment embedded into the shoulder-blade of an Airfield Safety Operator (AFSO) sergeant.
>
> A medical party came and took the injured away. Another party came and took control of the remains of Gopal. One of my boys from the BADC called out that the first wave of strike aircraft was about to return. I looked down at my wristwatch. It was not yet ten in the morning of 4 December 1971.

Major V.D. Sharma was awarded the Shaurya Chakra.[34]

It was not that all VPs were defended successfully by the ADA as the PAF raid carried out by a pair of F-104s led by Sqn Ldr Amjad Hussain managed to damage the radar antenna at Barnala, putting the radar out of action for nearly twelve hours.[35] The parts required for the repairs were not available locally and the delay in getting them from Delhi would have kept the radar off the air for that much longer. In order to ensure that the radar got back on the air at the earliest, Sqn Ldr Shreepad Prabhudesai, the chief technical officer, decided to have the parts fabricated locally. He recalls:[36]

> It would have taken a long time to fetch the parts back if they were sent to Delhi for repairs, so I decided to bestow my faith in the Punjabi people whom I always considered to be good mechanics and had the parts fabricated locally. They gave their 100 per cent and the radar was made functional by evening.

On 4 December itself, the first ADA battery reached from the east. It was a battery of 19 AD Regiment that was partly airlifted from Hashimara, using twelve An-12 and five C-119 Packet aircraft and was deployed at Agra. The battery coordinated the air defence layout with the L/60 battery already deployed there. As the radars could not be brought by air, the L/70 guns were to operate on local power control (LPC). It was not too soon that the AD battery was deployed as the PAF raided the airfield again on the night of 4/5 December and put the runway out of commission temporarily, resulting in the cancellation of some Canberra missions.[37]

The absence of SFM radars had adversely affected the effectiveness of the air defences. The other airbases raided by PAF during the night were Pathankot, Amritsar and Sirsa. No damage was caused during the raids and a PAF B-57 was hit by AD guns at Amritsar but it managed to escape.[38]

The IAF soon returned the compliment, carrying out thirty-five missions during the night. The raid on Masroor was particularly important as it was the main PAF airbase in their southern sector, responsible for all air defence missions, and any damage to it would have an effect not only on the overall PAF effort in the south but also on the air defence of Karachi. However, there is an interesting story about the grounding of the PAF at Masroor. Writing about his interaction with Air Cmde K.K. Badhwar who led the Canberras during the raid on Masroor (Karachi), ACM Lal notes:[39]

> The damage inflicted on the airfields by Badhwar's estimate was minimal. He believes that there was one lucky strike on a culvert at Masroor, on the very first night, which prevented some ten Pakistani B-57 aircraft from crossing over to the main runway and, thereby, rendering them inactive for a while. Apart from this,

he does not believe any damage was inflicted, though intelligence reports later indicated that a hangar was destroyed and with it an electronic countermeasure aircraft that had been parked inside it.

During these raids, two Canberras were lost during the night of 4/5 December. The first was lost as a Canberra piloted by Flt Lt L.M. Sasoon with Flt Lt R.M. Advani as navigator, was shot down by a Mirage III over Sargodha while the second was shot down by Pakistani AA artillery at Masroor. The Canberras were followed by Su-7s and MiG-21s for raids on Pakistani airfields during the night.[40]

The day of 5 December was an eventful one with the PAF mounting six raids on Indian airbases. The first raid came early morning, before daybreak, at Srinagar. At 0330 hours, a ground observation post (OP) picked up four aircraft headed towards Srinagar and passed on the warning to the ADA unit at the airfield. The aircraft could have managed to evade detection but for the moonlight that helped the OP pick up the Sabres. At the airfield, the warning was soon followed by the air raid sirens going off and that gave enough time for the gunners to be ready to take on the raiders. However, the orders issued for the AD guns were 'hold fire'. The reason behind them likely was to avoid giving out the layout of the runway.

Four Sabres came in pairs, flying low, followed by a C-130 Hercules. Some of the AD guns opened up as the PAF aircraft were overhead. Brigadier (then 2nd Lieutenant) Deepak Sharma was the troop commander of the AD Troop at Srinagar. He recalls:[41]

That night, they (PAF) brought in a C-130 Hercules. The air raid warning sirens had gone off but we got the orders 'hold fire' just as the sound of aircraft came that meant that the aircraft was already overhead.

Though the guns were not supposed to fire, some guns on the near end of the runway opened up. This must have confused the PAF pilots as they mistook the alignment of the runway and dropped the bombs in a nearby orchard. The C-130 was overhead for some time but could not get the correct alignment of the runway and just offloaded the bombs. They were of World War II vintage and most of them did not explode. One of the bombs fell just 50 yds. from one of our gun positions. It had USAF marking – one was marked '1945'. The bombs were lying there for days on end, and the last of them could be collected and defused only after the war was over.

The PAF returned at 0715 hours with four F-86 Sabres, managing to crater a part of the runway and get back without any damage. This was followed by another raid just minutes after the Sabres had left. At 0730 hours, five Sabres came in for a low-level attack. Like earlier, they were met by intense fire from the AD guns. The AD battery suffered a casualty as Gunner Armugam was killed in the strafing by the PAF Sabres.[42]

> Gunner Armugam was No 4 of a gun in 'B' Troop that was deployed next to the base ops (Base Operations Room) near the control tower though it (the control tower) was not being used during ops. The gun was one of the guns in the inner ring, about 20 yards from the ATC.
>
> As one of the Sabres dived onto the ATC tower, it was almost as if there were torrential rains of rounds coming down. Armugam's gun being near the tower was also subjected to some very heavy strafing. He was hit in the head. He continued to feed the ammunition even as he was bleeding and he refused to leave his post.
>
> Turning towards Gun No. 1, he said, 'Today we will not leave them. We will get them.'

Gunner Armugam succumbed soon after the raid was over and was awarded the Vir Chakra (posthumous) for his act of gallantry. His citation reading as follows:[43]

> On 5 December 1971, while manning an air defence gun deployed for the protection of Srinagar airfield, Gunner Armugam directed the fire of his gun accurately against an attack by nine enemy Sabre jet aircraft and shot down one enemy aircraft. Though seriously wounded, he continued to fire his gun till he succumbed to his injuries.

In this action, Gunner Armugam displayed gallantry and professional skill of a high order.

Besides some damage to the runway, the raid on Srinagar also resulted in the loss of a helicopter that was flying near the airfield that was shot down and both pilots seriously injured.[44]

Continuing its efforts to put down the Amritsar radar, PAF carried out a raid at about 1405 hours. Two F1-4 Starfighters came from the southwest at a height of about 200 ft. According to PAF records, it was a 'radar bursting project'.[45] 105 AD Regiment notes that 'before the aircraft could bomb the radar, the guns of 105 AD Regiment opened up and the aircraft flew towards Amritsar airfield'. Colonel (then 2$^{nd}$ Lieutenant) H.S. Sandhu who was the troop commander at the SU, recalls the raid:[46]

Two Starfighters came to the SU but instead of the radar they first came on to one of the AD sections. They tried to strafe the section but missed the guns. However, the SFM radar of the section was hit. Our guns continued to fire and hit one of the Starfighters in the tail. The stricken F-104 turned and went back.

It appeared as if the raid was over but the second Starfighter came back again targeting the guns. We had changed over to a manual mode of firing by now and as the Starfighter pulled up, its underbelly was exposed, presenting a good target. The guns did not miss and hit the Starfighter. The aircraft turned away and went towards the airfield.

The AD units deployed at the airfield claimed to have hit one F-104 Starfighter each. The first was claimed by Havildar Ramaswamy Chettiar of 27 AD Regiment. He was awarded the Vir Chakra, his citation reading as follows:[47]

Havildar (GD) Thapasi Chettiar Ramaswamy Chettiar was commanding a detachment of an air defence battery guarding the Amritsar airfield. On 5 December 1971, the enemy fighter aircraft raided Amritsar airfield on several occasions. Havildar Chettiar directed the fire of his gun accurately and shot down an enemy Starfighter and was instrumental in the capture of the enemy pilot.

Throughout, Havildar Chettiar displayed courage and professional skill of a high order.

Havildar Ajmer Singh of 105 AD Regiment shot down the second F-104 Starfighter and was also awarded the Vir Chakra.[48]

On 5 December 1971, while commanding a detachment of an air defence battery deployed for the protection of Amritsar airfield, Havildar Ajmer Singh directed the fire of his gun accurately and shot down one of the two Pakistani Starfighter aircraft raiding the airfield. In this action, Havildar Ajmer Singh displayed gallantry and professional skill of a high order.

The official history, and also the PAF, records the loss of only one Starfighter over Amritsar on 5 December. It was the specially equipped F-104 piloted by Sqn Ldr Amjad Hussain that was shot down. Hussain managed to eject and, as he landed, the AD gunners at the airfield rushed to take him prisoner, but Hussain refused to surrender and threatened to use his pistol. It was Major S.R. Prothi, the battery commander from 27 AD Regiment, who persuaded him not to resist and give himself up.[49]

Tufail erroneously notes that the Starfighter was shot down while strafing 230 SU and not the airfield:[50]

The Amritsar radar busting project came to a halt at midday on 5 December, when the specially-equipped F-104 flown by Sqn Ldr Amjad Hussain was shot down by AAA while carrying out a strafing pass over the radar. Amjad ejected and was hauled up as a PoW.

This 'kill' had many firsts – the first loss of Starfighter to be acknowledged by the PAF, the first kill of the war by a TA regiment and the first PAF pilot taken prisoner of war (PoW) after the formal declaration of war.[51]

Pathankot was raided by three Mirage IIIs in the afternoon but these failed to cause any damage. As it was repeatedly being targeted by Mirages, a detachment of four MiG-21s was shifted to Pathankot to augment the existing AD set-up.[52]

The IAF counter-air operations during the day were restricted to attacks on PAF airfields that were being used to support its army in the north. As a result, some aircraft were pulled back by PAF from Murid, Chander and Risalewala. The IAF raid on Sakesar proved to be a costly affair as two Hunters were lost to PAF during the raid even as one of the antennas of radar was hit and the radar put off for some time. A Su-7 was also shot down during the day while attacking the same target. The radar was defended by 20 LAA Battery of 53 LAA Regiment, PA, which claimed to have 'hit all the offending aircraft' though it failed to shoot down any aircraft.[53]

The third strike by No. 32 Squadron, IAF, on Shorkot Road also proved to be a costly affair as an Su-7 was shot down by Pak AAA. Owing to the shortage of drop tanks, this strike was to be carried out by two Su-7s only, with Flt Lt V.V. Tambay flying as No. 2 to Sqn Leader V.K. Bhatia. The strike was planned with TOT at midday on the assumption that the AA defences would be lax at that time. Bhatia describes the third, and last, strike against Shorkot Road:[54]

At pull up point (PUP) I eased up over and into my No. 2 to go for the attack. At the top of the dive, I suddenly noticed seven MiG-19S (F-6) stacked up on a tarmac far below and ahead of me. However, as I came closer, I realized that these must be dummy aircraft, which in fact they were. I diverted my attack onto a hangar firing a salvo of rockets. After the attack, I picked up Tambay who had gone in for the loop area. Tambay was lagging behind and, when I gave the 180° hard turn, I found that he landed up way ahead of me.

Realising that we were close to our PUP for the second attack, I quickly changed tactics and asked Tambay to go into attack first. I saw his aircraft shining like a silver streak as he pitched up for the dive. I pulled up behind him scanning the area to pick up a juicy target. The ack-ack must have been firing feverishly at us; however, in the bright sunlight, it was difficult to spot the tracer shells. The realisation of the presence of a hundred plus anti-aircraft guns which the enemy had deployed at Shorkot Road was driven home with sickening reality when Tambay's aircraft (B-839) suddenly began to spew out thick black smoke from its belly.

I immediately told Tambay on the R/T that he had been hit. Concentrating on his aircraft which by then had entered into a steep dive, I noticed that the smoke trail had thickened. I shouted on the R/T 'Tambay eject'. However, I was greeted with total silence. I must have given eight to nine calls for him to eject without eliciting any response from Tambay. The aircraft crashed near the runway edge in a huge ball of fire and smoke.

Blinded with fury and tears, I unleashed my rockets into the ORP area and then turned hard. I had descended so low that I could see the trees, which were in the vicinity of the airfield, coming up at me. Cursing myself, I steadied the aircraft and continued with the turn in the getaway direction.

The last strike over Shorkot Road was over.

The Pakistani AA defences had not missed the opportunity provided to them and made the best of it. Having the TOT at midday on a bright afternoon had proven to be a costly lapse for the IAF. Though IAF records two losses from two raids over Shorkot Road, the 264 LAA Battery of 75 LAA Regiment at Shorkot Road claimed three kills.[55]

The difference in the claims notwithstanding, there were no more raids on Shorkot Road. Tambay, the last man to be shot down over Shorkot Road, reportedly managed to eject and was taken prisoner. As per unconfirmed reports, Jayant Jatar, an Indian cricket board official who was related to Tambay, met him at an undisclosed location in 1989.[56]

The night of 5/6 December was rather eventful with PAF B-57s carrying out raids over multiple targets, mostly operating singly. PAF also used its C-130 for bombing missions over lightly defended targets during the night. A total of nine raids were executed during the night with the targets ranging from Pathankot, Amritsar, Adampur in the north to Nal and Bhuj in the southern sector but no serious damage was caused except at Okha where the oil depot there was hit and set on fire.[57]

This was a major success for the PAF as the previous raids had failed to cause any serious damage to any of the targets but the PAF also suffered a great setback as it lost three B-57s to ADA during the night. The first loss was over Amritsar as four B-57s came in at about 2215 hours IST – two each for Amritsar airfield and 230 SU. The troop of the 27 AD Regiment was able to shoot down one of the PAF B-57s. The pilot, Flt Lt Javed Iqbal, and the navigator, Flt Lt G.M. Malik, baled out but Javed's parachute did not open and he died as he hit the ground. Malik was injured in the fall and, though the AD gunners tried to take him to the Military hospital, he died enroute.[58]

The detachment commander, Havildar Gopala Krishnan, was awarded the Vir Chakra.[59]

> Havildar Gopala Krishnan was carrying out the dual duties of section commander and No. 1 of an air defence gun deployed for the protection of the air force signal unit at Amritsar. On 5 December 1971, enemy Canberras raided this station. Havildar Gopala Krishnan directed the fire of his gun in an accurate manner and shot down an enemy aircraft and was instrumental in the capture of an enemy navigator.
>
> In this action, Havildar Gopala Krishnan displayed gallantry and professional skill of high order.

The second loss of a PAF B-57 was over Jamnagar. The airfield was defended by an L/60 battery of 129 AD Regiment (TA). The regiment had been deployed at the same airfield in the 1965 war, too, and was familiar with the layout and the approaches normally taken by PAF. The night with an almost full moon offered good visibility not only to the PAF raiders but also to the AD gunners who otherwise had no fire control radar to help them track the aircraft.

As the B-57 came overhead, the AD guns opened up and scored a direct hit on the B-57 piloted by Squadron Leader Khusro with Sqn Leader Peter Christy as the navigator. Both had joined Pakistan International Airlines (PIA) but when war became imminent had re-joined their squadron. Unfortunately for them, this was to be their last missions as the fire of AD guns of 129 AD Regiment (TA) proved to be deadly, totally destroying their aircraft and not giving them time to eject. Both Khusro and Christy were officially declared to be 'missing in action' by the PAF. For their 'courage and devotion to duty' they were awarded the Sitara-e-Jur'at.[60]

The third 'kill' was over Bhuj when a B-57 of the day was shot down by 129 AD Regiment. Squadron Leader Ishfaq Hameed Qureshi, pilot of the ill-fated B-57 (Tail No. 3943), had also joined PIA and reverted back to PAF just before the war. As he was carrying out his bombing run over Bhuj airfield, his aircraft was hit by the AA fire of the L/60 guns of 129 AD Regiment (TA).[61] It was, creditable performance by the TA gunners to have shot down two B-57s in one night and using manually operated AD guns of Second World War vintage at that.

For the Indian ADA, it was a satisfying performance with three B-57s shot down in one night but, surprisingly, these kills find no mention in the official history of the war with a mention of a B-57 being hit by the AD fire at Amritsar airfield.[62]

During the night, the IAF Canberras revisited Shorkot, Murid, Mianwali and Masroor airfields. Of special satisfaction was the raid on Masroor as the Canberras scored hits on the bulk petroleum installation (BPI) and the airfield infrastructure in face of heavy AA fire. But tragically, No. 35 Squadron, IAF, lost a Canberra over Masroor (Karachi) to Pak AA fire.

The strike was planned during dusk to have an element of surprise and reduce the chances of detection by the enemy. Flt Lt Sandal, guided by his navigator Flt Lt K.S. Nanda reached over the target and successfully carried out the attack and managed to destroy one blast pen. However, the attack exposed the aircraft to Pakistani AD guns and the aircraft came under heavy firing from them. The aircraft took direct hits and crashed in the enemy territory.[63]

The fighting on 6 December saw a change for the previous pattern of PAF operations as they refrained from attacking Indian airbases during the daytime. Mirages and F-86 Sabres attacked Amritsar and Srinagar airfields as dusk fell. Each raid was made up of six aircraft and managed to cause 'slight damage' to the runways though they were soon repaired and put back into service.[64]

The first raid on IAF surface-to-air missile sites was carried out on 6 December. These sites were protected by troops from 104, 126 and 144 AD Regiments (TA) equipped with L/60 guns. Three of the missile sites were attacked on the night of 6/7 December but the AD guns managed to protect the SAM sites, with the PAF inaccurately dropping bombs, away from the missile sites.

The night raids by PAF continued as before, with as many as ten raids against the airfields at Amritsar and Pathankot and the radar at Amritsar. PAF had some satisfactory results at Pathankot as it was able to damage a missile preparation shed and hit one aircraft servicing hangar. One Vampire aircraft inside the hangar was partially damaged. The missile preparation shed was not seriously damaged and the fire was put out before it could spread to the missile storage sheds.[65]

Four PAF aircraft attacked Ambala airfield about 1815 hours with the aircraft dropping flares in the first run and, as the flares illuminated the targets on the airfield, the PAF aircraft dropped the bombs in the second run. But the illumination by the flares helped the AD gunners in picking up targets and they claimed one aircraft to have been hit. In face of the AD fire, the PAF was not able to deliver the bombs accurately, and the airfield remained unharmed. Some of the newspapers reported erroneously that two PAF aircraft had been shot down and that 'wreckage was sighted near Rajpura'.[66] The raid carried out by four Mirages at the Chandigarh airfield was also successfully repelled by the L/60 guns of 144 AD Regiment (TA) as was the raid on Bhuj airfield by a lone B-57.[67]

On 6 December, twenty-two counter-attack sorties were carried out by the IAF against PAF bases to prevent them from interfering with the ground operations. Chander and Risalewala were targeted during the day while Sargodha and Chaklala were attacked during the early hours of the night of 6/7 December. With the demand for close support now increasing, IAF reduced the counter-air operations to focus on close air support (CAS) tasks. During the day on 7 December, IAF raided only Risalewala and Chander. The Hunters from Pathankot raided Murid and Kohat airfields. No serious damage was inflicted and the IAF aircraft came back without any major incident with the Pak AAA proving to be ineffective in causing any damage.[68]

Though incessant PAF raids on 230 SU had been repelled successfully to date, the frequency of these raids had put a strain on the ADA detachments as they continuously manned the guns. The AD troop of 27 AD Regiment had a narrow escape on 7 December while engaging in a PAF raid. All guns were firing when there were blasts on three of the guns. A round had prematurely exploded in each of the three of the guns, blowing off the front, top and bottom covers. The guns were damaged but, thankfully, the crew manning all the three guns were not injured. On checking, it was found that the ammunition used on the three guns was of the same lot. Lt Sandhu, the troop commander, immediately ordered for ammunition of the same lot to be segregated to avoid any further accident. But the problem was that he was now short of an L/70 gun and that would have adversely affected the ADA efficacy at the SU. He approached his battery commander (BC) to check if a gun could be shifted from the other troop at the airfield but, given the intensity of PAF raids, it was not a workable option for his BC. The regimental headquarters, in turn, informed that it could shift one gun but it would take 5 to 6 days. This was too long a delay and Sandhu decided to get the covers fabricated from a local workshop. Col Sandhu recalls the incident:[62]

I took the broken parts to a local railways workshop and asked the foreman if he could fabricate the same parts. I was not disappointed as he, with the typical 'never say no' attitude of Punjabis, assured me that the parts will be as good as the original, if not better. The parts were ready in three hours. But it was not the end of the problem. I had to pay Rs. 250/- for the parts and I did not have that much money on me. Remember, those days the pay of a 2$^{nd}$ Lt was Rs. 300/- per month!

I could not ask the regimental headquarters for the money, as there was no chance in hell that an 'official' sanction would have been given to me to get the parts fabricated locally. I told the foreman about my predicament and he gallantly refused to take any money. 'How can I take money from you. I thought it would be the *sarkar* that would be paying, hence asked for Rs. 250.

But I could have not paid him and gave him all that I could pay at that time. It was Rs. 50/- and I paid by cheque and took a receipt, hoping someday I would be reimbursed that amount.

The next thing was to check if the same would work, without any damage or injury to the gun or the crew. I took the parts and had them fitted under my personal supervision. Then I took permission from the CO of the SU to check my guns by firing in the air. After getting the permission, I loaded one round in the first gun. I then asked the crew to get away to a distance and only then I fired. The gun worked fine and there was no mishap. I repeated the process, of firing a single round, three times, and then put the gun at 'auto'. Now I fired three short bursts of three rounds each. It was perfect firing with no stoppages or mishaps. The gun was as good as new.

I repeated the process with the other two guns and it took me about five hours to check all the guns. They were all fine and ready to take on the next raid.

I reported to my battery commander that all guns were OK but, as things are, the matter was reported to the commanding officer. Promptly came a message from the regimental headquarters, 'Do not use these guns. Hold Fire' I was told that the guns were not to be fired till such time they had been inspected by a team of officers from the regimental headquarters comprising of the commanding officer. The OC, Workshop, and a representative from the brigade headquarters would be arriving the next day (8 December).

As things turned out, there was a raid by the PAF in the night and two of the guns were used to engage the PAF aircraft, firing 50-60 rounds.

The next morning, when the team of officers arrived, I was surprised to find that the brigade commander had himself decided to come visiting.

I informed the CO that two of the guns had been used in the night and had fired about 60 rounds each. More importantly, both were OK. On hearing this, the brigade commander told the CO and said, 'Saldhana (Lt Col H.W. Saldhana, the CO), if the guns have fired and are OK, it is fine by me. I think there is no problem if they are used normally.' Then turning towards me, he said, 'I am really proud of you. God bless you' and he hugged me.

The OC, SU, was also present during the visit and he said to Col Saldhana, 'I want to do something for the young man.' Before the CO could say anything, the brigade commander told him, 'Leave it to me. I will be glad to do the needful.'

The guns continued to be used throughout and there was never any problem with them, even when used with the radar in radar power control (RPC) mode.

Col H.S. Sandhu was awarded the Sena Medal but the story did not end with the visit of the brigade commander. It was followed by the visit of the mobile ammunition repair section (MARS) to check the ammunition. The ordnance officer wanted to check the entire lot by firing the suspect ammunition from all the guns. Sandhu refused as he did not want to take the risk. After much discussion, it was decided to fire three rounds from a single gun. But as the first round was fired, the same fault occurred and the gun was damaged. Lt Sandhu had to get the parts fabricated again and they were found to work fine with no problems, all through the operations. The MARS team, rather reluctantly, agreed to backload the suspect ammunition without any further firing.

Meanwhile, the night campaign of PAF continued unabated. Uttarlai was raided thrice during the night and the AD guns could not prevent the PAF from causing damage to the runway, though it was not serious. The raids on Pathankot were more of a nuisance as PAF raided the airfield eight times during the night, each raid by a solitary aircraft. The battery of 128 AD Regiment did not miss out on this repeat opportunity and, all the while preventing any damage to the airfield, the vintage L/60 guns shot down one F-86. Hav. Kans Raj of 128 Air Defence Regiment was awarded the Vir Chakra for his act of gallantry.[70]

> On 7 December 1971, Lance Havildar (GD) Kans Raj was performing the duties of Gunner No. 1 of an air defence gun deployed for the protection of an airfield. During an enemy air raid, he directed the fire of his gun accurately and shot down one enemy aircraft. In this action, Lance Havildar (GD) Kans Raj displayed gallantry and professional skill of a high order.

An early morning raid by a B-57 on Amritsar airfield was repulsed by the ADA. As Prasad put it, 'the B-57 that overflew Amritsar was chased away by the AA fire'. It was already the morning of 8 December.[71] It was an eventful day as the IAF achieved its biggest success in the counter-air operations during the war when it destroyed five F-86 Sabres on the ground at Murid during the raid by the Hunters of 20 Squadron.

Murid lies about 120 km inside Pakistan but has a vulnerability that a surprise attack can be launched against it from the north-easterly direction as the raiders can exploit the route from Pathankot to nestle against the Parmandal range, before swinging in from Naushahra-Rajauri side and then home on to Murid. To counter this susceptibility, PAF usually had F-86Fs from No. 15 Squadron providing CAP but all the defensive measures including the AD guns deployed at the airfield proved to be of no use.

The mission was led by Sqn Leader R.N. Bharadwaj with Flying Officer V.K. Heble, Flying Officer B.C. Karambuya and Flt Lt A.L. Deoskar caught the PAF by surprise and scored IAF's single biggest 'kill'. Karambuya recalls:[72]

> We were a four-aircraft formation. Aircraft 1 and 2 went ahead on schedule. Aircraft 3 and 4 were asked to delay their attack by a minute and a half. There was a lot of ack ack fire in the sky. We broke radio silence and the lead aircraft told me 'I just clobbered a four-engine aircraft in the pen'.

The *History of Pakistan Artillery 1947-1971* acknowledges the loss of the Sabres and also mentions that there was no damage inflicted on the IAF Hunters.[73]

On 8 December five of our own aircraft were lined up for taking off when caught by a low-level enemy attack. There had been no early warning and the hostile aircraft got away with a score of five.

The other missions during the day included PR sorties launched by the IAF to try and locate a Pakistani radar believed to be in the Lahore airfield. Also, Su-7s of TACDE raided Risalewala and lost one aircraft. The raid had been launched in the afternoon by two Su-7s and, as they were exiting after attacking the airfield, two F-6s of No. 23 Squadron, PAF, that were on a patrol, were vectored on to the Sukhois. Wg Cdr S.M.H. Hashmi caught up with one of the aircraft, about ten miles east of the airfield, and let off a Sidewinder at the straggler. The missile homed in on the Sukhoi and hit the aircraft with the Su-7 exploding above the tree-tops.[74]

In the pursuit for the second Su-7, Hashmi reportedly shot down his wingman Flt Lt Afzal Jamal Siddiqui instead in a case of mistaken identity as Hashmi took the F-6 to be an Indian Sukhoi. The official PAF version, however, claims that Siddiqui was shot down by 'own ground fire'. He was awarded the Sitara-i-Basalat with his citation reading as thus:[75]

Flight Lieutenant Afzal Jamal Siddiqui displayed outstanding keenness, enthusiasm and aggressiveness during the 1971 war right till the time he was shot down and killed by our own ground fire, while chasing an enemy Su-7 aircraft on 8 December 1971. By then he had flown six operational missions. His cheerful, bold and selfless attitude contributed largely to the high morale of his fellow pilots and inspired them to fight the enemy with greater tenacity. For his spirited and aggressive approach towards operational commitments, his sustained display of courage and enthusiasm in the air and on the ground, he has been awarded the Sitara-i-Basalat.

Counter air operations during the night by IAF were restricted to the Karachi area with the airfield at Drigh Road and the oil storage tanks at Karachi harbour targeted by Canberras.

Pakistan Air Force carried out four raids on 9 December. The first was at 0950 hours at Srinagar as four F-86 Sabres raided the airfield and managed to hit the runway in face of stiff AA fire from the gunners of 151 AD Regiment. The bombs caused six small craters on the runway which were repaired by nightfall. The raid on Pathankot was even less successful as the six PAF Mirages that raided the airfield failed to cause any damage.

The PAF raid on Pathankot was carried out in the afternoon. The regimental records note that the Mirages carried out strafing only and were accompanied by a B-57 that dropped delayed-action bombs. The AD guns claimed to have downed a B-57 and Naib Subedar Rati Ram of 26 AD Regiment was awarded the Sena Medal for the same. No wreckage of the B-57 was, however, found or the kill confirmed by other sources.[76]

PAF again tried to target the Indian SAM sites as two B-57s raided one of the sites twice in the night, but the only casualties were civilians of a nearby village. It was suspected that the PAF aircraft were being guided by some agents and a search was launched to apprehend them but no suspect was caught.

The Indian counter-air campaign was again low key on 9 December with Western Air Command focusing on CAS, particularly in the Chhamb sector. To prevent the PAF from interfering with Indian ground operations, the IAF attacked Chander and Risalewala airfields to try and keep PAF grounded. With a total of twenty-two counter-air sorties launched during the day, IAF also attacked the Hyderabad, Nawabshah and Jacobabad airfields. Jacobabad was defended by two batteries of the 58 LAA Regiment and the official history of Pakistan artillery notes that 'there was little activity over Jacobabad'.[77] Even the Indian records do not mention any serious damage caused over the airfields in south Pakistan.

An HF-24 was lost to Pakistani AAA during the raid on Hyderabad. This was the third and last loss of an HF-24 to AAA, the previous two having occurred during close support missions. Sqn Ldr A.V. Kamat managed to eject and was injured in the fall. He was taken prisoner.[78]

The PAF carried out night raids on Amritsar and Pathankot but without any luck. One B-57 'tried to attack Agra'. It was picked up by the radar at the airfield and the AD guns were alerted of the intruder. The lone B-57 tried to weave his way through the tracers streaking across his path. The AD guns claimed to have hit the B-57, damaging one engine, but the B-57 managed to get back. The regimental records of the 19 AD Regiment mention that an aircraft crash was reported by a nearby railway station master and the wreckage was found and claimed by the regiment, but this crash does not find mention in any official record. A lone B-57 attacked Ambala airfield at about 0045 hours, dropping the bombs in a single low-level pass and failing to cause any damage.[79]

On 10 December, one troop of 25 AD Regiment was deployed at Srinagar airfield. This troop had been moved from the east and was now to reinforce the ADA defences at Srinagar. Pathankot was again raided by PAF and it managed to cause three craters on the runway but missed the two Hunters that were about to take off. No hits or kills were claimed by the AD gunners. The Amritsar airfield was attacked during the night as the PAF targeted the control tower, dropping four bombs, but the damage was light. One Mirage was claimed by the ADA gunners but the kill was never confirmed. Uttarlai was also targeted by the PAF but without any success.[80]

For the first time, there was no counter-air operation by the IAF during the day but the low-key PAF effort against its own ground troops was an indicator that the earlier counter-air missions had borne fruit.

PAF carried out a few counter-airstrikes on 11 December and during the raid by two F-104s at Uttarlai, IAF lost an aircraft on the ground for the first time as the defences were caught off guard. One of the two HF-24 about to take off were hit and though the pilot, Sqn Ldr M.S. Jatar managed to escape, the aircraft was destroyed.[81] Srinagar, Amritsar and Jammu were also raided by PAF during the day and the AD gunners claimed to have shot down an F-86 Sabre over Amritsar but the same was never confirmed.

One of the tasks of IAF for 11 December was to try and locate a PAF radar that was suspected to be located near Zafarwal. Another radar at Walton airfield near Lahore had also not been located by the IAF and a PR mission was launched to locate the same. The IAF suspected that the radar at Walton was being used to track and intercept IAF aircraft operating from Amritsar. It was a case of 'Hunt for Fish Oil' as PAF had been trying to locate and destroy the radar at Amritsar. The Indian efforts also ended in a similar fate as the radars remained elusive.[82]

Pathankot remained a prime target for PAF and the increased activity of Mirages was becoming a cause of concern, as the Gnats were found to be ineffective in intercepting the Mirages. To strengthen the air defences at Pathankot, seven MiG-21s were shifted from Chandigarh to Pathankot on 12 December. In another redeployment, four MiGs were shifted from Hindon to Uttarlai where they replaced the Gnats. This was prompted by the use of F-104s by PAF during its raids on Uttarlai and the inability of the Gnats to take on the Starfighters.[83]

Srinagar was another airfield that continued to be targeted, as five F-86s attacked the airfield at 1128 hours causing five craters in the runway. The craters were repaired within an hour and it did not delay operations for long.

The main mission of the day for the IAF was a strike by MiGs of No. 47 Squadron, IAF, against the PAF FPS-20 radar at Badin. It was one of the two high-level radars covering the PAF's southern AD sector, the second being a P-35 radar at Malir. The Badin radar had been attacked earlier on 4 December by IAF and had suffered serious damage with the aerial head and other vital components destroyed, along with extensive damage inflicted on the powerhouse and fuel stores. The radar was recovered, with degraded performance, after a day. On 12 December, two MiGs from Jamnagar first carried out a PR mission of the radar complex and, later at 1242 hours, four MiGs attacked the radar with bombs. The result of the raid led by Wing Commander H.S. Gill, however, could not be ascertained, but it was decided to pay the radar a revisit the next day. Apparently, the bombs had not damaged much.[84]

PAF attacked the frontline airfields at Jammu, Pathankot and Amritsar but the airfields remained operational. IAF, on its part, carried out seventeen counter-air missions during the day including on Talhar and Badin. Two of the three Hunters that attacked Talhar were shot down by Pakistani F-86. The IAF, too, suffered a loss during the raid on the Badin radar complex as a MiG was shot down by AA guns. The raid was again carried out by No. 47 Squadron, IAF, with Wing Commander H.S. Gill.

No. 47 Squadron had carried out a strike in the morning using 57 mm rockets against the underground ops room and the communication centre in which one MiG had been hit by the AA fire and suffered some damage. During debrief, it was decided that the more powerful S-24 rockets would be used in the next mission, but, before the aircraft could be loaded with the new ammunition, the

Western Air Command ordered the squadron to carry out one more urgent strike. The second attack was carried out by Sqn Ldr Viney Kapila and Gill with Flt Lt Boparai and Flt Lt B.B. Soni as an escort. After Kapila and Gill had attacked the radar complex, Gill decided to make one last lone pass over the complex and it was then that his aircraft got hit by the AA fire. It was not clear if Gill was able to eject or not with the initial accounts only mentioning that his aircraft was shot down. He was awarded the Vir Chakra.[85]

PAF launched six raids against Indian airfields on 14 December, two by day against Pathankot and Jammu, and four by night against Pathankot and Amritsar, all raids being carried out by a single aircraft. The main action of the day was, however, at Srinagar as it was raided by four PAF Sabres. Flying Officer Nirmaljit Singh Sekhon of No. 18 Squadron, IAF, was on the runway when the PAF Sabres attacked. At great personal risk, he took off, even as the runway was under attack and engaged the Sabres against all odds. He shot down one Sabre and set another on fire before he was shot down.

Kaiser Tufail wrote about Sekhon that he 'turned out to be a hard nut to crack' and that 'his was a commendable effort indeed, as he had kept the field single-handedly to the very end'. Sekhon was awarded the Param Vir Chakra, posthumously, the only aviator to be so honoured.[86]

Brigadier Deepak Sharma, the ADA troop commander at Srinagar, recalls Sekhon:[87]

> I remember Sekhon well as my Troop was at the far end and we would often chat as the pilots waited at the ORP. Just two days before that fateful day, Sekhon had ferried a Gnat from Amritsar and I met him as he landed. He had brought home-cooked paranthas for me. Handing them over, he said, 'Deepak, I have been enjoying the dosas made by your boys. Today, I have brought these for you.'
>
> Sekhon was a simple, down-to-earth guy and it was really sad that we lost him that day. He was a real braveheart.

During the PAF raid on Jammu, the AD gunners claimed to have hit a Mirage III. With the war almost winding down, PAF launched only three raids during the day with just one against an airfield. One Vampire was hit on the ground inside a blast pen at Srinagar.[88]

The IAF operations were low key during the day with just one strike against a Pakistani airfield at Pasrur with four Su-7s using S-24 rockets. A photo-recce of the Gujarat airfield was also carried out.

Srinagar continued to be targeted with a PAF raid in the afternoon on 16 December that killed five civilians and damaged the runway. The nearby airfield at Avantipur was also attacked but it was not damaged. During the night of 16/17 December, the radar at Amritsar was again attacked as a lone B-57 dropped eight bombs. They fell just 200 yards from the radar site but no damage was caused.

On 17 December, the IAF attacked the airfield at Skardu for the first time. This was a unique mission with the IAF using three Canberras and one An-12 cub transport aircraft for the raid. The Cub proved to be very accurate. This was amongst the last of missions by either side as the war came to an end at 2000 hours on 17 December with the acceptance of the ceasefire offer by Pakistan.

## NOTES

1. The SA-2 was first used during the Vietnam war and as the India-Pakistan war of 1971 was being fought, the SA-2 continued to be used by the Viet Cong against the United States. The Viet Cong also deployed AA guns near their missile sites but it was done as part of overall AA defences and not for the defence of the SA-2 sites.
2. Interview with Colonel H.S. Sandhu.
3. Tufail, *In the Ring and on its Feet,* pp. 55-7 and Sultan M. Hali, 'B-57 The Intrepid Bomber of PAF', *Defence Journal,* http://www.defencejournal.com/may99/b-57.htm, accessed on 4 October 2019.
4. Prasad and Thapliyal, op. cit., pp. 212-13.
5. Lal, *My Years with the IAF*, p. 249.
6. Wg Cdr, T.K. Sen, *Hectic Days at Halwara-4: The Enemy Shows Up*, accessed on 4 October 2019 at https://tkstales.wordpress.com/2010/04/04/hectic-days-in-halwara-4-the-enemy-shows-up/
7. Anchit Gupta & Jagan Pillarisetti, 'The S-75 Dvina: India's First Surface to Air Guided Weapon', *Bharat Rakshak,* 19 October 2018 accessed on 16 July 2020 at http://www.bharat-rakshak.com/IAF/aircraft/past/949-s75-dvina-sagw.html#gsc.tab=0
8. Tufail, *In the Ring and on its Feet*, p. 57 and Lal, op. cit., p. 270.
9. Lal, op. cit., p. 270.
10. Wg Cdr Divakar Chaudhri, 'Sirsa's War', *Bharat Rakshak,* 23 August 2011 accessed on 17 June 2020 at http://bharat-rakshak.com/IAF/History/1971War/1095-Sirsa-War.html#gsc.tab=0
11. Lal, op. cit., p. 287.
12. Wg Cdr Anil 'Tootsie' Ghosh, 'Night Intruder: A Personal Tribute to the Canberra', *Bharat Rakshak,* 13 June 2017 accessed on 17 June 2020 at http://

www.bharat-rakshak.com/IAF/history/1971war/1268-anil-ghosh.html#gsc.tab=0

13. Anchit Gupta & Jagan Pillarisetti, 'The S-75 Dvina: India's First Surface to Air Guided Weapon', *Bharat Rakshak*, 19 October 2018, accessed on 16 July 2020 at http://www.bharat-rakshak.com/IAF/aircraft/past/949-s75-dvina-sagw.html#gsc.tab=0
14. Tufail, *In the Ring and on its Feet*, p. 56.
15. Prasad and Thapliyal, op. cit., pp. 213-14.
16. Wg Cdr Anil 'Tootsie' Ghosh, op. cit.
17. Shaukat Riza, *History of Pakistani Artillery 1947-1971*, pp. 454-5.
18. Prasad and Thapliyal, op. cit., pp. 214-15.
19. Air Marshal V.K. Bhatia, 'Shorkot Road Attack', *Bharat Rakshak*, 02 April 2015 accessed on 2 March 2020 at http://www.bharat-rakshak.com/IAF/history/1971war/1280-vinod-bhatia.html#gsc.tab=0
20. Ibid.
21. Shekhar Gupta, 'Two Indian Air Force Prisoners of War on their Audacious Escape Plan from a Rawalpindi Jail in 1971', *The Print*, 15 December 2017, accessed on 7 March 2020 at https://theprint.in/opinion/indian-prisoners-of-war-escape-plan-pakistan-1971/22727/
22. Martin Bowman, *Cold War Jet Combat: Air-to-Air Jet Fighter Operations 1950-1972*, Pen & Sword, Barnsley, 2016, p. 98.
23. The Hunter was hit by AA fire but it was not destroyed and it managed to reach back to base. Prasad and Thapliyal, op. cit., pp. 214-15.
24. This was just an exaggerated claim and is not corroborated by any other evidence. The reported wreckage was also never found. Shaukat Riza, *History of Pakistani Artillery 1947-1971*, p. 453.
25. Riza, op. cit., p. 457.
26. Kaiser Tufail, 'F-6 at War', *Defence Journal*, 31 October 2009, accessed on 11 April 2020 at http://kaiser-aeronaut.blogspot.com/2009/10/f-6s-at-war.html
27. Prasad and Thapliyal, op. cit., pp. 214-15.
28. Tufail, *In the Ring and on its Feet*, p. 57.
29. Ibid., p. 60.
30. Ibid.
31. Citation for Lance Naik Shreepati Singh's Vir Chakra can be accessed at 'Gallantry Awards', Ministry of Defence Government of India website https://www.gallantryawards.gov.in/Awardee/shreepati-singh
32. Wg Cdr T.K. Sen, *Hectic Days in Halwara-6: The 'Thing' Explodes*, 10 April 2010, accessed on 25 July 2020 at https://tkstales.wordpress.com/2010/04/10/hectic-days-in-halwara-6-the-thing-explodes/
33. Ibid.
34. Citation for Maj V.D. Sharma can be accessed at https://www.gallantryawards.gov.in/awardee/2058
35. Prasad and Thapliyal, op. cit., p. 213.
36. 'The Goan Who Repaired Radars', *The Herald*, 29 May 2016, accessed on 17

July 2020 at https://www.heraldgoa.in/Review/Goa-Social/The-Goan-who-repaired-radars/102459

37. Prasad and Thapliyal, op. cit., p. 213.
38. Ibid., p. 214.
39. Lal, op. cit., p. 295.
40. Prasad and Thapliyal, op. cit., p. 214.
41. Interview with Brigadier Deepak Sharma.
42. Ibid.
43. The Kill is not acknowledged by PAF as it denied losing any Sabre over Srinagar on 5 December nor is it mentioned in the semi-official '*The India Pakistan War of 1971: A History*'. Reference: Gazette Notification 77 Pres/72,17-6-72.
44. Prasad and Thapliyal, op. cit., p. 214.
45. Tufail, *In the Ring and on its Feet*, p. 60.
46. Interview with Colonel H.S. Sandhu.
47. Government of India Gazette Notification 73 Pres72, 17-6-72. The citation can be accessed at https://www.gallantryawards.gov.in/awardee/4269
48. Citation of Havildar Ajmer Singh accessed at https://www.gallantryawards.gov.in/awardee/1809
49. Prasad and Thapliyal, op. cit., p. 214.
50. Tufail, *In the Ring and on its Feet*, p. 60.
51. Two PAF pilots were taken POW on 22 November 1971 after their F-86 Sabres were shot down at Boyra but it was before the formal declaration of war on 3 December 1971.
52. Prasad and Thapliyal, op. cit., p. 214.
53. Riza, op. cit., p. 458.
54. AVM V.K. Bhatia, 'The Shorkot Raid Attack', *Bharat Rakshak*, 2 April 2015, accessed on 8 August 2020 at http://www.bharat-rakshak.com/IAF/history/1971war/1280-vinod-bhatia.html#gsc.tab=0
55. Riza, op. cit., p. 458.
56. Shail Ittaman, 'Uncle Claims seeing POW in '89', *Times of India*, 10 June 2007, accessed on 8 August 2020 at http://timesofindia.indiatimes.com/articleshow/2112112.cms?utm_source=contentofinterest&utm_medium=text&utm_campaign=cppst
57. Prasad and Thapliyal, op. cit., p. 214.
58. Interview with Colonel H.S. Sandhu and Tufail, op. cit., p. 59. Tufail, in his book *In the Ring and on its Feet* claims that both the pilots survived the fall though they were injured with one of them in a coma. An article in *The News* published in 2014 also claims that they were admitted to Military Hospital where they succumbed to their injuries. They were buried in the Nijam-ud-din Auliya graveyard in Delhi. ('The Untold Story of a PAF Martyr buried in Delhi', *The News*, Karachi, 29 December 2014, accessed on 9 September 2020 at https://www.thenews.com.pk/archive/print/545502-the-untold-story-of-a-paf-martyr-buried-in-delhi)

59. The official history of war only records that '*One B-57, although hit, managed to get away*'. It is a surprising lapse as not only was the wreckage found and reported, both the pilot/navigator was captured and taken prisoner. Citation for the award of Vir Chakra to Havildar Gopala Krishnan can be accessed at https://www.gallantryawards.gov.in/awardee/1801
60. Tufail, op. cit., p. 59 and Gp Capt Sultan Hali, 'B-57 The Intrepid bomber of PAF', *Defence Journal,* accessed on 4 October 2019 at http://www.defencejournal.com/may99/b-57.htm. The citation for the Sitara-i-jurat can be accessed at http://www.pafmuseum.com.pk/heroes/1971-shuhada
61. Tufail, op. cit., p. 59 Gp Capt Sultan Hali, 'B-57 The Intrepid bomber of PAF', *Defence Journal*
62. It was almost a repeat of the previous war of 1965 when the credit for shooting down of the B-57 on the night of 6/7 September 1965 was not given to by 129 AD Regiment (TA) in the official history. Incidentally, no B-57 was shot down by the IAF during the entire war with only one RB-57 destroyed on the ground. [Prasad and Thapliyal, op. cit., p. 214.]
63. Flt Lt Sandal is one of the 'Missing 54' with no confirmation of his being a prisoner of war in Pakistan and remains so till date. Simmi Waraich, 'War of Memory: Dead or Alive', Spectrum, *The Tribune*, 17 December 2006, accessed on 23 April 2019 at https://www.tribuneindia.com/2006/20061217/spectrum/main1.htm
64. Prasad and Thapliyal, op. cit., p. 215 and Tufail, op. cit., p. 61.
65. Ibid.
66. 'Wreckage of 2 Pak Planes Sighted', *The Tribune*, Chandigarh, 7 December 1971.
67. Prasad and Thapliyal, op. cit., p. 215.
68. Ibid.
69. Interview with Colonel H.S. Sandhu.
70. The claim for the F-86 is not mentioned in the official history nor is it supported by any other record. Citation for Vir Chakra for L/Hav Kans Raj can be accessed at https://www.gallantryawards.gov.in/awardee/2792
71. Prasad and Thapliyal, op. cit., p. 216.
72. Vishnu Som, 'Exclusive Details of How Air Force Raided a Pak Air Base, Destroyed 5 Jets', *NDTV*, 23 January 2018, accessed on 13 May 2019 at https://www.ndtv.com/india-news/exclusive-details-of-how-air-force-raided-a-pak-air-base-destroyed-jets-1803601
73. The loss is mentioned and duly acknowledged by Tufail in his book *In the Ring and on its Feet* also though India's official history makes no mention of the raid. Riza, op. cit., p. 454
74. Tufail, *In the Ring and on its Feet*, p. 91.
75. Tufail, however, acknowledges the shooting down to be a case of fratricide. [Tufail, op. cit., p. 144.] The citation for the award of however claims that Siddiqui was shot down by 'own ground fire'. He was awarded the Sitara-i-Bisalat

to Siddiqui are given at 'Citations for PAF', *Defence Journal* and can be accessed at http://www.defencejournal.com/sept98/citation_paf3.htm

76. Maj Gen Jagjit Singh in his book 'Indian Gunners at War: The Western Front-1971' notes that during the raid on Pathankot 'our air defence gunners claimed having hit five aircraft – but none could be downed'. [Maj Gen Jagjit Singh, *Indian Gunners at War: The Western Front-1971*, Lancer, New Delhi, 1994, p. 213].
77. Riza, op. cit., p. 457.
78. Kamat was awarded the Vayu Sena Medal (Gallantry). The citation that can be accessed at http://www.bharat-rakshak.com/IAF/Database/6009 reads thus: 'Squadron Leader Arun Vithal Kamat was commissioned in the Indian Air Force in December 1960. He has flown 1400 hours on operational aircraft. During the Indo-Pak Conflict of 1971, he was employed as a Flight Commander in one of the fighter squadrons operating from an advance base in the Western Sector. On the 9th December 1971, he was detailed to lead a section of two aircraft, their target being a Pakistani airfield. This was his 4th operational mission over enemy territory. He commenced the attack in the face of heavy fire from the enemy's anti-aircraft guns and light machine guns. His aircraft was badly hit. Finding that it was impossible to control the aircraft, he abandoned the aircraft. He broke both his legs on impact with the ground.
    Squadron Leader Arun Vithal Kamat thus displayed courage, determination and exceptional devotion to duty in the best traditions of the Air Force.'
79. Prasad and Thapliyal, op. cit., pp. 217-18.
80. Ibid.
81. Prasad and Thapliyal, op. cit., pp. 217-18 and Pushpinder Singh, 'No 10 Squadron, IAF', *Bharat Rakshak*, 14 June 2017, accessed on 20 April 2019 at http://www.bharat-rakshak.com/IAF/units/squadrons/10-squadron.html#gsc.tab=0
82. Prasad and Thapliyal, op. cit., pp. 217-18.
83. Ibid.
84. Prasad and Thapliyal, op. cit., p. 218.
85. He was awarded the Vir Chakra posthumously though Wing Commander Gill is one of the 'Missing 54' – Indian armed forces personnel believed to be still held as POW by Pakistan. [Dogra, Chandra Sutra, *Missing in Action*, Harper Collins, New Delhi, 2019 and 'The Trauma of a Long Wait', *Times of India*, New Delhi, 13 May 2007, accessed on 20 April 2019 at https://timesofindia.indiatimes.com/india/The-trauma-of-a-long-wait/articleshow/2039269.cms
86. Kaiser Tufail, 'A Hard Nut to Crack', *Aeronaut*, 21 November 2008, accessed on 4 October 2019 at http://kaiser-aeronaut.blogspot.com/2008/11/hard-nut-to-crack.html
87. Sekhon was awarded the Param Vir Chakra posthumously.
87. Interview with Brigadier Deepak Sharma.
88. Prasad and Thapliyal, op. cit., p. 219.

CHAPTER 7

# Case West: With the Field Army

In the western sector, India and Pakistan had a near parity in armour and artillery, though India had a superiority in infantry. West Pakistan had ten infantry divisions, a few independent infantry brigades, two armoured divisions, and two independent armoured brigades. Of these, 12 Infantry Division was deployed in the northern sector of Pakistan occupied Kashmir (PoK), while the 23 Infantry Division was deployed against Chhamb. Its 1 Corps was responsible for the area opposite Chhamb to Dera Baba Nanak, between the Chenab and Ravi rivers. It had 6 Armoured Division, 8 Independent Armoured Brigade and 8, 15 and 17 Infantry Divisions. 6 Armoured and 17 Infantry Divisions were in reserve while the 8 Independent Armoured Brigade was to act as a mobile strike force in Shakargarh.[1]

Pakistan's 4 Corps was responsible for the Lahore-Amritsar axis and the area opposite Khem Karan. It had two infantry divisions (10 and 11). Its 2 Corps was responsible for the area down south up to Fort Abbas. It had 33 Infantry Division and two infantry brigade groups. The sector opposite India's Southern Command was under Pak 18 Infantry Division with two regiments of armour. Pakistan's GHQ reserve, consisting of 1 Armoured Division and 7 Infantry Division, was held in the Okara-Montgomery area, close to its 2 Corps.[2]

The Indian formations in the west, starting from the north, were 15 Corps deployed in Jammu & Kashmir. It had five infantry divisions (3, 19, 25, 10 and 26) and three Independent armoured brigades. The area from Anupgarh to Dera Baba Nanak (north of Amritsar) was the responsibility of 11 Corps which had three infantry divisions (15, 7 and Foxtrot sector) and 14 Independent Armoured Brigade. The responsibility of the Shakargarh Bulge was that of 1 Corps with its three infantry divisions. Further south, 11 Corps was deployed in the area from Dera Baba Nanak to Fazilka, its 15 Infantry Division holding the positions north of the Grand Trunk Road and 7 Infantry Division holding those to the south. Indian Army Headquarters reserves, comprising 1 Armoured Division and 14 Infantry Division, were positioned south of the Sutlej.[3]

India's Southern Command had two infantry divisions, viz., 11 and 12 Infantry Divisions deployed in the Jaisalmer and Barmer areas.[4]

Though India's strategy in the west was primarily defensive, a number of offensive actions were carried out to seize vulnerable salients with the aim of improving the defensive posture and denying any strategic advantage to Pakistan. Of these, the main offensive was to be launched by 1 Corps – to drive into the Shakargarh salient with the aim to unhinge any Pakistani attempt to thrust north between Jammu and Pathankot. With three infantry divisions and two armoured brigades, 1 Corps was to push into the salient from the north and east to shield vulnerable parts of India, to tie down Pakistani mechanized forces and seize as much territory as possible. The limited offensive operations planned by India were as under:[5]

- An advance by 1 Corps into the Shakargarh Bulge with a view to capturing Zafarwal, Dhamthal and Narowal. The corps was subsequently to secure the line Marala-Ravi Link Canal-Degh Nadi and later take Pasrur.
- A two-pronged move by 15 Corps, with 10 Infantry Division advancing north of the Chenab towards Tanda and Gujarat, and 26 Infantry Division advancing south of that river to threaten Sialkot.
- A feint towards Qila Sobha Singh by simulating a crossing over the Ravi in the general area of Gill Ferry.

The rest of the Western Command was to maintain a posture of offensive defence. In case 1 Corps' offensive succeeded in diverting Pakistan's GHQ reserve to the Shakargarh Bulge, the Indian reserve formations were to be launched across the Sutlej so as to secure Pakistani territory up to the line Raiwind-Rajajang-Luliani, south-west of Lahore.[6]

The Pakistan Army, on its part, had its own offensive plans

though there was a sharp difference of opinion in Pakistan's general headquarters on the manner in which the offensive was to be launched. While one group was for an all-out offensive, the second group favoured preliminary operations by holding formations and thereafter launch its strike formation. According to the plan for a phased offensive, the Pakistan Army was to launch offensive operations five or six days after an Indian attack in the east. These were to be secondary operations, essentially distractions, designed to fix the enemy and to divert his attention away from the intended site of the main attack by 2 Corps. With one armoured and two infantry divisions, 2 Corps was to strike into India from the Bahawalnagar area, approximately three days after the secondary attacks, and was to drive east to cross the international border, before turning to the north-east to push for Bhatinda and wishfully, head for objectives beyond Bhatinda. It was expected that most of India's armoured reserves would have become embroiled in Pakistan's defences in the Shakargarh salient, during this three-day interval between the secondary attacks and the main effort.[7]

With both sides initially planning 'fixing' operations to facilitate a later offensive by the offensive or strike formation, it was always going to be a battle between the two sides to 'fix' the battlefield as per their plans. That the outcome turned out to be quite different for both is a different matter altogether and a matter of separate study. With the focus of employment of ADA, the scope of discussion of different battles hereafter is limited to highlight air defence aspects. The limited scope will be apparent as the allotment of ADA by both armies to their field formations was rather modest and, during some of the famous and well-known battles, e.g. the Battle of Longewala, there was no ADA with the integral formation, though the other anti-aircraft weapons were used with telling effect. More of that later.

The allotment of ADA by India with the field army in the west may have been modest, but was still an improvement over the previous war, as almost six AD regiments were allotted to the field formations. This included composite regiments as also batteries or troops detached from their regiments deployed on rear areas. 3 (Independent) Armoured Brigade of 15 Corps was allotted an ADA troop of the 27 AD Regiment. 1 Corps had two AD regiments with 45 AD Regiment providing a battery each to the 2 (Independent) Armoured Brigade, 16

(Independent) Armoured Brigade and 39 Artillery Brigade, while 29 AD Regiment provided ADA cover to 36 and 54 Infantry Divisions. 49 AD Regiment was affiliated to 11 Corps and was deployed at ten locations; having created an ad hoc ADA troop ('K' Troop) from within its own resources. 1st Armoured Division had 50 AD Regiment while 152 AD Regiment provided ADA cover to 11 and 12 Infantry Divisions of the Southern command. There were additional ADA troops deployed on ammunition depots, bridges and other VPs within the corps zones, adding to the overall ADA cover.

## CHHAMB

One of the Pakistanis' main objectives was Chhamb in 10 Division sector of 15 Corps. In 1965, the Pakistanis had succeeded in capturing this place with a surprise attack and they also did so this time around. Indian 10 Infantry Division was initially deployed for the offensive and was fairly well-equipped, having four infantry brigades, two regiments of armour (9 HORSE and 72 Armoured Regiment), two engineer regiments and six regiments of artillery (two medium, three field and one light), besides elements of air defence artillery. 28 Brigade was deployed in the hill sector north and north-east of Chhamb, while 191 Brigade held the firm base in the plains west of the Munawar Tawi. Covering troops held positions supporting BSF posts on the border. The first phase of the attack was to be put in by 68 Brigade, held around Akhoor. The division's fourth brigade (52) was near Jaurian. The division had initially been given an offensive task but at the last hour it was was tasked to take up defences. This was conveyed to the formation only on 1 December. By then it was too late to bring about any worthwhile changes or re-adjustments.[8]

In this sector, there was a fairly good concentration of ADA with 64 AD Battery of 45 AD Regiment at Sambha, 65 AD Battery (45 AD Regiment) and a battery of 151 AD Regiment with 10 Infantry Division. Both these batteries were allotted to 10 Artillery Brigade which had 39 Medium Regiment, 216 Medium Regiment, 12 Field Regiment, 18 Field Regiment, 81 Field Regiment and 86 Light Battery (in Sundarbani with 28 Infantry Brigade).

'E' Troop along with Battery HQ was giving air defence cover to 39 Medium and 216 Medium Regiments, deployed only 4 km short of frontline, very close to River Munawar Tawi. 39 Medium Regiment was deployed on the left side of the road and 216 Medium Regiment on the right side of the road closer to Munawar Tawi near the foot of Buchamandi hills.[9]

On 3 December, a massive artillery bombardment of border posts began shortly before 2100 hours. Then, around 2130 hours, came simultaneous attacks by Pakistan all along the line. Indian troops stood their ground except at one or two places. The attack was mounted by Pakistan's 23 Division.

Regarding the fateful day, then 2nd Lieutenant Arvind Nautiyal recalls:[10]

> During 1971 Ops, I was a 2nd Lt having about 2 years' service and was posted with 64 AD Battery in Sambha area of J&K. Around mid-Nov. 1971, I was shifted to 65 AD Battery deployed under 10 Infantry Division in Chhamb-Jaurian sector to replace 2nd Lt Rakesh Mehta who was transferred to Deolali to a new raising missile Battery.
>
> ADA unit with Arty Bdes were 65 AD Battery under Maj. K.N. Khanna and battery of 151 AD under Maj. Kaul. 'E' Troop under command, Capt. Chander Bhushan Behl, a course senior to me, along with Bty HQ was giving air defence cover to 39 Med and 216 Med Regts. The 'F' Troop of the battery, under command Capt. V.M. Joseph, was allotted to the armoured formations of the division and was in the concentration area about 5 km behind 'E' Tp with 9 Horse and 72 Armoured Regiment. 2nd Lt K. Waran, my course mate, was Tp Ldr of 'F' Tp.
>
> On joining 65 AD Bty, I was assigned responsibility of 'command post officer'. Soon after I joined, the situation started getting critical. Beginning December, there was an absolute lull in the area but it was more of a lull before the storm than anything else. Lt Col Tapan Bose, our commanding officer visited my command post on 2 Dec. at 5 p.m. while I was all alone. When I questioned him about the lull in the activities, he told me that something was expected to happen in a day or two.
>
> It was on 3 December evening, around 8 p.m., I, along with Maj. Khanna, were in a makeshift bunker, planning to have our dinner, when he asked me to pick up his transistor radio from his bunker to listen to the latest news. Radio Pakistan was giving the news that Indian forces have attacked Pakistan, resulting in their strong retaliation all over our western border. Radio Pakistan mentioned that they had bombed many of our (Indian) air fields in Punjab and Rajasthan

and that Pakistani forces had launched a massive attack in the Chhamb-Jaurian sector and that their troops are advancing towards Akhnoor after crossing the river, Munawar Tawi. This news surprised us and we took it as propaganda of Pakistan. At 8.30 p.m. when the broadcast was over, Maj. Khanna asked to examine progress of work with regard to digging of trenches around the command post and come back quickly for dinner. While I was hardly 100 yards away from the bunker, Pakistani shelling started and one of our JCOs present in that area confirmed to me that war has broken out. I was very excited and immediately rushed back and noticed Maj. Khanna standing outside bunker. He hugged me and said, 'I was like you in the 1965 war, cool down, soon you will get used to war.'

Within a few minutes, our artillery guns started responding. It appeared that we were taken by surprise by the enemy. The Pakistan army, with massive armoured support, attacked us with a ratio of 9 is to 1. Throughout the night heavy shelling went on.

Three PAF squadrons of F-86E/F at Sargodha, Murid and Peshawar were used to provide close air support to Pakistan's 23 Infantry Division in the Chhamb sector. In addition, T-6G trainers were used for strafing convoys in moonlit nights. F-6, the better-endowed fighter for tank killing, remained committed in the more critical Shakargarh sector and was not used in the Chhamb sector.[11]

The offensive was launched by two infantry brigades on the night of 3/4 December. The command and control of the widely separated AD sections deployed right up on the international border were a challenge as ADA guns were deployed ahead of field artillery guns, nearer to the IB.[12]

Section 2 of our 'E' Troop was deployed at the bank of River Munawar Tawi near the foot of Buchamandi hills, a little ahead of the 216 Medium Regiment and was very close to the front line. Across River Munawar Tawi were the Mandyala heights held by 5 Sikh. One of the companies of 5 Sikh was being commanded by Maj. H.S. Pannu, who was our instructor in Officers' Training School (OTS). Maj. Pannu was the first officer to be killed in the Chhamb-Jaurian sector on 3 Dec. 1971. The situation was heating up as a fierce battle was being fought a couple of kilometres away from our location, across River Munawar Tawi by 5 Assam and 3/4 GR with the advancing Pakistani army.

My cousin Maj. Sushil Hatwal was 2nd in command of 5 ASSAM. Keeping the vulnerability of our gun position of Section No. 2 to enemy ground attack in mind, Maj. K.N. Khanna told me to shift my base to that section. As I was about to leave, he changed his mind and, instead of me, sent our battery senior JCO, Sub. Varghese to Section No. 2 till further orders. Our gunner Hav. Jacab

Sultan, being senior most, was in charge of Sec. No. 2 till then. Sometime in the evening, Hav. Sultan called and informed us that their gun position was frequently coming under enemy small arm fire and Sub. Varghese was feeling uncomfortable.

Around 7 p.m., Capt. Chander Bhushan asked me to accompany him to visit our forward position to take stock of the situation and to boost up the morale of our troops. The safest way to our respective gun positions from the command post after darkness was to follow the field telephone cable. On reaching our gun position, we could hear small arm fire in the vicinity. After spending over an hour with Sub. Varghese, Hav. Sultan and the troops, we came back to command post.

While we were returning to our command post, we could hear the sound of small arm firing and some shouting in the vicinity and were wondering where and what was going on. Around 9.30 p.m. while Capt. Behl and I were in command post, having a bite, a tall infantry man came there, introducing himself as Capt. Mohan Bhandari [later Lt Gen.] of 7 Garhwal Rifles. He told us that his company has been detailed for protection of 216 Med Regt and he was looking for their command post. After offering him a bite, we advised him to follow our field telephone cable to our Sec. 2 and that on the way he would be able to see the 216 Medium gun area and their command post.

Thereafter, even I left the command post to visit own troops, moving from trench to trench and boosting their morale.

The other ADA troop deployed in the area was the 'Echo' Troop of 151 AD Regiment of which four guns were deployed for the AD of 81 Field Regiment, on the west bank of Munawar Tawi. The remaining two L/60 guns were deployed at Akhnoor under a JCO to provide AD to the bridge over the Chenab River. Early next morning, the PAF came in to support Pak 23 Division and attack the forward-defended localities and the gun positions.[13]

Early morning around 8 a.m. on 4 December, Pakistani air attack came in our area. Our guns opened up on enemy aircraft and they very quickly pulled up and vanished but not before dropping two 1,000 pounder bombs. From the command post, I could see two bombs coming down and hit the ground, resulting in a very big crater near us. However, there was no damage to us.

The PAF raids were met by intense AD fire and though Lt Nautiyal may not have observed any hits on attacking aircraft as 'they quickly pulled up and vanished', not all Sabres were fortunate that day. In all, six raids were mounted by PAF in the morning of 4 December. One of the PAF aircraft was claimed to have been shot down by AA fire and another was claimed as hit.

One of the PAF aircraft hit over Chhamb was flown by Flt Lt Isar Ahmad. His aircraft was hit by AA fire and he was seriously injured although he was lucky to get back to base. Ahmad was awarded the Sitara-i-Jurat, Pakistan's third highest gallantry award. His citation gives the details of the damage to his aircraft, and the injuries inflicted on Ahmad:[14]

> On 4 December 1971, Flight Lieutenant Israr Ahmad was detailed to fly a bombing mission over the Chhamb-Akhnoor sector. While over the battle area, his aircraft was hit by enemy ground fire and he was seriously injured. In spite of his injuries, he climbed to height, flew the aircraft and landed at a base during an air raid warning. When he was removed from the cockpit, it was found that his right upper arm bone was shattered and he was suffering from serious loss of blood. Flight Lieutenant Israr showed tremendous courage and determination in flying the aircraft back and landing at his base in spite of his injuries. In doing this, he displayed sterling qualities of devotion to duty, and courage and determination. In recognition of his performance, he has been awarded the Sitara-e-Jur'at.

In face of a determined Pakistani offensive, the Indian forward brigade was pushed back. 'F' Troop suffered its first casualty of the war, as a radar operator was injured during the artillery shelling.[15]

> Heavy enemy shelling continued and around 8.30 a.m. gunners from our Sec. No. 1 brought Officer V. Raja Manickam in a 1 ton vehicle who had sustained a head injury due to splinter from an enemy artillery shell. Maj. Khanna asked me to rush him to the medical centre. I, along with our workshop JCO, immediately took him in the same 1-ton vehicle, keeping his head on my lap, to the divisional medical centre, but midway he expired on my lap, giving to me the greatest shock of my life. He was the first of our buddies to have fallen in the first and only deadly war I faced in my life.
>
> Before I could decide what to do next, I noticed 2/Lt Waran, my course mate from our 'F' Troop on the roadside, he had probably been communicated with the details and he was waiting for me. I handed over Raja Manickam's body to Waran for further necessary action and returned back to my post. Throughout the day, we were having intermittent enemy shelling, and our artillery guns also kept responding.

Around 1040 hours, a Pakistani L-19 Bird Dog flew in from the south-west towards the gun area. The ADA guns of 151 AD Regiment opened up, hitting and shooting off its tail.

It was not only the PAF that the ADA troop had to contend with as the Pak artillery shelling continued throughout. With the Indian defences increasingly coming under strain, the IAF was asked to provide close support. No. 101 Squadron, IAF, at Adampur carried out the early CAS missions in the sector, with Flt Lts Gurdip Singh and J. Bhattacharya amongst the first to do so.[16]

Our squadron was assigned the task of supporting the ground troops in Chhamb sector. So, as we landed after the first mission, Flt Lt J. Bhattacharya and I were assigned for a Close Air Support mission in Chhamb sector. We both went to our GLO who thoroughly briefed us on all aspects, targets to be attacked, precautions to be taken and alternate targets, etc. And there we were, fully briefed and raring to go once again.

My memory fails me for exact timings but it must have been approximately about 9-9.15 a.m. when I, as No. 2 took off from Adampur airfield, skirting Pathankot and the Shakargarh Bulge to approach the battlefield area of Chhamb. As is well known on the night of 3-4 Dec., the Pakistanis had tried their armour thrust with the aim of cutting off Kashmir from the rest of India and had succeeded in entering Indian territory, hence the need for urgent air support.

Dot on time we contacted the FAC Flying Officer V.G. Kumar, another pilot from Adampur base itself, we being well known to each other. He tried his best to guide my leader, but somehow or the other, he was not able to make contact with the tanks. We carried on orbiting making efforts to locate the targets. Although I had contact with the enemy tanks, I also tried to guide him besides the FAC but without any success. As we had already spent enough time in orbiting and locating the targets and were also getting low on fuel without yet having achieved the main aim of attacking their tanks.

My leader asked me to overshoot him and carry on with the attack as I was in contact with the enemy tanks. In the meanwhile, having already warned the enemy about our presence, it gave them sufficient time not only to hide themselves under a grove of trees but also be ready to take shot at us. So having overshot my leader, I turned around and pulled up for the attack. We had selected four rockets to be fired at a time from all four pods so that 16 57 mm rockets are released each time which would have given us four passes with 16 rockets in each pass besides the gun passes if required.

I think it was almost simultaneous because as I released the rockets at the proper range more or less at the same time I heard some thuds on my aircraft, which I soon realised were ack ack gun hits from the same tanks which I had fired upon and destroyed (confirmed later on by army troops as well as the FAC). So as I looked inside to check the after-effects of those thuds, what I saw stunned me. Numerous red lights were flashing and gauges were giving erratic readings, indicating engine failure and fire in the aircraft. I was obviously heading in a direction which would have taken me deeper into Pakistan territory. But that intuition, sixth sense and presence of mind made me turn towards Indian territory while pulling up to gain maximum height so that I could glide as much into Indian side as possible. Because ejecting immediately would have been asking for a sure place in PoW camp if captured alive. After all, we are all trained to be able to defend our nation while fighting the enemy, and if an eventuality arises, must try to come back safely which will not only be better as an individual but a morale booster for colleagues, too.

So there I was having almost climbed to one km plus (~3300 ft AGL) and hopefully heading towards the Indian side as all instruments were not behaving properly and I believed in them with a pinch of salt. While I was trying to make RT calls to declare my emergency and intentions of ejecting, I was also making an attempt to relight the engine which could take me to nearest airfield Pathankot for an emergency landing. Because under the circumstances going back to Adampur was asking for too much. I tried an May Day call but as even R/T had packed up it was a futile one. My leader did not see me ejecting or had any knowledge about my whereabouts or fate.

This was the first IAF aircraft lost in CAS in the western theatre to AA fire. The loss was, however, to the tank mounted AA machine guns of 26 CAVALRY and not to Pak ADA. As Major General Syed Ali Hamid recalls:

I was adjutant 26 Cavalry in Chhamb sector during the 1971 War and went and saw the wreckage of your aircraft. I was intrigued to see how intact the airframe was and now I know why . . . because you ejected so close to the ground at stalling speed. I really enjoyed your article as I could relate to so much of your narrative. From your account and the location of the crash site I can conclude that you were looking for tanks in the area genline south of Chhamb, whereas the bulk of our armour on the morning of 4 Dec. was opposite Mandyala in the North.

Only two squadrons of Shermans of my regiment were operating in the area you were probably searching and there was good cover available from the mango trees. It is also likely that the .50 Brownings of our tanks shot you down as there were no AA guns supporting the division.

That very morning I was leading a convoy of ammo and POL vehicles of my regiment when a pair of SUs passed overhead . . . fortunately for us they did not attack. It may well have been you. I had a sketch made of the aircraft for the book I wrote on the war history of my regiment that I would like to dedicate to you.

Glad you survived and God bless.

The other sorties launched by IAF were also met by intense AA fire and a number of aircraft were hit. Amongst them was a Hunter of No. 27 Squadron, IAF, flown by Flying Officer G.D. Bomboat. On 4 December, while carrying out search and strike mission in the Chhamb sector, the enemy AA hit and damaged his aircraft's hydraulic system but he managed to bring the aircraft back to base.[18]

After the initial sorties, there was a break in providing close support to the beleaguered 10 Infantry Division by the IAF during the day. The reasons of the IAF keeping away are not known though A.V.M. Tiwary does mention that:[19]

> The 191 Infantry Brigade was totally pinned down in its present position. Flt Lt V.G. Kumar, the FAC with the brigade, had his tentacle shot up in the artillery pounding. Even the mast aerial fitted on the GU-734 R/T set was destroyed. There was utter confusion to say the least.

The total air effort earmarked by IAF in this sector was 45 sorties per day but only 20 sorties were demanded on 4 December by the formation. The confusion and damage to the R/T set mentioned above may have been the reason for the same. As regards PAF, its Sabres supported Pak 23 Division but they were not very effective as 'weapon-target compatibility left a lot to be desired as neither the F-86's 0.5-inch guns, nor were the general purpose bombs effective against armour'.[20]

Meanwhile, with the defences becoming untenable, the ADA troops deployed forward were threatened by the advancing Pakistanis.[21]

> Sometime early evening on 4 Dec., a company of 13 Azad Kashmir Rifles, supported by another company of 47 Punjab of Pakistan army, crossed over the border in between Mandyala heights and the Buchamandi hill feature and parked themselves in Buchamandi hill area. That area was not manned and was covered only by mines. There was not even an artillery OP covering that unmanned area. I believe, Pakistanis used 'charpoys' (cots), collected from nearby abandoned village to cross over the minefield. It was learnt that they were spotted by the HQs artillery brigade but were mistaken as 47 BSF withdrawing from the front line. In fact, when we were in our forward gun position, the enemy was already lining at FUP a couple of hundred yards away on the right flank our gun area at the foot of Buchamandi hill. Soon after, Capt. Chander Bhushan and I left the gun position for our command post, probably around the same time the enemy launched its attack. As already mentioned, while we were on our way back, we could hear a lot of noise and small arm firing in the vicinity, but we were not able to visualize what was actually happening as the same was least expected.

The enemy ran over very close to the right flank of our gun position, killing one of our men, Gunner (DSV) Louis Vages, and, thereafter, attacked the gun position of two batteries of 216 Medium Regiment, 200 yards short of our gun positions. Both medium batteries were at rest at that point of time. The enemy burnt 11 out of our 12 130 mm guns and in hand-to-hand fight killed about 65 gunners of the 216 Medium Regiment. Since the enemy was not expecting our gun positions so close to the front line to fall on their way, they were not carrying proper charge required to blast the barrels of medium guns. They succeeded in only burning rubberized parts of the guns, putting the guns temporarily out of action. Out of the 11 damaged guns, the workshop team of 216 Medium Regiment was able get 10 guns in action before ceasefire was declared.

The ground situation was very fluid with a breakdown in communication adding to the confusion. The location of own and enemy troops was not always known with certainty and the Pakistani troops, having breached the defences, were operating in small groups.[22]

After the attack on the gun area, Pakistani troops had spread all over in small groups of 10 to 12 men and were in hiding, probably familiarizing themselves with the terrain and planning further attacks.

As our command post was about 800 yards from the ill-fated medium regiment gun position, we could hear small arm fire regularly. Around 1.30 a.m., one squadron of the 72 Armoured Regiment arrived and lined up about 50 to 60 yards ahead of our command post.

Artillery brigade headquarters and all artillery units were operating on 'Delta 5' net. In fact, those days on 'Delta 5' net, one could get running commentary of operations of the entire division as all OPs are also hooked to the same net. Unfortunately the 'Delta 5' net failed at that point of time resulting in total commotion due to lack of correct information.

Some of our gunners manning our local defence panicked, mistaking our tanks as the enemy and opened small arm fire on them. The tanks retaliated with MMG fire on us thinking us as the enemy. I rushed to our local defences, trench to trench, and ordered them to hold fire. As mentioned earlier due to failure of the 'Delta 5' net, we were incommunicado with rest of the army. Maj. Khanna and I were sitting under a nearby tree adjacent to one of our bunker, keeping a watch on developments and thinking about how to get out of the mess. Around 3.30 a.m., sensing the situation was getting out of hand, Maj. Khanna told me that, since our wireless communication has failed, we have to somehow personally contact someone in the tanks, lined up in front of our location, before there is any damage to us, and tell them that we are Indian troops. Being the junior officer, the task of contacting the armoured units fell on me.

My battery commander told me to take along our troop havildar Major

Jesudasan, VrC, who was a veteran of the 1965 War. We started walking towards the tanks. As expected, after about 15 to 20 yards, came one MMG burst close to me on my left side. I ducked instinctively. After a while, I again started walking next to him and he immediately kept his hand on my shoulders (unheard of in uniform) saying 'Sa'ab, nothing will happen. Until there is a bullet with your name on it'.

I got the feeling of 'a hen covering her chicks under her feathers sensing danger'. All this happened in the fraction of a second. Hats off to the bravest of brave soldier Hav. Maj. Jesudasan, VrC. As we kept walking, shouting 'DD' 'friend, Indian Army', tanks fired two more MMG bursts at us and in the pitch dark we could see dust coming off the ground. When we were closer to the tank, someone from another tank shouted, asking us to come towards his tank. There was a Sikh gentleman on top of the tank, pointing his pistol at us, asked me to climb up. On my climbing up, he rested his pistol against my chest and asked for my identity. Thereafter, he asked me the names few more officers of my unit to verify. Since the 'Foxtrot Troop' of our battery was in support of armoured units, I immediately mentioned the names of Capt. V.M. Joseph and 2/Lt K. Waran of our 'F' Troop. Hearing their names, he withdrew his pistol, hugged me and said, 'You are lucky son, we fired to kill you'. I felt like crying. He introduced himself as Maj. Amarjit Singh Hundal, squadron commander and asked my purpose for coming. Upon my explaining, he informed his squadron on wireless not to fire in our direction and asked me to call my battery commander. Since the distance was about 50 to 60 yards, I shouted for my BC and soon he was there. Maj. Khanna also told him to stop firing at us. Maj. Amarjit Singh told Maj. Khanna that he is waiting for 7 Kumaon for the last one-and-half hour, which was supposed to accompany him for an attack.'

'F' Troop survived the confusion but it was not the last time the troop had a close call and Nautiyal did not have to wait long for his first brush with direct enemy fire.[23]

Early winter morning of 5 Dec., it was still pitch dark, and our command post was receiving intermittent small arm fire. Capt. Chander Bhushan Bahl, troop commander, Echo Troop, observed that fire was coming from the top of a nearby tree. He, with the help of one of our men, took a light machine gun and blasted the tree, and within no time a Pakistani dropped dead from the tree.

Early morning, we started taking stock of the situation and had come to know about the 216 Medium Regiment debacle. We were worried about fate of our Section No. 2. As Pakistani troops in small groups were spread all over the area. There was no response from Section No. 2 and we came to know that, during attack on 216 Medium Regiment, troops of our Sec. No. 2 had abandoned gun position and their whereabouts were not known. We also noticed that men from some of our local defence trenches guarding the right flank of our battery headquarter and command post had also abandoned their post.

Although, through field telephones, we received an all OK report from our other AD sections, Battery Commander Maj. K.N. Khanna asked me to visit the nearby Section No. 1 deployed on the left side of the road behind 39 Medium Regiment to get first-hand ground information. Around 7.30 a.m. I along with four of our men, proceeded towards Section No. 1.

After the previous night's gun area attack, the remaining enemy had taken up position on Buchmandi hill, and some of them were present in small groups all over that area. While we were couple of hundred yards away from our command post, on an uncultivated farm land, we came under direct enemy small arm fire from a close range from the Buchamandi hill direction. We immediately took position behind a divider in the field and returned the fire. We engaged enemy for about 4 to 5 minutes. When this encounter was going on, my personal weapon, a sten carbine, did not fire and I had to strip the gun, clean its breech block with my handkerchief, reassemble it and, by the time I opened fire, the enemy had escaped.

My first experience of encountering the enemy directly was a great lesson learnt and I realized the importance of weapon cleaning which was highly emphasized during our academy days. During this encounter one of our men had a miraculous escape as he got a direct hit of the enemy bullet on his helmet making a hole in it. Thereafter, we returned back to command post.

In view of the Pakistani raid on the medium gun area and the threat to the ADA sections, the battery commander decided to consolidate the battery HQ, command post and all other AD guns with Section No. 1 gun position and deploy all guns in a straight line, like the field artillery, against the established norms of air defence gun deployment. It was an unconventional layout but, given the threat, was a better option than to have the ADA guns strung out, exposed to ground attack(s).

While doing so, the guns and other equipment of No. 2 Section were still at their location and were yet to be retrieved. As leaving the guns was never an option, the battery commander decided to send a party to retrieve the guns. It was a tough call as the position had been overrun by the Pakistanis and no information was available about the enemy.[24]

It was a tough task as it amounted to entering in to enemy's den for retrieving our assets from the bank of River Munawar Tawi. Our AD guns and generators were operationally deployed and well dug in inside gun pits and they had to be pulled out, towed with the gun tower vehicles and driven away from the area which was under direct enemy fire. Capt. Chander Bhushan Bahl took a number of gunner drivers and a few more men with him in a 3 ton vehicle mounted with light machine guns and proceeded for the task. We all were keeping our fingers crossed.

On reaching the gun position of Sec. 2, we came under enemy fire from the direction of Buchamandi hill. Leaving some of our men engaging enemy with light machine guns, the rest of the crew started towing and pulling the guns and generators out from the gun pits with the help of the vehicles of the section, already parked in the nearby hideout. The entire operation was conducted by Capt. Chander Bhushan very effectively without any collateral damage excepting that of Gunner (DSV) Louis Vages who had fallen to enemy bullets the previous night during gun area attack. Capt. Chander Bhushan informed us that he noticed several enemy dead bodies lying all around our gun position.

Around 12 noon, Capt. Chander Bhushan arrived with the convoy of vehicles towing AD guns and generators loaded with ammunition and other equipment. On the arrival of our guns, the scene became very emotional as troops started hugging and kissing the guns and some even cried in joy. Losing guns to the enemy would have been a big stigma on us.

While the guns and other equipment were being retrieved, the troop headquarters and Section No. 1 came under fire from Buchamandi Hill which was about 4 to 5 hundred yards from the gun position. Enemy movement could be observed on the hill. Around 11 a.m., Lt Col Gauri Shankar, commanding officer 39 Medium Regiment, came to the ADA gun position and asked for the ADA guns to be fired in ground role on the enemy movement on Buchamandi Hill. Lt Nautiyal personally manned one L/70 gun and started firing, using the reflector sights. The devastating power of the L/70 air defence gun firing 40 mm shells soon got enemy bodies 'flying in the air due to our effective engagement'. This continued for about half-an-hour. It later came to light that it was an enemy observation post that had been destroyed by the guns of 45 AD Regiment.[25]

During the night of 4-5 December, a small bridgehead was formed by Pakistani infantry elements to enable the armoured brigade to break through. Heavy enemy air and artillery attacks, however, forced them back with heavy losses to armour.

On 5 December, the field regiments moved to occupy new positions to the east of Munawar Tawi. Captain (later Colonel) Deepak Kaul, the troop commander of 'Echo' Troop/151 AD Regiment, was able to move and deploy three of the guns as the fourth gun had been disabled due to enemy shelling. Having deployed the three guns, Kaul went back to retrieve the fourth gun.[26]

I went back across the Mandyala Bridge to try and retrieve my fourth gun. I was travelling in an open jeep with three or four gunners.

Earlier that morning, Pakistan's 4 AK Brigade had launched an attack across the Munawar Tawi along the Sukh Tao Nala and had run into medium guns of our 216 and 39 Medium Regiments, who engaged them by firing with direct sights. They were also attacked by our infantry and armour, and had withdrawn in complete disarray.

When I was returning from the Sakrana gun area, I came across a Pakistani officer with two others hiding behind a hedge. The officer fired at me with his sten gun; while two bullets whizzed past me. One grazed my left forearm near the wrist. I immediately fired back at him and injured his knee. He then put up his hands and surrendered with his party. I took him into custody and noticed that they were all injured in their earlier action. I took them to the advance dressing station (ADS) of the 191 Infantry Brigade, and left without taking any receipt. The officer was Lt Colonel Basharrat Raja, Commanding officer of 13 AK Rifles.

Meanwhile, I applied a First Field Dressing on my bleeding left arm, and continued to lead 'Echo' Troop through the war. I ignored my injury and did not report sick; I was afraid of being evacuated as I did not want 'Echo' Troop to be left leaderless as my JCO was far away in Akhnoor.

I still carry a scar from my injury. Incidentally, since I did not report my injury to the ADS, I did not even get a wound medal!

The PAF mounted a number of sorties against the guns area and the armour as also the bridge at Mandyala on 5 December during which 45 and 151 AD Regiments claimed to have shot down two Sabres.[27]

The IAF was also carrying out CAS missions over the sector; with 28 sorties on 5 Decemebr and 30 on 6 December. All these were hotly contested by Pakistani AA defences and a number of Indian aircraft came back with hits from AA fire. Luck ran out for Flt Lt Jagdish Bhattacharya of 101 Squadron on 6 December as he was attacking Pakistani armour in Chhamb. His Sukhoi was shot down by AA fire.[28]

During the operations against Pakistan in December 1971, Flight Lieutenant Jagdish Bhattacharya, as a pilot of a Fighter Bomber Squadron, carried out many operational missions. On 6 December 1971, while he was attacking the enemy near Munawar River, his aircraft was hit by enemy ground fire. As his aircraft went out of control, he ejected in enemy territory. The enemy sent a detachment to capture him but in spite of spinal injury, he evaded the enemy.

Flt Lt V.K. Wahi of 101 Squadron, IAF was also providing close support in the same sector. He faced heavy AA fire while attacking the ground targets but he continued with the attack. He managed to survive the ground fire but was shot down by a PAF Mirage III while returning from the mission. He was able to eject but sustained fatal injuries. He was awarded the Vir Chakra.[29]

Pakistani AA defences remained active throughout, putting up a stiff resistance to the IAF. On more than one occasion, the IAF aircraft sustained hits from the AA fire while providing close support to the army, though most of the aircraft managed to return safely back to base. Amongst the IAF aircraft subjected to heavy ground fire were the Sukhois of 101 Squadron.

In an unfortunate incident of fratricide, a Sukhoi-7 strafed its own gun position on 7 December, killing one JCO and nine gunners of the 39 Medium Regiment besides injuring an officer and a JCO. Two ammunition vehicles were also destroyed. Capt. Nautiyal was present at the location and recollects:[30]

On 7 December around 1300 hrs., while I was in our gun area, an Indian Air Force mission comprising of five Su-7s and an MiG-21 appeared in our area about which we did not have any advance information.

Lt Col Gauri Shankar, CO of 39 Medium Regiment, who was nearby, asked me regarding identity of the aircrafts. The presence of our fighter aircrafts is always highly morale boosting and as they saw the aircraft overhead, Khalsa (Sikh) troops of 39 Medium Regiment came out of gun pits and local defences and started dancing.

All five Sukhois kept hovering over us for some time and suddenly, to our horror, they started diving and strafing us. All of us jumped and took shelter in nearby trenches and gun pits. They dropped one 1,000 pounder bomb which landed in between our two AD guns creating a huge crater which covered our guns with mud and slush. Empty cartridges ejected by the aircrafts were falling all over us and some fell inside the trench in which I had taken shelter. They were flying so low that we could see IAF markings on the aircraft very clearly. They played merry hell with us for a couple of minutes and, thereafter, pulled up and flew away.

Lt Col Gauri Shankar, who was with me all the time, started shouting at me saying that how I could make such a blunder in recognizing the aircraft. However, I was firm on the identity of aircrafts and later he, too, agreed with me about having noticed the IAF marking on the aircraft. Lt Col Gauri Shankar immediately contacted Brig. Srinivasan, commander, 10 Artillery Brigade over the 'Delta 5' net but was told by him that there was no IAF mission in our area at that point of time and that we had probably mistaken the MiG-19 aircraft of Pakistan as SU-7. There is, of course, some resemblance between these two aircraft, but SU-7 is much bigger aircraft than MiG-19.

After about 20 minutes, while Lt Col Gauri Shankar was still trying to convince the commander, the mission returned with same five 'Sukhois', 4 in steel grey colour and one having camouflage marks. Noticing this, Lt Col Gauri Shankar told me that, since IAF is mistaking us as enemy, I should personally open fire from only one gun to scare them away and not shoot them. Before the aircraft could start diving on us, I personally opened fire to scare them and, to our pleasant surprise, the entire mission immediately pulled up and flew away. After about 5 minutes, the lone camouflaged Su-7 again came and dived on us, I again opened restrained fire and the aircraft immediately pulled up after firing a few bursts without causing any damage.

During this, the IAF had blown two, 10-tonner Kraz gun towing vehicles fully loaded with artillery ammunition, killing one EME JCO and 9 gunners of the 39 Medium Regiment and injuring Capt P.P. Singh and the Granthi (Sikh religious teacher) of the regiment.

We collected a sand bag fully of ejected 20 mm empty cartridges having Indian ordnance factory markings, fired by the IAF on us, which was handed over by Maj. Khanna to the commander in support of our claim being fired, by IAF. Subsequently, I believe, an inquiry revealed that the IAF mission had been correctly briefed that all troops across River Munavar Tawi are enemy. There is a dry nallah called Lauki Khadd about 7 to 8 km short of Munawar Tawi and the IAF mistook the Lauki Khadd as Munawar Tawi and in the process, we got screwed.

On 8 December, the IAF mounted twenty-eight sorties by Su-7s and Hunters in the Chhamb area and accounted for a number of Pakistani tanks and vehicles.[31]

On 8 December, IAF lost another aircraft to AA fire as Sqn Ldr Denzil Keelor's MiG-21 was shot down over Chhamb. The other aircraft flown by Flt Lt Apramjeet Singh was also badly hit. This was, in fact, how things can go wrong and AA fire can be brought down to a deadly effect as the pilots commit minor lapses. There are two accounts of the incident and both bring out good lessons. As per Apramjeet:[32]

On the morning of 8 December 1971, Denzil Keelor came from the operations room, where he had been briefed by the station commander and, on entering the OPR, said 'we are going hunting, let's go'.

As per the flying programme Sqn Ldr Sonpar was to lead the mission and I was to be his wing man. But Denzil pulled him down from the stairs and said 'AJ – follow me, we are going hunting'.

That was my briefing! I did not know of the actual briefing Denzil had received from the station commander. I did not know what the aim of our mission was! Before I knew what was happening, we were airborne heading towards the battle area and clearing each other's tail.

At this stage, things started going wrong. We were on an air defence mission, but we flew straight over Pakistani army concentrations at a height of 300 ft. The Pak army convoy was escorted by tanks with ZSU-23 mm air defence guns. Then for inexplicable reasons, Denzil decided to make a second pass over them.

During this second pass, both of us got shot up by the anti-aircraft guns. We were both in a dive when hit by the fire. As soon as I got hit, I started pulling up, and Denzil was pulling up as well. There was a thick cloud and I couldn't see him. Both of us lost contact with each other. That was the last I saw him. I had lost my R/T (due to the AA fire) and there was no contact. In fact, Denzil's aircraft was shot down, and he ejected and came down in no-man's land.

My aircraft, on the other hand, was shot up badly. The only damage that I could see was the wing. The front leading edge of the left wing was split open. The aileron control rods were in the leading edge and it was broken. I had lost the left aileron and was operating only on the right aileron.'

It seems an avoidable loss with the MiGs taking unnecessary risk. What is of interest is that Pakistan did not have ZSU-23 mm air defence guns and that the MiGs were engaged by a mix of 12.7 mm and 0.50 Browning anti-aircraft machine guns of the Pakistani tanks of 26 Cavalry. The aircraft were engaged by Major Shamshad Ahmad.[33]

I had just climbed on to the tank, when I saw two enemy aircraft swooping down on my squadron. This was not new to us as we had been targeted since the beginning of the war and as an MiG-21, whizzed past, I happily engaged it with the Five O. Not having the foggiest idea of the pilot's intentions, I emptied the entire box of ammunition.

As the plane was about to disappear from sight, I saw to my horror that it was taking a U-turn for aligning back with our tanks. I suddenly realized that I was out of ammunition. Holy Caramba! I was caught with my pants down. I kicked the gunner in his butt and shouted for the ammunition box while keeping an eye on the aircraft as it completed its turn. In the next few precious seconds, I grabbed the box from the gunner, ripped it open (like opening a tin of sardines), dropped it into the cradle, opened the body cover of the Browning, placed the ammunition belt with a zig-zag movement in the slot to hold the bullet; slammed the body cover shut, yanked the loading lever and sensed the bullet enter the chamber. If I had made any error in the sequence, surely somebody else would have been writing this story. When I pressed the butterfly trigger, I half-feared I would hear a dull 'click'. The Brownings were in super condition, but of Second World War vintage. However, the gods were on my side. As I thumped the trigger, the gun barked into action.

The pilot had brought the plane down to tree top level and I could see his white helmet. I could also see from the tracers of the bullets hitting the target. However, at the back of my mind, I somehow felt that this was doomsday for me. One short burst from his 30 mm cannon or a salvo of rockets, and I would be blown into smithereens. Luckily, I got him first, because he pulled the plane straight up and ejected when he had gained enough height.

The pilotless aircraft plummeted towards the ground while a parachute drifted lazily towards the Tawi.

There was rejoicing all around my tank, with 4th Punjab officers and men throwing up their helmets and berets in jubilation.

The loss of the MiG was due to misplaced bravado on the part of the pilot while it needs to remembered that the AA machine guns and other AA weapons are very effective at low level and should never be discounted. Even if the adversary air force does not offer any opposition, the ground-based weapons can continue to cause attrition. This simple fact was repeatedly forgotten by both the air forces and they paid a heavy price for it.

If the IAF lost a MiG over Chhamb and had another close shave, it was a bad day for PAF as well. The Pakistan Army had launched an attack across the Munawar Tawi in the area of Chhati Tahli and the PAF was very active overhead. At about 1050 hrs., the supply depot at Jaurian was attacked, followed by another raid at Akhnoor. As the Sabres flew overhead, one of the F-86 Sabres was shot down by the gun detachment of Havildar Uttam Jawalge of 151 AD Regiment. Capt. Deepak Kaul was at the gun site when the Sabre was shot down. He recollects:[34]

On 8 December, while I was sitting on the No. 3 layer's seat of one of the gun detachments (whose No. 1 was Havildar Uttam Jawalge), I saw two Pakistani Sabres in hot pursuit of three of our Su-7s, who were returning from a mission over enemy territory. I immediately ordered the detachment to load, at the same time guiding the No. 2 to lay on the leading Sabre for 'elevation' while I laid for 'line'.

As soon as I had in my sight, I ordered 'Fire'. We fired four rounds, all of which hit the fuselage of the leading Sabre, which went down in front of our eyes, killing the pilot.

Coincidentally, this engagement had been observed by Lt Gen Sartaj Singh, the corps commander and Maj. Gen. Jaswant Singh, the GOC, who were on their way forward from the divisional headquarters.

Havildar Uttam Jawalge was awarded the Vir Chakra. His citation for Vir Chakra mentions that his gun was deployed for protection of divisional headquarters.[35] In a rare admission of the loss of a F-86 Sabre to ground fire, PAF accounts mention that the aircraft was lost as the AA fire 'presumably hit a bomb fuse, causing the aircraft to explode'. Flt Lt Fazal Elahi, the PAF pilot, was awarded the Sitara-e-Jur'at.[36]

By 9 December, IAF had flown almost 200 sorties and the close support continued even after the 9th. On 10 December, IAF mounted forty-two close support sorties against tanks, guns, fuel dumps and bunkers while some thirty air defence sorties were flown in the area to keep the PAF at bay. In this, both air forces suffered losses to ground-based air defences. Sqn Ldr M.K. Jain of No. 27 Squadron was leading a two-aircraft strike mission to the Chhamb sector. While carrying out an attack on Pakistani positions, his Hunter was hit by AA fire and crashed. Flying Officer Jai Singh Gahlawat, his No. 2, saw Jain's Hunter being hit by ground fire and crashing, but he remained unperturbed and pressed home his attack on the enemy concentration. Gahlawat managed to get back without any damage.[37]

In another mission, the Hunter flown by Sqn Ldr R.N. Bharadwaj of No. 20 Squadron as well as that of his number two were hit by ground fire, and as they pulled out of the attacks they were engaged by enemy Sabres. Bharadwaj guided his number two out of danger, and then returned to the fray shooting down a Sabre which crashed near the Chhamb bridge. By this time, Bharadwaj was alone, but he returned to attack the Pakistani tanks and troops, causing extensive damage to these targets before nursing his damaged aircraft back to base, where he landed safely.[38]

Pakistani AA fire remained as intense, and deadly as it was on the first day and was continuously taking its toll. With all the action and the continuously changing ground situation, there was always a possibility of fratricide and, though Pakistan had had a couple of incidents of shooting down of its own aircraft by its AA and ground fire, there had been no such case with the IAF and Indian ADA. Unfortunately, the IAF again slipped up in this respect and an IAF Sukhoi-7 attacked the positions of 45 AD Regiment. Thankfully, there were no casualties. It was almost the last of close missions over Chhamb as the situation had stabilised by now.

Pakistan, on its part, flew a total of 146 sorties in Chhamb sector, which was 20 per cent of PAF's total tactical air support effort. A total of 89 sorties were considered successful while 57 were rated as failures. There were no CAS sorties by PAF after 10 December when it flew just six sorties. On many occasions, the pilots found no enemy activity on reaching the target area, resulting in wasted missions.[39]

While the IAF may claim credit for establishing a favourable air situation over Chhamb, the role of the ADA in challenging every mission and inflicting continuous attrition were a major factor in keeping the PAF at bay.

## AKHNOOR-POONCH

26 Infantry Division had been alloted a Troop of 27 AD Regimnet augmented by a few guns of 151 AD Regiment. On 4 December, a section of the troop was deployed to cover the armour and infantry being ferried across the Machhal crossing. Keeping in mind the large distance to be covered, the guns were deployed at a distance of almost 2 km between them. As expected, the crossing was contested by the PAF, but the ADA guns, firing without radars at local power control (LPC), managed to keep the PAF at bay and no damage could be inflicted on own troops. During the battle, 27 AD Regiment claimed a F-6 on 6 December.[40]

The IAF had Vampires of No. 121 Squadron at Srinagar and four Harvards at Poonch for rendering close support to the army and these were used extensively during the operations. The Vampires operated in the Kargil sector while it was the Harvards that were used in Poonch. No aircraft was lost to Pak AAA in the sector though they suffered hits from ground fire on more than one occasion. Amongst these 'close shaves', Flt Lt Shivinder Singh Bains on No. 121 Squadron had his Vampire hit by ground fire but he brought the aircraft back to base safely.[41]

## SHAKARGARH

Keeping in view the overall strategy of maintaining a defensive posture in the west, the initial orders for 1 Corps in early October were to concentrate the field forces in Punjab so as to adopt a defensive posture at short notice. The Corps was accordingly poised in a defensive posture as follows:[42]

- 36 Infantry Division to cover the approaches to Pathankot across the Ravi in the general area of Gurdaspur-Dinanagar.
- 39 Infantry Division in the general area of Madhopur-Kottia Parol-Bamial-Ujh River Dyala Chak to cover the approaches to Madhopur and protect rail and road communications in the area.
- 54 Infantry Division in the general area of Samba between the Bein River and the Degh Nadi.
- The Ramgarh-Nandpur-Samba area between the Aik Nullah and the Degh Nadi was held by about two brigades under an ad hoc headquarters.

The defensive plan was to strongly hold the likely routes of ingress in depth and have suitably positioned reserves for counteraction in the rear. Contiguous to the zone defended by 1 Corps, the shoulders of the Bulge were held in the north between the Chenab and the Aik Nullah by 26 Infantry Division under 15 Corps, and the 15 Infantry Division under 11 Corps covered in the south the Ranian and Dera Baba Nanak area, including Gill Ferry. With the expected offensive by Pakistan not materializing, it was decided by India to launch its 1 Corps with the following aims:[43]

- 1 Corps, with the 36 and 54 Infantry Divisions and armoured brigades, to attack between the Degh Nadi and Ravi to capture the Pakistani strong points of Zafarwal-Dhamtal-Narowal-Quila Sobha Singh. It was hoped that this would force the enemy to commit its reserve formations (6 Armoured and 17 Infantry Divisions) south of the Degh Nadi.

- After the enemy's reserve formations had been committed thus, the 39 Infantry Division, supported by one armoured regiment, was to break out of the general area of Nandpur-Ramgarh towards the enemy's rear in the Pasrur area.
- Dovetailed with the above, 15 Corps, with the 10 and 26 Infantry Divisions supported by the affiliated armoured brigade, was launching a two-pronged offensive simultaneously, or shortly before or after, with one thrust on either side of the Chenab.
- In addition, depending upon the Pakistani reaction to these thrusts, if the rear areas of Pasrur and Quila Sobha Singh were vacated by the Pakistani reserve formations moving to meet either of the above thrusts and towards the Chenab, XI Corps, with two infantry brigades and an armoured brigade, was to develop an offensive through Gil Ferry in the south towards Quila Sobha Singh and Pasrur, making Narowal fortress en route.

Holding the defences was Pakistan's 1 Corps with the help of the 8 and 15 Infantry Divisions supported by 8 Independent Armoured Brigade. Pakistan's 15 Infantry Division held the northern border covering the approaches to Sialkot and Chawinda, and Pakistan's 8 Infantry Division manned the Zafarwal, Dhamtal and Narowal fortresses and the approaches to Pasrur through the Gil Ferry north of Ajnala. From its base at Sialkot, a line of defences ran eastwards. An anti-tank ditch covered the international boundary up to the Degh Nadi. Thereafter, the Supwal Ditch covered the gap between the Degh Nadi and the Basantar. All major towns had anti-tank ditches, which were integrated into a belt of defences running from the Degh Nadi to Zafarwal, Dhamthal and further down.[44] The Pakistani ADA resources in the sector included 112 LAA Battery of 67 LAA Regiment and the 109 and 211 LAA Batteries of 29 LAA Regiment.[45]

Allotment of ADA to 1 Corps included 29 AD Regiment and a Battery of 45 AD Regiment that was assigned both mobile and static tasks. 29 AD Regiment was deployed for the air defence of Headquarters 1 Corps, gun areas of 31 (Independent) and 41 (Independent) Artillery Brigades, the medium regiments of 39 and

54 Infantry Divisions and the ammunition point at Samba. The regimental headquarters was established alongside the Joint Operations Centre (JOC) of 1 Corps.

45 AD Regiment was allotted to the Independent armoured brigades with 63 and 64 AD Batteries allotted to 2 (Independent) and 16 (Independent) Armoured Brigades, respectively. The third battery was allotted to 39 Artillery Brigade. A troop from this battery was later grouped with 54 Infantry Division.

The regiment had already converted to L/70 and it was always going to be a challenge to operate with the armoured formation(s). Colonel (then Major) H.S. Chaudhary, who was the battery commander of 63 AD Battery, talking of his experience, recollects:[46]

> My battery was with 2 (Independent) Armoured Brigade. I had one troop under (then) Lt Venkateshwarlu at Shakaragarh/Nainakot and the second troop under (then) Captain Rajiv Vig with 7 Cavalry.
>
> I realised that the towed guns with radars and generators would find it difficult to keep pace and had planned to first shed radars if the going got tough and have the guns fire at LPC. The new reflector sights of L/70 were far better than those of the L/60 and that in itself was an advantage that we had over the older L/60 guns. At times, we ended up using the guns without generators as the latter could not be taken along. But we ensured that the AD guns never lagged behind and continued to provide the AD cover to the affiliated units.
>
> Another challenge was the deployment pattern to adopt while providing AD. It was obvious that the older 'two rings' deployment could not be followed and we often deployed the guns in a linear pattern. With this, we tried to ensure that at least 8 of the 12 guns could engage the enemy aircraft.

It was for the better that Major Chaudhary had anticipated these issues and planned for the operations as the ADA troops were soon to face these challenges when 1 Corps launched its offensive on night 5/6 December. The offensive started well with 39 Infantry Division crossing the international border from a north-easterly direction on the evening of 5 December and capturing the initial objectives.

54 Infantry Division, on its part, crossed the international border as per plans, with 64 AD Battery covering the advance. The formation had two artillery formations, viz., 54 Artillery Brigade and 41 (Independent) Artillery Brigade. These were covered by 29 AD Regiment. At 0825 hours, the first enemy air raid came on the

medium gun area and was engaged by the ADA guns. It was claimed that one F-6 had been shot down by the ADA. The advance of 39 Infantry Division ran into trouble as it hit the first belt of a well-laid out minefield at Thakurpur-Parni on 7 December. The advance was contested by PAF making it more difficult for the formation. The PAF strikes, the heavy artillery fire and air attacks frustrated the attempts to make any headway.[47]

It was then decided to attempt a breakthrough from the north, at Harar Khurd (see Map 7). The attempt from the north the following day failed when a second belt of the minefield was encountered. 2 (Independent) Armoured Brigade could not establish a bridgehead and the corps commander then decided to abort his plan of investing Shakargarh and decided to redeploy 39 Division in another sector with HQ 39 Infantry Division taking over the responsibility of Ramgarh sector.[48]

The advance partly failed due to the intensive air support provided by the PAF from its bases at Murid, Sargodha and Risalewala. It had five squadrons for CAS in the sector – two squadrons of F-6 and three of F-86E/F. A Pakistani account mentions:[49]

> As the Indian 39 Division ran into the first minefield belt, PAF's F-6s and F-86s managed to get some good hits at the stalled armour. For the most part, however, PAF had to make-do with sporadic and reactionary air support.

The PAF was not always successful especially during night as Tufail admits 'the vital and vulnerable bridgehead operations and subsequent breakout of all three divisional offensives, escaped punishment from the air as these took place under cover of the night'.[50]

Another reason was that the ADA was taking its toll though there were some raids that were left unattended due to miscommunication. On 7 December, two PAF aircraft raided the gun area of 39 Artillery Brigade but it had been wrongly reported that own (Indian) aircraft would be operating in the area and the ADA guns of 29 AD Regiment were accordingly told to 'hold fire'. The PAF raid was not contested by the ADA, giving PAF a free run. Another raid by two F-6s followed and it was also not engaged initially due to the same confusion, but as soon as the orders were given, the ADA guns opened up and claimed one F-6.[51]

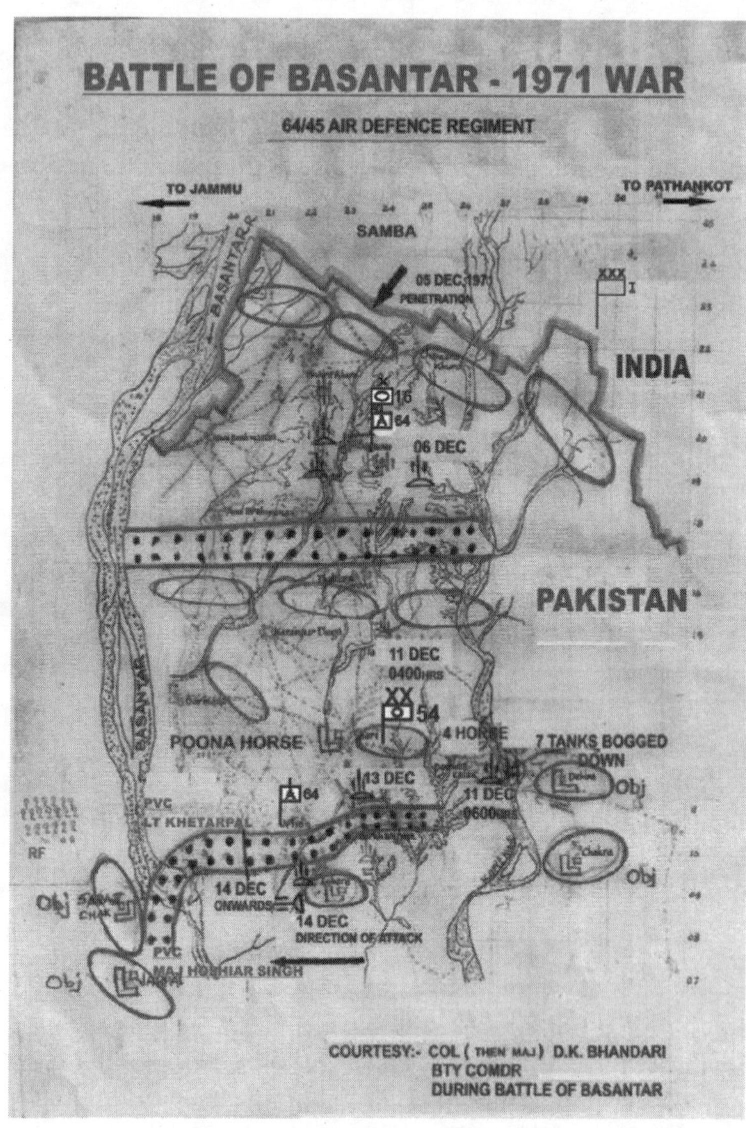


Map 7: The Battle of Basantar – 1971 War.
*Source:* Col. (then Major) D.K. Bhandari

Later in the evening, 217 Medium Regiment gun area was attacked by two F-6s. As the AD guns of 29 AD Regiment opened up, the F-6s turned towards them and tried to strafe them. Despite being under enemy fire, Gunner Bhadreswar Pathak continued to supply ammunition to his gun and the regiment claimed to have shot down a F-6:[52]

> Gunner Bhadreswar Pathak was carrying out the duties of ammunition manager in a detachment of an air defence regiment deployed for the protection of a medium regiment gun area in the western sector. On 7 December 1971, the medium regiment gun area was attacked by two enemy MiG-19 aircraft. The air defence gun immediately opened intense fire on the enemy aircraft. To silence the gun, the enemy aircraft started strafing the gun at low level. Throughout the attack, Gunner Pathak, with complete disregard for his life and safety, kept on supplying ammunition to the gun, resulting in the destruction of one of the enemy aircraft.

One of the Pakistani accounts mention that, during one of its CAS missions on 7 December, four F-6s of No. 11 Squadron, PAF, tried to engage the Sukhois over Zafarwal, when they came under AA fire. The No. 2 aircraft of the PAF mission was hit by AD fire and had to pair up with another aircraft and recover back.[53] 29 AD Regiment claimed another F-6 during the day and Naik Bal Bahadur, the detachment commander, was awarded the Vir Chakra.[54]

The PAF was active over 39 Infantry Division too as it was moving on the left flank of 54 Infantry Division. Amongst the raids carried out on 7 December was one on 7 CAV. 63 AD Battery of 45 AD Regiment, affiliated to 7 CAV engaged the F-6s and claimed to have shot down one aircraft. Later in the day, 1 HORSE was attacked and the battery claimed to have shot down two more aircraft. These claims were, however, not verified.

As 1 HORSE moved towards Tugailpur village to break out from the minefield that had reportedly been breached, the AD guns of 45 AD Regiment had to struggle to keep pace with the tanks churning up the mud track. As the towing vehicles repeatedly got stuck in the churned-up tracks, it was decided to move off the track even though there was a risk of mines along the track. This enabled the AD guns to move faster and they manged to marry up with the armour at Tugailpur village. The guns were still 'on wheels' as the PAF Sabres came in over the village in the evening. The AD troop with 1 HORSE and the adjoining AD troop that was deployed at a distance, both engaged the PAF aircraft, hitting two of them.

Similar action was taking over 36 Infantry Division, as four F-6s came in for a raid at about 1240 hours on 7 December. The battery of 29 AD Regiment deployed at the gun area engaged the F-6s and claimed one aircraft besides hitting two more aircraft.

As per Pakistani accounts, they lost only two aircraft on 7 December to AA fire. An F-6 flown by Flt Lt Wajid Ali Khan of No. 11 Squadron was shot down by AAA as he was attacking ground targets near Marala. He ejected and was taken PoW.[55] The same day, Sqn Ldr Cecil Chaudhry of No. 18 Squadron, PAF, was hit by own AAA, near Zafarwal. He was lucky to fall into Pakistan Army hands as he parachuted down after ejection, only a few hundred yards away from Indian positions. A PAF accounts gives out the details of the incident:[56]

> We took-off and proceeded towards the battle area heading east at low level, with Cecil leading the mission. He was flying at about 200 ft AGL, regulation height. This was not a problem as long as we were over Pak territory.
>
> Once we were approaching the battle area, I asked Cecil to get down lower. He responded by saying there were too many birds around. Birds are the biggest menace against fighter aircraft, especially during low-level missions. A bird hit is no less than an ack-ack shell hitting an aircraft; depending on where the bird impacts and how big it is, it determines the danger to the aircraft and the pilot.
>
> I called a second time urging the leader to get low owing to my experience that, in an ack-ack-infested battle environment, the fighter at 200 ft is most vulnerable if spotted by the gunner observer post. That was when he responded and sounded slightly anxious; addressing me, he said, 'I have been hit, am going to eject'.
>
> How ironical, the choice between a bird and a shell! I instantly told him to pull up and egress. The next thing I saw to my utter relief was Cecil hanging by the silk cord (as we say for a pilot descending down with his parachute). I asked his No. 3 to take over lead and continue with the mission as I watched over Cecil's landing.

The gun area of 217 Medium Regiment was attacked the next day, i.e. 8 December by five F-86 Sabres and, in a repeat of the previous day, the Sabres strafed the ADA gun positions. In this raid, Gunner Pathak was injured but he refused to be evacuated and stayed on his post till he succumbed to his injuries. Prasad was not the detachment commander but an ammunition number and was only the second such gunner to be awarded the Vir Chakra.

With 39 Infantry Division moved to its new area of responsibility, 36 Infantry Division now commenced its operations in the Lasian enclave, with the 18 Infantry Brigade Group having some armour crossing River Ravi and establishing a bridgehead. 115 Infantry Brigade and 14 HORSE used this bridgehead to advance on Nurkot-Shakargarh at 2200 hours on 8 December.[57]

The AD guns were moved forward for the AD of the pontoon bridge being constructed over the river and were in position by 8 December. Surprisingly, no PAF raid came on to the bridge at this critical juncture and the movement across the bridge carried on unhindered. On 10 December, IAF lost a Sukhoi at Zafarwal as it carried out a mission against a watch tower. Flt Lt D.K. Parulkar's Sukhoi was hit be AA fire forcing him to eject. He was taken as PoW.[58] The first raid on the bridge came on 11 December when four F-86 Sabres swooped down on a convoy crossing the bridge about 1600 hours. The F-86s fired rockets and guns, damaging a portion of the bridge. The AD guns opened up and, though they did not hit any PAF aircraft, further damage to the bridge was prevented. The PAF claimed to have 'destroyed the pontoon bridge' but admitted that the raid was carried out too late as the 'crossing by the main elements of Indian 39 Division had already taken place' and 'the destruction of the bridge did not induce any delay in the commencement of this (*36 Infantry Division's*) offensive'.[59]

At the same time, a raid was mounted by four Sabres on the nearby medium gun area and the AD troop successfully deterred the PAF and it also claimed a kill. The same day, in a first-of-its-kind incident, a Sukhoi was shot down by a wire-guided missile near Shakargarh.[60]

On 11 December, 2 (Independent) Armoured Brigade less 7 CAV was placed under command 36 Infantry Division and the division continued to exploit its success along the axis. The armoured brigade had a battery less troop of 45 AD Regiment with it. The formation succeeded in securing the entire east bank of Bein River by 14 December. The PAF made another attempt to destroy the bridge on the Ravi River on 14 December with three F-6s and three F-86 Sabres carrying out the attack. The bridge was not damaged but a convoy that was assembled near the bridge was starfed and attacked with rockets. The AD troop was able to not only deter the PAF but also claimed two aircraft – one each of the attacking F-6 and Sabres. These claims were however were never verified or confirmed.

36 Infantry Division subsequently tried to capture Shakargarh or Nurkot but failed and suffered heavy losses in the process. The main battles were to come the way of 54 Infantry Division. The task allotted to 54 Infantry Division was the destruction of Pak 8 (Independent) Armoured Brigade and the capture of Zaffarwal. As the offensive progressed, 54 Infantry Division made good progress west of Karir, almost according to the plan, but the Pakistani defences at Dehlra village needed to be reduced for the subsequent operations. 39 Infantry Division had contacted Dehlra on 7 December and learnt that it was considerably strengthened by a protective minefield. Also, the defences at Dehlra were linked with another fortified position around Chakra village that was on dominating ground, with two streams on its immediate flanks acting as partial anti-tank obstacles. While a frontal assault would have been disastrous, the division's capacity to take this position at Dehlra from the rear was impaired because of the failure of his abortive attempt to breach the second minefield west of Harar Khurd. Not to hold up the advance any further, the reduction of the Chakra-Dehlra position was entrusted to 54 Infantry Division.

One squadron of 4 HORSE from 16 (Independent) Armoured Brigade was also tasked for the same and it was required to cross the Karir Nadi to put in the attack along with the infantry. On 10 December, the squadron moved out but only eight tanks managed to cross the river with the rest of the tanks and some vehicles getting bogged down in the Nadi during the night move. It was but obvious that these tanks would be 'sitting ducks' to Pakistan Air Force in the morning.

At 0100 hours on 11 December, Major D.K. Bhandari, the battery commander, was called by Commander, 16 (Independent) Armoured Brigade and was asked to ensure air defence of the tanks and vehicles stuck in the river, by first light on 11 December. Considering the sub-allotment of the troops, Major Bhandari decided to task 'D' Troop for the same. It was going to be a challenging task as the troop was deployed almost 8 km away and would have to move cross-country in uncharted, hostile territory with no ground protection, cross a river and then deploy and be ready by first light; all under four hours.

Still working out the details of the planned move and deployment, Major Bhandari moved to 'D' Troop location and briefed Captain Dabral about the new task. As per the plan, the troop was to move to village Tarakwal from where guides were to be provided by 6 MADRAS. The troop, with the guns coming out of action, moved out at 0200 hours.

With the area under enemy shelling, it took almost two hours for the column to traverse the distance and reach village Tarakwal where it was met by two guides of 6 MADRAS, but they were not sure about the exact location of the bogged down tanks and vehicles. With time at premium, Major Bhandari proceeded on a reconnaissance of the exact location of the tanks, leaving Captain Dabral to organize the troop for the crossing.

Having located the tanks, Major Bhandari led the Troop to the west bank of Karir Nadi where it was deployed in its new location by 0600 hours on 11 December. The AD gunners were more than ready for the Pakistani Air Force and they did not have to wait long as six F-86 Sabres came in at about 0825 hours expecting to have an easy picking of the Indian tanks, oblivious of the AD troop that was waiting for them.

As the F-86 Sabres moved in and tried to target the bogged down tanks and vehicles, the AD guns opened up, forcing the Sabres to break off. Colonel (then Captain) R.C. Dabral recalls:[62]

> When I reached Chakra, there was heavy shelling and I could see the village burning across river. There was an intense battle going on across the river that was just about 200 yards ahead of us. The first thing I did was to deploy three guns at a distance of 10 to 20 yards from each other.
>
> As it was not possible for the men to stand and dig trenches because of the heavy shelling and firing going on all around us, I asked them to keep their heads down and dig whatever trenches and pits possible. We spent the night under heavy firing and, by first light, had hardly been able to prepare the trenches.
>
> In the morning, I could look across the river and saw some tanks and 3-4 1-ton vehicles bogged down in the river. I remember the bogged down 1-ton vehicles very clearly.
>
> At 0800 hours or so, the first PAF raid came. There were four F-86 Sabres, and as they came in range, all the three guns opened up. The Sabres tried to attack the bogged down tanks and vehicles but fire from the AD guns was so intense that they failed to execute any successful attack. I observed one Sabre getting

hit, with smoke emitting from the stricken aircraft but it managed to get away. A second raid came in later but was unsuccessful, as the Sabres could not hit a single tank in face of our firing.

The air raid was a complete failure, with not a single tank or vehicle hit by the Pakistani Sabres. The troop remained deployed ahead of the tanks till late evening, even as the tanks fired over the AD guns, on to the enemy defences at Dehlra. About 1800 hours, some of the our tanks came near the ADA troop location and started firing from a raised platform into enemy defences at Dehlra. With the ADA guns deployed ahead of the tanks, the shells were going over the gun location! The gunners kept their heads down as the firing continued for some time. Things turned for worse as the Pakistani tanks responded to own tanks and the AD troop was caught between the tank-to-tank firing that was going on. Thankfully, it did not suffer any casualties.

The Troop was ordered to withdraw from the west bank of Karir Nadi at 1915 hours as all the tanks and vehicles had been recovered. Captain Dabral, the troop commander, organized the reeling up and move back, with the troop getting back to the east bank. It was not too soon as the Pakistani counter-attack to take back Dehlra came in at 2200 hours.[63]

The counter-attack came in and we were again caught between cross-fire. There were star shells bursting all over the place and heavy firing was going on. Captain Dabral manged to reel in his troop and started his move back but the tracks made by the engineers had by now been obliterated. With firing going on all around the troop and the noise of tanks and vehicles making the orientation difficult, it was a challenge to maintain the direction while moving back.

We took almost twelve hours to get to our new location.

Chakra may have been captured but a minefield to the south was holding up the advance. While the engineers were tasked to breach the minefield, the battery was ordered by 16 (Independent) Armoured Brigade on 13 December, at about 1430 hours, to be deployed in area Sadwal, Lohra to provide air defence to the bridgehead established across the minefield in the area.

The battery gun group reached general area of Village Sadwal at about 2300 hours on 13 December. As the minefield was still being breached by 9 Engineer Regiment and an intense tank-vs-tank battle was going on across the minefield, the battery spent the night 'on wheels' and was able to get to its new deployment location by early hours on 14 December, coming into action by 0600 hours.

As had happened at Chakra, the Pakistan Air Force came in at about 0800 hours, once again six F-86 Sabres, trying to pick up easy targets but they were in for a rude surprise as the AD guns opened up almost instantly and, though no aircraft was shot down, one Sabre was hit and it was seen flying away in flames. In the bridgehead, the ADA troop was deployed right on the forward edge on the bridgehead while the armour was yet to breakout and was *behind* the ADA guns.[64]

When we reached the bridgehead, we were received and guided to our locations. Little did I realise at that time that we were the forwardmost troops.

Only when own tanks started moving out of the bridgehead did we come to know that we had no troops deployed ahead of us!

As the battle was progressing, came a new task for the ADA – deploy a section of AD guns in the FDLs in village Hamral to give the direction of attack to the armour and infantry. Captain Dabral was tasked for this and he personally led the section and was in position at 2200 hours. The guns opened up, firing tracers at the appointed time, but were soon picked up by enemy artillery and came under heavy shelling. Undeterred, the section continued firing, giving direction to own tanks and infantry. As if the enemy shelling were not enough, the Pakistani Air Force made an appearance in the morning, but the section under Captain Dabral fought off the F-86 Sabres and ensured no damage was inflicted on own troops.[65]

At about 0300 hours, when I was in my trench, CO 75 Medium Regiment came to my location and told me that my guns were required to give direction of attack in the night to two infantry battalions and the armour that are going for an attack. He (the CO) told me that I was required to fire one round every five minutes between 2300 hours and 0200 hours on 15 December.

I took two AD guns (D-5 and D-6 guns) of No. 3 Section. The detachment commander of D-5 gun was Havildar Appania and that of D-6 gun was Havildar Kycharla Mahalakshmia. Taking the two guns, I reached the FDL and I still remember the objective was at 264 degrees. I had the guns deployed and applied 10 degrees elevation. The 3-ton towing vehicles were parked just behind the guns in case we were required to move at short notice.

The attack went in the H-Hour, I fired the first round at 2300 hours. I could see the objective. As the first round was fired, the flash must have been picked up by a Pak OP as we were soon under artillery shelling, the rounds were falling all around us.

We stayed at our location, firing the tracer rounds every five minutes – and inviting enemy fire on to us. Those three hours were the most harrowing experience I have ever had but we stayed put, doing our job.

In one of the last PAF raids in Shakargarh sector, a F-86 Sabre was claimed by the Indian ADA on 17 December. Havildar Kycharla Mahalakshmia, of D-6 gun detachment of 45 AD Regiment, was awarded the Vir Chakra for shooting down the Sabre. His citation reads:[66]

On 17 December 1971, while commanding a detachment of an air defence battery deployed in the Shakargarh Sector, Havildar Kycharala Mahalakshmia directed the fire of his gun in an accurate manner, resulting in the shooting down of one of the four enemy aircraft attacking his gun. In this action, Havildar Mahalakshmia displayed gallantry and professional skill of a high order.

This was one of few losses admitted by the PAF. Flt Lt Syed Shahid Raza, the ill-fated pilot, was officially declared missing in action and was awarded the Tamgha-i-Juraat.[67]

PAF flew a total of 296 sorties in Shakargarh sector which made up. 41 per cent of PAF's total tactical air support effort. The missions were mostly close air support and armed recce. Even by its own records, almost 40 per cent of the sorties ended up in failure, with only 183 of 296 sorties claimed to be successful by PAF war records.[68]

## PUNJAB

11 Corps was responsible for Punjab sector that included Punjab, Haryana and the Ganganagar district of Rajasthan. It had four formations – 15 Infantry Division defending the Amritsar Sector, 7 Infantry Division which was to defend the territory south of Bhuchar headworks including Ferozepur, 14 Infantry Division responsible for the area between Ferozepur and Fazilka and HQ 'F' Sector to defend Fazilka-Abhor-Ganganagar sector. Opposite 11 Corps was Pakistan's 4 Corps with Pak 10 and 11 Infantry Divisions. Pak 11 Corps with 1 Armoured Division and 33 Infantry Division was deployed in the general area of Montgomery-Bhawalpur.

Besides 49 AD Regiment, under 11 Corps, that was deployed at ten VPs, there were a number of other ADA troops deployed in the sector, especially on rear targets including bridges, ammunition depots and administrative areas. With only localized operations taking place in the sector, the ADA troops did not face many PAF raids, with Pakistan focusing mainly on the airfields and radars in the area. One of the early operations was in Dera Baba Nanak (DBN), Khemkaran and Hussainiwala, and at Abhor-Fazilka near Ganganagar. 49 AD Regiment had a troop deployed for the protection of the independent artillery brigade in DBN sector and a troop at Hussainiwala.[69]

The gun area of 15 Artillery Brigade in Amritsar sector was attacked by PAF on 5 December but was repulsed by the AD troop of 49 AD Regiment with Havildar Ram Kishan claiming a PAF aircraft. The gun area was later reportedly attacked again in the night by a B-57. The IAF carried out sorties in support of the army in the DBN sector. In this No. 222 Squadron, the IAF with its Su-7s played a major role. Air Marshal Narayan Menon who flew Sukhois during the war recalls:[70]

> At DBN, the attack was against gun emplacements. The entire area of interest to us used to be covered in the dust thrown up by convoys and tanks on the move. Target acquisition became difficult but under the guidance of the FAC we were able to accomplish most of the allotted tasks. There was intense activity on the ground and the entire airspace was full of lead ejected from guns of various calibres. After the first day's missions were over, 13 out of 16 Sukhois of the squadron had small arms bullet damage, all of which was repaired overnight and the fighters were ready early morning the next day.

Squadron Leader Sahin's Sukhoi was amongst those that were hit by the AA fire, forcing him to land at Pathankot. Sqn Leader D.S. Jafa, on attachment from the office of the CAS, had his Sukhoi damaged by the enemy AA, forcing him to eject.[71] On 6 December, another Sukhoi was lost in DBN sector when Flying Officer K.C. Kuruvilla's aircraft was hit by Pakistani AA fire as he was making a second pass over enemy tank concentration.[72]

On 7 December, 14 (Independent) Armoured Brigade moved from Amritsar to Abohar. Anticipating a strong reaction for the PAF, it was allotted an ADA Troop but the move went in wihout any incident. The medium regiment of the formation was however attacked at about

0800 hours the same day, during which one of the attacking aircraft was claimed to have been hit. The PAF came again on 8 December to attack the gun area when another F-86 Sabre was claimed by the AD troop.

The PAF attacked the gun area at Fazilka on 14 December and a Sabre was claimed to have been hit by the ADA. On 16 December, PAF attacked the gun area near Kot Kapura, south of Ferozepur, where the armoured division and 14 Infantry Division were concentrating. The ad hoc 'K' AD Troop of 49 AD Regiment engaged the PAF aircraft, hitting one of them.

## 1 ARMOURED DIVISION

50 AD Regiment was the affiliated AD regiment with 1 Armoured Division. It was the only regiment with the L/60 AD guns mounted on Ford Morris trucks and thus suitable for operating with mechanized formations. As the location of the formation was of prime interest to Pakistan, it was important to 'hide' the formation's location and deny it, at times even to own troops. This often led to some unintended confusion as Captain Pimplekhute of 50 AD Regiment found out:[73]

I was posted at School of Artillery, Deolali, as an instructor when the mobilization was ordered. With time, the courses were curtailed and the instructional staff was posted to the units. I was earlier with 19 AD Regiment and was the adjutant during the 1965 War but this time around I was posted to 50 AD Regiment.

When I received my posting order, I was told to report to Jhansi but, on reaching there, I was directed to go to Moga in Punjab. I took a train from Jhansi and somehow reached Moga but there was no reception centre of any detachment to receive me at the railway station. The railway staff was clueless about the location of the division headquarters of my regiment. I stayed there at the railway station for the night in the waiting room. Thankfully, I met an officer in the morning who turned out to be the aide de camp (ADC) to the general officer commanding. But when I asked him about the location of the division headquarters, he refused to tell me, saying that it was a secret!

I managed to get the location of the nearby transit camp from a party of jawans who had reached the station in the morning and then, taking a lift, reached the camp and then on to my unit.

## SOUTHERN COMMAND

The Southern Command was divided into four sectors. From north to south, these were Bikaner, Jaisalmer, Barmer and Kutch. The 1971 campaign was, however, largely confined to the Jaisalmer and Barmer sectors due to the poor surface communications in the other two sectors. The Jaisalmer sector was under 12 Infantry Division with the divisional headquarters was at Tanot, about 120 km north of Jaisalmer. The Barmer sector was under 11 Infantry Division that had its headquarters at Ranasar, about 11 km short of the border at Gadra Road. The divisional centre lines were about 240 km apart in these two sectors. There was no corps headquarters with an advanced headquarters of Southern Command exercising control over the operations in the sector. The Indian plan was to cut-off Karachi from Lahore by capturing Rahimyar Khan with 12 Division. At the same time, 11 Division was to advance to the Naya Chor-Umarkot area and pose a threat to Hyderabad (Sindh).[74]

The ADA allotment to 11 and 12 Infantry Divisions was a battery each from 152 AD Regiment with the subunits deployed with the artillery brigades. 11 Artillery Brigade was located at Magra and Harsani with 12 Artillery Brigade at Ranch and Ghantiyah. The third battery was retained as command reserve.

## LONGEWALA

The Battle of Longewala was one of the first major engagements in the western sector, fought at the Indian border post of Longewala, in the Thar desert. The concept of Pakistan Army's plan was rather bold with 38 CAV, with a battalion from 206 Brigade tasked to capture Ramgarh, and 22 CAV less one squadron with a battalion from 51 Brigade to neutralize Jaisalmer airfield. However, the roles were reversed; with 206 Brigade tasked to follow the advance and capture Longewala with one battalion and establish a firm base there. The plan was to make the approach march to the IB from the concentration area south of Reti at night and the next night advance to the assigned objectives. The PAF was expected to provide air cover during the entire operation.[75]

At 4:00 a.m. on 5 December, the enemy armour was seen enveloping a prominent dune south of BP-638, ostensibly to overrun the Longewala defences. These forces were later identified as 22 CAV, plus a squadron of US-built Shermans. The enemy armour was first engaged by the recoilless (RCL) guns but with the enemy threatening to overrun the defences, the company commander requested for reinforcements and immediate close air support.

The Hunters from Jaisalmer were the ones that were tasked for the CAS mission and, as the first mission of two Hunters appeared over Longewala they spotted tanks all over, some on the sand dunes, some heading towards Ramgarh and some just bogged in the sand. Flying low, the mission leader fired a rocket at the first tank, a T-59 creeping up towards the defended locality and scored a direct hit. He then knocked out five other tanks. In Wing Commander K. Suresh's words:[76]

> On 5th morning, the first pair, i.e. D.K. Dass and Ramesh Gosain, took off in the darkness and were over the target at 07:02 hrs. Major Atma Singh, who was airborne in his small Krishak aircraft, confirmed that the tanks that were spotted around Longewala were indeed those of the enemy. This was another unique development that emerged so successfully, viz. air observation post (AOP) pilots acting as airborne forward air controllers (FAC), and a very high degree of co-ordination was achieved during the war.
>
> Our strike force had a field day bashing tanks, although up against intense ground fire.

The Hunters were not contested by the PAF and all that was between them and an outright slaughter of the Pakistani force were the tanks of 22 CAV. They did take evasive, albeit futile, manoeuvres, mostly in circles, in order to ward off direct hits but also used their AA machine guns. One tank fired its main gun at Wing Commander Suresh's Hunter and almost knocked it off:[77]

> I took off later in the morning with Sherwin as my leader. It was an awesome sight at Longewala, with several tanks on fire and some still smouldering. We had carried twelve T-10 rockets to be fired in three passes, to be followed by 30 mm cannon attacks. Tanks were going round and round in crazy circles, kicking up dust to hide themselves to the extent possible. During a gun attack, one of the tanks whose main gun was pointing towards me fired a shell. Although the shell did not hit me, the flash and dust blinded me and my aircraft just fell out

of control. I hit a sand dune at 420 Knots and I am living to tell the tale. During those fleeting moments, I remembered my entire life. As the dust cleared, I found myself flying very low but the aircraft was just about controllable. Sherwin had by then started heading home and I called out to him, since I could not catch up, as the speed was not building up above 250 knots, even with full throttle. He quickly joined up with me and his talking to me eased all the tension. I flew the aircraft back to base and landed safely with his encouragement.

Throughout the day on 5 and 6 December, IAF Hunters were over the target continuously and pounded the Pakistani armour. This was possible since there was no aerial opposition. Whatever little opposition the armoured regiment could offer was not enough, except to score some non-consequential hits on the Hunters. Longewala became a graveyard of Pakistani armour. It may be just a hypothetical question but it is still something worth pondering – if the Pakistani column had integral ADA, would it have made a difference?

## NAYA CHOR

11 Infantry Division's plan envisaged the capture of Khokhropar and Gadra City on D plus one day. A firm base was thereafter to be established by the leading brigade for a divisional attack on Naya Chor, the main enemy position before Umarkot. The leading brigade was to complete this task by D plus two days, and Naya Chor was expected to fall in the next six days. The main axis of advance was to be Munabao-Khokhrapar-Parbat Ali, while a subsidiary thrust was to make for Khinsar and Chachro.[78]

The ADA was involved in the operations right from the start, as a L/60 gun was used to during the pre-H-Hour operations to destroy an enemy observation post in Munabao area. It fired forty-nine rounds and destroyed the post, facilitating the initial movement across the IB. The IAF was used in the sector against the Pakistani defences and on 5 December suffered its first loss to AAA as a HF-24 of No. 220 Squadron, IAF, was shot down near Naya Chor and Flt Lt J.L. Bhargava was taken prisoner.[79]

On 5 Dec. 71, with Air Cmde K.K. Bakshi as my leader, I was in a 2 ac formation attacking Naya Chor Area. It was my first sortie. Over the target I was hit by ground fire and I experienced numerous emergencies, one after another –

hydraulic failure followed by controls reverting to manual, port engine flaming out, ASI zero, R/T failure and finally starboard engine JPT rising above the red mark and RPM fluctuating. I decided to eject. My parachute barely opened when I touched down. I probably damaged my spine during this ejection. When I settled down on a sand dune, time was 0920 hours (IST). I looked for a map but to my surprise I had none. There was no map in the survival pack. I thought that I was north of the railway line (Khokhrapar to Naya Chor) and close to Khokropar whereas I was actually south of this line and near Vasarbha, which is nearly 15 km west of Khokropar. I knew for certain that I was in Pak territory. I changed my watch to PST.

As the advance progressed, an ADA troop located aa Munabao was moved ahead on 7 December to provide AD to the rail track being laid ahead of Khokhrapar. The troop reached its new location at 1615 hours and, as it was in the process of deploying the guns, a PAF raid came in. The guns were unhooked and, while still on wheels, engaged the F-86 Sabres. Though no Sabre was hit, the raid was repulsed.

Pakistan had No. 19 Squadron with 26 F-86E/F, No. 9 Squadron with 7 F-104 (9 more RJAF F-104 became available from 14 December onwards) and a half-strength No. 7 Squadron with 8 B-57 bombers. No. 2 Squadron with 11 T-33 trainers was also used for strike missions. A small detachment of 4 F-86E was stationed at the forward base of Talhar. In absence of the low-level radar cover, PAF had mobile observer units to provide early warning.[80]

The PAF remained active in the sector as it carried out repeated strike to disrupt the rail link. On 8 December, Gadra Road was attacked with the ADA guns beating back the Sabres (*the details of PAF raids on rail network are covered in the subsequent* chapter). The focus of PAF remined on disrupting the communications even as Indian operations progressed with 11 Division capturing Parbat Ali on 13 December. On 15 December, the ADA guns at Gadra Road were moved forward to protect an IAF radar. The ADA resources in the sector were reinforced with the arrival of 179 AD Battery of 48 AD Regiment that reached Gadra Road on 16 December.[81] The troops were deployed at the Gadra Road and Munabao railway stations. The last ADA troops to arrive in the command was a troop of 129 AD Regiment (TA) that was placed under 12 Infantry Division on 16 December 1971.

In all, PAF carried out 175 sorties (including 24 night sorties by B-57, T-33 and C-130 in support of Pak 18 Division in Chor, Ramgarh and Kutch Sectors. In addition, 40 combat air patrol sorties were flown by F-86E and F-104. It did not acknowledge the loss of any aircraft to ground fire while three Indian HF-24 Maruts were lost to AA fire in the sector.[82]

## NOTES

1. Prasad and Thapliyal, *The India-Pakistan War of 1971: A History*, Natraj Publishers, New Delhi, 2014, pp. 104-11 and Major K.C. Praval, '1971 Operations: Case West-I', *Indian Defence Reviews*, 14 March 2011 accessed on 6 July 2019 at http://www.indiandefencereview.com/spotlights/1971-operations-case-west-i/
2. A.H. Amin, 'The Western Theatre in 1971: A Strategic and Operational Analysis', *Defence Journal*, accessed on 17 May 2020 at http://www.defencejournal.com/2002/february/theatre.htm
3. Prasad and Thapliyal, op. cit., pp. 108-10.
4. Ibid.
5. Major K.C. Praval, '1971 Operations: Case West-I', op. cit.
6. Ibid.
7. Prasad and Thapliyal, op. cit., pp. 111-13 and A.H. Amin, 'The Western Theatre in 1971: A Strategic and Operational Analysis', *Defence Journal*, Karachi, 2002, accessed on 19 May 2019 at http://defencejournal.com/2002/february/theatre.htm
8. Prasad and Thapliyal, op. cit., pp. 140-2, Major General Sukhwant Singh, '1971 War: Battle of Chhamb', *Indian Defence Review*, 1 December 2018, accessed on 23 May 2019 at http://www.indiandefencereview.com/spotlights/1971-war-battle-of-chhamb/, Major K.C. Praval, '1971 Operations: Case West-II', *Indian Defence Reviews* and Major General A.J.S. Sandhu, *Battleground Chhamb, The India Pakistan War of 1971*, Manohar, New Delhi, 2018.
9. Interview with Captain Arvind Nautiyal.
10. Ibid.
11. Tufail, *In the Ring and on its Feet*, p. 100.
12. Interview with Captain Arvind Nautiyal.
13. Ibid.
14. Citation for Sitara-e-Jur'at for Flt Lt Israr Ahmad can be accessed at https://www.pafmuseum.com.pk/heroes/
15. Interview with Capt Arvind Nautiyal.
16. Gp Capt Gurdip Singh, 'Ejected Over No Man's Land!', *Bharat Rakshak*, 22 December 2018, accessed on 19 May 2019 at http://www.bharat-rakshak.com/IAF/history/1971war/1375-ejection-over-no-mans-land.html#gsc.tab=0

17. Major General Syed Ali Hamid, 'The View from the Other Side', *Bharat Rakshak*, 22 December 2018, accessed on 19 May 2019 at http://www.bharat-rakshak.com/IAF/history/1971war/1376-ejected-over-no-man-s-land-the-view-from-the-other-side.html#gsc.tab=0
18. Flying officer GD Bomboat was awarded the Vayu Sena Medal (Gallantry). Gazette of India dated 7th October 1972, No.108, Pres/72, dated 23rd September 1972 refers. It can be accessed at http://www.bharat-rakshak.com/IAF/Database/Awards/awards.php?qunit=27%20Sqn
19. AVM A.K. Tiwary, *Indian Air Force in Wars*, Lancer Publishers, New Delhi, 2013, pp. 194-5.
20. Tufail, op. cit., p. 100.
21. Interview with Capt Arvind Nautiyal.
22. Ibid.
23. Ibid.
24. Ibid.
25. Ibid.
26. Major General A.J.S. Sandhu, *Battleground Chhamb: The India Pakistan War of 1971*, op. cit., pp. 140-50.
27. Claim made by the Regiment's veterans but no record or acknowledgement exists for these claims and were most probably just hits on the PAF aircraft and not kills.
28. Bhattacharya was awarded the Vayu Sena Medal (Gallantry). Gazette of India dated 7th October 1972, No. 108, Pres/72, dated 23rd September 1972 refers. It can be accessed at http://www.bharat-rakshak.com/IAF/Database/7739
29. Gazette of India, 17th June 1972, No. 79, Pres/72, dated 1st June 1972, accessed on 11 August 2020 at https://www.gallantryawards.gov.in/Awardee/flight-lieutenant-vijay-kumar-wahi
30. Interview with Capt Arvind Nautiyal.
31. Prasad and Thapliyal, op. cit., p. 224.
32. Gp Capt Apram Jeet Singh, 'Mission to Chhamb', *Bharat Rakshak*, 16 June 2017, accessed on 14 August 2019 at http://www.bharat-rakshak.com/IAF/History/1971War/1089-Chamb.html#gsc.tab=0
33. Maj Gen Syed Ali, 'MiG-21 Down', *Friday Times*, 8 March 2019, accessed on 21 March 2019 at https://www.thefridaytimes.com/43224-2/
34. Sandhu, op. cit., p. 260.
35. The citation can be accessed at https://www.gallantryawards.gov.in/Awardee/uttam-jawalge
35. Flt Lt Ahmad had earlier taken part in the strike missions on Srinagar airfield. Accessed on 18 March 2019 at http://www.pafmuseum.com.pk/heroes/1971-gallantry-awards
36. Tufail, op. cit., p. 101. The citation that can be accessed at https://www.pafmuseum.com.pk/heroes/ reads:

    'On 8th December, his aircraft was hit by ground fire in Chhamb-Jaurian sector; the ground fire presumably hit a bomb fuse, causing the aircraft to explode.

Flight Lieutenant Fazal always volunteered to fly irrespective of the danger of the mission. He displayed exemplary courage and determination at his young age in spite of limited experience. He was awarded the Sitara-i-Juraat.'

37. Sqn Leader M.K. Jha was awarded the Vir Chakra. His citation can be accessed at https://www.gallantryawards.gov.in/awardee/157
38. B. Chakravorty, *Stories of Heroism: PVC & MVC Winners*, Allied Publishers, New Delhi, 1995, p. 112.
39. Tufail, op. cit., p. 102.
40. Prasad, op. cit., p. 223. In an interesting incident, an infantry battalion, 3/5 Gurkha Rifles, claimed to have shot down the F-6 but the claim, after verification, was rightly given to 27 AD Regiment.
41. Bains was awarded the Vir Chakra. Gazette of India, 29th July 1972, No. 92, Pres/72, dated 18th July 1972 refers. The details can be accessed at https://www.gallantryawards.gov.in/awardee/264
42. Major General Sukhwant Singh, '1971 War: Battle of Shakargarh Bulge', *Indian Defence Review*, 10 October 2017, accessed on 19 April 2019 at http://www.indiandefencereview.com/spotlights/1971-war-battle-of-shakargarh-bulge/, A.H. Amin, *The Western Theatre in 1971: A Strategic and Operational Analysis* and Prasad and Thapliyal, op. cit., pp. 157-60.
43. Prasad and Thapliyal, op. cit., p. 160 and Major General Sukhwant Singh, *1971 War: Battle of Shakargarh Bulge.*
44. A.H. Amin, *The Western Theatre in 1971: A Strategic and Operational Analysis.*
45. Riza, op. cit., pp. 408-9.
46. Interview with Colonel H.S. Chaudhary.
47. Prasad and Thapliyal, op. cit., p. 161.
48. Ibid., pp. 162-3.
49. Tufail, op. cit., p. 106.
50. Ibid.
51. This is an unverified claim though the official history does mention that three PAF were shot down by ADA on the TBA.
52. Citation for Gunner Bhadreswar Pathak's Vir Chakra (Gazette Notification: 77 Pres/72,17-6-72), accessed on 13 July 2020 at https://www.gallantryawards.gov.in/awardee/4273
53. Tufail, op. cit., pp. 106-7.
54. Gallantry Awards, Ministry of Defence accessed at https://www.gallantryawards.gov.in/awardee/2816
55. Tufail, op. cit., p. 108.
56. Tufail claims that Cecil Chaudhary's aircraft was '*hit by a bird or by own AAA*'. Tufail, op. cit., p. 108 and Hussain Sajad, *Flight of the Falcon*, Vanguard Books, Lahore, 2010, p. 111.
57. Prasad was not the gun detachment commander but an ammunition number the second gunner to be awarded the Vir Chakra.
57. Prasad and Thapliyal, op. cit., p. 165.
58. Flt Lt D.K. Parulkar was repatriated a year later, after the war.

Air Marshal Narayan Menon, 'Recollections of the 1971 War', *Indian Defence Review*, vol. 24, no. 4, 4 October-December 2009, 10 December 2019, accessed on 20 February 2020 at http://www.indiandefencereview.com/spotlights/recollections-of-the-1971-war/

59. Kaiser Tufail, 'Air Support in Shakargarh: 1971 War', *Aeronaut*, 14 April 2010, accessed on 16 March 2020 at http://kaiser-aeronaut.blogspot.com/2010/04/air-support-in-shakargarh-1971-war.html
60. Air Marshal Narayan Menon, 'Recollections of the 1971 War', *Indian Defence Review*, vol. 24, no. 4, 4 October-December 2009, 10 December 2019, accessed on 20 February 2020 at http://www.indiandefencereview.com/spotlights/recollections-of-the-1971-war/
61. Interview with Col D.K. Bhandari.
62. Interview with Colonel R.C. Dabral.
63. Ibid.
64. Ibid.
65. Ibid.
66. The citation can be accessed at https://www.gallantryawards.gov.in/awardee/1583
67. Flt Lt Syed Shahid Raza's citation for Tagma-i-Jurat can be accessed at https://www.pafmuseum.com.pk/heroes/
68. Tufail, *In the Ring and on its Feet*, p. 110.
69. Lt Gen K.P. Candeth, *The Western Front*, Allied Publishers, New Delhi 1984, p. 149.
70. Air Marshal Narayan Menon, 'Recollections of the 1971 War', *Indian Defence Review*, vol. 24, no. 4, 4 October-December 2009, 10 December 2019, accessed on 20 February 2020 at http://www.indiandefencereview.com/spotlights/recollections-of-the-1971-war/
71. Jafa was awarded the Vir Chakra. The citation can be accessed at https://www.gallantryawards.gov.in/awardee/163
72. Gazette of India, 16th June 1973, No. 37, Pres/73 dated 26th January 1973, accessed on 23 April 2020 at https://www.gallantryawards.gov.in/awardee/181
73. Interview with Colonel M.R. Pimpalkhute.
74. Prasad and Thapliyal, op. cit., pp. 191-3.
75. Major General Kuldip Singh Bajwa, 'Battle of Longewala', *Journal of the United Service Institution of India*, vol. CXXXVIII, no. 574, October-December 2008.
76. Wg Cdr Suresh, Battle of Longewala: 5th and 6th December', *Bharat Rakshak*, 12, accessed on 13 March 2020 at http://www.bharat-rakshak.com/IAF/history/1971war/1282-kukke-suresh.html#gsc.tab=0
77. Ibid.
78. Prasad and Thapliyal, op. cit., pp. 197-8.
79. Air Cmde J.L. Bhargava, 'How I got Captured', *Marutfans*, accessed on 14 June 2020 at https://marutfans.wordpress.com/2010/08/31/how-i-got-captured-air-cmde-jl-brother-bhargava/
80. Tufail, *In the Ring and on its Feet*, pp. 113-17.
81. Chhetri, *Meandering Memories*, p. 102.
82. Tufail, *In the Ring and on its Feet*, pp. 113-17.

CHAPTER 8

# Air Defence of Depth Areas

ADA of both armies was tasked to defend military and civilian installations and assets, including dams, bridges, depots, harbours and ports. Some of the known Indian ADA deployments were as under:

| *Installation* | *Allotment* | *Regiment* | *Remarks* |
|---|---|---|---|
| Akhnoor Bridge | Troop | 128 AD Regiment (TA) | L/60 |
| Madhopur Bridge | Troop | 26 AD Regiment | L/60 |
| | 2 × Troops | 140 AD Regiment (TA) | L/60 |
| Mirthal Bridge | Troop | 140 AD Regiment (TA) | L/60 |
| Ucchi Bassi | 2 × Troops | 140 AD Regiment (TA) | L/60 |
| Thein Dam | 2 × Troops | 140 AD Regiment (TA) | L/60 |
| Harike | Troop | 26 AD Regiment | L/60 |
| Okha | Troop | 129 AD Regiment (TA) | L/60 |
| Dwarka Port | Troop | 129 AD Regiment (TA) | L/60 |
| Bhabha Atomic Research Centre | Battery | 103 AD Regiment (TA) | L/60 |
| Tarapor Atomic Power Station | Troop | 130 AD Regiment (TA) | L/60 |
| Baroda Oil Refinery | Troop | 130 AD Regiment (TA) | L/60 |

The subsequent allocation changed with the progress of operations and the arrival of ADA troops from the east as they were relieved from their tasks in absence of any PAF activity. Some ADA troops were shifted from the east and were deployed on logistic installations and economic targets. The re-adjustments and late deployment were because the ADA resources were at a premium and there were not adequate resources to be deployed at all assets *ab initio*. It was the same with the defence of the naval installations and the Navy had to augment the defences at its important installations, especially on the west coast, from within its own resources.[1]

> Additional batteries ashore were installed – two 4-inch guns at Okha, two 40/60s at Jamnagar, one 40/60 at Valsura. At Bombay, the existing batteries were augmented by putting two additional 40/60 guns each at Colaba Point and Worli. Three additional 40/60 guns were installed at Oyster Rock and Middle Ground. Four 40/60 guns were installed at critical points in the naval dockyard.

Pakistan ADA was similarly deployed on several installations and VAs but there was a difference in the allocation of responsibility. For the defence of air force installations and the naval dockyard at Karachi, the responsibility lay with the 3 AA Brigade. The field formations controlled the organic AA units while the logistic areas were provided by AA Mujahid companies for all other tasks. Due to the inadequacy of AA resources, most of the oil installations and railways remained largely unprotected. To make up for the deficiency, several Mujahid AA companies were raised but the equipment of some of the AA companies was found to be defective, seriously undermining their efficacy.[2]

The ADA resources remained woefully short of the requirement and Pakistan, in particular, had to pay a heavy price for this. Keeping in mind its overall strategy for the pre-emptive strikes, PAF only attacked selected IAF airfields on 3 December and did not target any other installation. In fact, it was India that first attacked the strategic targets, as Hunters of the Operational Conversion Unit (OCU) based at Jamnagar attacked Karachi and its reserve oil tanks at 0850 hours IST on 4 December. The attack was successful with many a target set ablaze.[3]

Wing Commander Donald Melvyn Conquest, the then commanding officer of the OCU, recalls:[4]

> As per SOP (standard operating procedure) we dipped our noses off Karachi and fired a few rounds into the sea to test our guns. Mukherjee's guns had jammed, so three of them (Squadron Leader S.N. Medhekar and Flight Lieutenant S.K. Gupta) pressed on at 500 ft along the coast. As they neared Karachi, its large oil tanks loomed out of the coastal sky, its silver paint shining in the sunlight. We made two runs without difficulty. After the first, there were huge balls of fire and volumes of smoke that came out of the storage tank. As the smoke and haze made flying dangerous, we aborted other runs and flew back.

Karachi harbour was famously attacked on 4 December as the Indian Navy launched Operation Trident that saw the first use of anti-ship missiles in the region. Pakistan lost a minesweeper, a destroyer and a cargo vessel carrying ammunition. Another destroyer was badly damaged and had to be eventually scrapped. As the report of the Hunter's raid had not yet been officially sent to Air Headquarters, it was unaware of the IAF's role in the damage caused at Karachi and the credit for the raid was given to the Navy alone. It was much later when the details of the IAF raid came to be known that its role was acknowledged.[5]

The IAF's OCU at Jamnagar airbase, with its Hunter aircraft, had no assigned role for the morning. Wing Commander Don Conquest asked his commander Air Commodore Pete Wilson whether the new Hunters Type 56A and 235-gallon drop tanks could be used on Karachi. Wilson was busy planning to hit Badin and Drig Road with MiG-21s at first light on December 4 and allowed Conquest to go ahead with his plans.

Four OCU Hunters took off on the morning of December and made two runs over 'the large oil tanks looming out of the skyline, their silver paint shining in the rising sun'. In Conquest's words, 'after the first [run], there were huge balls of fire and volumes of smoke coming out of the storage. The smoke haze made flying dangerous; we aborted the other runs and flew back.'

Before Conquest could file his reports about Karachi on landing, his squadron was ordered to fly to Jaisalmer. With air headquarters unaware of any action by OCU at Karachi, the hits were recorded in the navy's count until it was clarified a few years later and credit duly accorded.

Expanding the scope of the airstrikes, IAF attacked Mangla Dam early in the day on 4 December. It was carried out by four IAF Hunters of No. 20 Squadron, IAF, from Pathankot at 0742 hours.[6]

As with other targets in the depth, they faced no opposition from the AA defences and managed to get back without any incident. Pakistan had deployed AD guns for the defence of the dam but in absence of a radar cover, they received no warning of the raid and were caught napping. As there was no confirmation of the damage caused to the dam, it was again attacked by two aircraft of the same squadron later in the day at 1655 hours. Even during this raid, the AA defences failed to achieve any hits.

It was only after Indian Navy's raid on Karachi on the night of 4/5

December that PAF decided to carry out an attack on Okha for which a B-57 from Masroor was used on the evening of 5 December. While it was clear that any strike by PAF would be unlikely to find the Indian Navy missile boats still at Okha, it was decided to go ahead with an airstrike to hamper any future missile boat operations from the port.[7]

In the wake of the missile attack, Pak Navy felt – almost as an after-thought – that the home base of the missile boats at Okha needed to be taken out. In all likelihood, the tit-for-tat raid serving as retribution of sorts would have been uppermost in the minds of the naval staff. In any case, the necessity of tackling the threat of missile boats also sank in at PAF's COC and it was agreed to attack Okha harbour. Of course, it was not expected that the missile boats would still be berthed at the quayside in Okha. As a matter of fact, these had already been dispersed to smaller locations along the Saurashtra coast, even before the war had started. None the less, it was the considered opinion of the Pak Navy that a hit on the infrastructure could hamper missile boat operations to some extent.

Okha port had a troop of 129 AD Regiment (TA) with another troop at Dwarka. While only two dispersed L/60 troops were not enough to ensure an effective defence, they were expected to at least deter the PAF aircraft from trying to attack the port. In the end, the PAF sent just one B-57 against Okha and it proved to be 'one too many'. The raid has been described by Tufail in his book, *In the Ring and On Its Feet.*[8]

On the evening of 5 December, Flt Lt Shabbir A. Khan was standing out on the B-57 tarmac watching preparations for the night missions, when he was informed about being detailed for a strike on Okha harbour. He, along with his navigator, Sqn Ldr Ansar Ahmad, rushed off to the operations room to start planning the mission. Two hours after moonrise seemed like a good selection of the TOT, as the glimmering sea would clearly outline the edges of the darkened harbour.

Taking off at 2210 hrs, the B-57 got a fiery send-off as the AAA opened up in the nearby Karachi harbour, signalling an air raid. Continuing the take-off, Shabbir and Ansar settled down to watch – with unnerving anticipation – the moonbeams dazzling the creeks and estuaries of the Kutch coast to their port side. Finally, turning to the attack heading, they picked up a sizeable flotilla on their radar, about 20 nm to their starboard. There was a temptation to go for the ships, but discipline prevailed and they continued for the designated target. Reaching the pull-up point, Shabbir pushed the throttles to 100 per cent power, while Ansar started to guide him into the attack. Just when Shabbir pressed the bomb release button and there was no release, Ansar realised that he had forgotten to arm the release switch. In a fraction of a second he flipped the switch on and Shabbir pipped the button again, pulling out of the dive narrowly. After some 10-odd seconds, there was a tremendous flash of light and the aircraft shook up with the blast. A direct hit had been achieved as nine 500-lb bombs slammed into fuel tanks and other stores at the harbour. In the meantime, AAA had started to fire and the sky seemed ablaze. Shabbir and Ansar saw the shells continuously exploding along the aircraft's flight path but luckily, the bomber escaped unscathed.

The AA defence at Okha put up by the manual L/60 guns of Second World War vintage did not prove to be very effective and the PAF raid was a partial success. No missile boats were found but PAF succeeded in the destruction of oil tanks which brought an end to the use of Okha as the advance missile base. As the *History of Indian Navy* notes:[9]

From 5 December onwards, Okha received concentrated attention by the Pakistan Air Force aircraft and was bombed almost every day. Our special oil fuel tank was blown up in the very early stages of the war and our use of Okha as an advance base came to an end.

During the 'almost daily' raids, PAF, suffered a setback as it lost an F-86 Sabre to Indian ADA. Though the PAF accounts do not mention the details of any raid by the F-86, a Sabre was claimed by Indian ADA on 5 December at a military installation (Okha) defended by 129 AD Regiment. Naik Dhondi Ram Bhansode of the regiment was awarded the Vir Chakra for the same.[10]

Attock oil refinery was targeted by the IAF on 6 December with four Hunters from Pathankot detailed to carry out the strike. Due to a technical fault, one of the Hunters had to abort with only three aircraft going in for the strike. They struck the refinery at 0741 hours causing serious damage with the complex set ablaze.[11]

By the time the Pakistani AA defences opened up, the Hunters had already executed the attack. They managed to get back without any damage.[12]

This target was defended by a good network of anti-aircraft guns controlled by the nearby airfield of Chaklala which was about 20 miles away. Destruction of the refinery or, at the very least, hampering its operations, would impose a severe crunch in the POL reserves of the Pakistanis.

It was planned to send a four-ship strike to Attock. Wg Cdr Parker, along with Sqn Ldr Bajpai and Flying Officers DeMonte and Karumbaya, were the pilots on this mission. Technical snags prevented Karumbaya's Hunter from starting. Finally, Parker, DeMonte and Bajpai took off to attack the refinery.

The actual routing of the Hunters took them over for a diversionary attack on to Chaklala, then executing a turnabout and hitting the Attock oil refinery from the west. The AA guns were caught napping at first. The refinery was shrouded in camouflage, and the AA guns were defending it to the inch. Parker was the first to dive in. The Hunters carried cannon ammunition, and the first burst set fire to the fuel tanks.

The fire spread quickly through the refinery fuelled by the vapours. The blaze spread so fast that their height was reaching the Hunters which were making their second run. The ack-ack fire could not make its presence felt, and all the aircraft were recovered safely. Gun camera pictures of the raid prove the accuracy of the damage to the facilities. PR recce confirmed the damage to the refinery. The fire in the refinery resulted in a beautiful blaze lasting several days and nights. Indian bombers flying in the stealth of the night reported the flames which served as a navigational aid for some days to come.

The failure of Pakistani AA defences at Attock, as at other targets in the depth areas, was primarily due to the absence of a radar cover and an early warning system.[13]

Two strafing runs by the Hunters set fire to several fuel tanks. The AAA defences were taken by surprise, but by the time the guns opened up, the damage had been done. The Hunters survived the AAA barrage, and with no interceptors on patrol, they made good their escape.

The war was just a couple of days old and with news of PAF raids coming in daily, almost all major cities regularly carried out air raid warning drills and civil defence practice. Bombay (now Mumbai) was no exception. A routine practice on 6 December had an unintended effect on the civil population of the metropolis as 'balls of fire' were seen over the city creating panic among the people. It was reported that 'radar men' had sighted a flight of Pakistani jet planes sweeping in from the Arabian Sea and the AA guns had opened up to protect the city. A United News of India (UNI) dispatch from Bombay said that hundreds of rounds were fired but it was not clear whether the PAF planes had attacked the city or a nearby naval base. To add to the panic, UNI quoted hospital sources as having reported that 'fifteen persons were wounded by shrapnel from the antiaircraft guns'. Other air raid warnings were reportedly sounded in towns and villages in the area around Bombay.[14] Michael Patrao, a Mumbai resident, remembers the day well:[15]

I had no fear of enemy attack on the city until one night fear gripped me with its icy hands as it did all the residents in Vakola locality of Santacruz. The reason: a series of red balls of fire had floated in the air moments after a blackout, and this was something the people had never before witnessed. Many thought it was the enemy bombing the city. Although it was dark, I was still playing in the bylanes with a neighbourhood friend when I saw the red balls of fire. I was scared stiff, as also my friend. This is our end, I thought. We both decided to rush to the nearest shelter, which happened to be a Hanuman Mandir.

We waited with bated breath until we heard the all-clear siren and the lights were switched on. The next day, the fiery red balls were the talk of the town.

The city was never attacked by PAF and all the confusion was due to incorrect reporting. As regards the firing of AA guns, it was never clear if the ADA troops had fired or if it was the AA guns of the navy.

While there were more rumours than actual news about the PAF raids on depth areas, there was nary a doubt about the IAF raids on Pakistani strategic targets as they continued uncontested. The next target was an attack on Mangla dam on 7 December.[16]

The next economic target on the list of No. 20 Squadron was the Mangla Hydel Dam which was attacked on the morning of December 7th. The strike was scheduled to be a four aircraft mission. Sqn Ldr R.N. Bharadwaj led the raid, with C.S. Dhillon, Chowfin and Heble as his wingmen. All the Hunters were equipped with 2 × 68 mm rocket pods.

Mangla Dam had been assigned as a target for the squadron as far back as October 1971. Parker was briefed about the position and location of the dam, and the objective was given as the destruction of the hydroelectric station at the foot of the dam. With no pictures to go by, and instructions to knock out the hydel station, a trip for Parker was arranged to the Joginder Nagar Dam in Punjab.

This dam was supposed to simulate the actual layout of Mangla Dam, and Parker was allowed to study the area in detail. Later, Parker and Bharadwaj, flew a dummy sortie to the Joginder Nagar Dam, to try and test their tactics. All the training paid off, when Bharadwaj led the actual raid on the Mangla Dam, he found the target exactly as they imagined it, with the hydel station at the foot of the dam and two AA guns on top of it.

Again the enemy AA defences were caught napping. They could not respond effectively to stop the Hunters which, by that time, had set fire and damaged the hydel station. The Hunters suffered several cannon stoppages and failure of the rocket pods to fire, but all in all, the power station was badly knocked about.

A second strike was planned later in the day. Bharadwaj was deputed to lead the air raid again, accompanied by Dhillon, Sharma and Chowfin. But Bharadwaj's aircraft suffered problems, the engine refusing to start and the remaining three carried out the raid, without damage or loss. Sqn Ldr Rozario led a four-aircraft mission to Kohat, with DeMonte and Karumbaya as his wingmen. The fourth aircraft, flown by Deoskar, returned to base as soon as it suffered some technical snags after take-off. The raid was successful.

Pakistani AA defences were almost helpless against such raids as they could only react after the raid and to no avail.[17]

Another three-ship raid was flown the same afternoon, and some damage was claimed. The dam was defended by AAA, but the attackers were able to catch them unawares by ingressing low. Lack of early warning also precluded the possibility of an interception.

Karachi had been targeted by both the IAF and Indian Navy on 4-5 December and the fire at the oil tanks was still raging when the IAF paid a revisit on 8 December. It was a 'low-key' raid by a solitary Canberra that attacked the oil storage tanks at Karachi and obtained direct hits. Four of the tanks were seen going up in flames. It was estimated that 60 per cent of the oil resources held by Pakistan in Karachi were lost to air attacks.[18]

Karachi reportedly had a heavy presence of AAA being a high priority target with the responsibility of coordinating its AD directly under 3 AA Brigade, PA. The naval dockyard and the airbase at Masroor were defended by 41 Heavy AA Regiment, 74 Composite Light AA Regiment and 310 Independent Light AA Battery with a mix of AA guns, but all these guns were not able to effectively defend against the IAF raids.[19]

With a good radar cover at Karachi, it was expected that there would have been a warning available, as the low-level radar cover at Karachi was provided by a Civil Aviation ASR-4 approach radar at Karachi Airport and an AR-1 radar at Pir Patho. With limitations of the latter, direct flight tracks from Jamnagar to Masroor remained outside the radar cover in case of the aircraft coming in hugging the coast. Similarly, the Mobile Observer Units (MOUs) could be avoided by taking a seaward approach. This meant that the Pakistani AA defences practically had no warning of any IAF raid and it was this constraint that resulted in their failure to offer any worthwhile resistance.

Trying to up the ante, and ensure a safe passage for its aircraft, the PAF changed tacks on 9 December as it decided to send F-104 Starfighters for a raid on Okha.[20]

> Two F-104 Starfighters were again sent to Okha to attack the OSA missile boats on the Indian Navy. No missile boats were seen and the Starfighters targeted the oil tanks at the base.

It was the first time that the Starfighter was observed in this sector and they may have been located to the south to strengthen the Pak air defence around Karachi which had been a regular target for the IAF. Using F-104s for the raid, however, did not end well for the PAF. The raid was a partial success only, as the oil tanks were targeted by the Starfighters and hit, setting them on fire while the missile boats remained elusive. An F-104 Starfighter was claimed by Battery Havildar Major Babu Mall of 129 AD Regiment (TA) during the raid.[21] As with the credit of setting the oil tanks ablaze at Karachi initially going to the Indian Navy, the shooting down of the F-104 is credited to the 'naval air defence' in the official history of the India-Pakistan war.[22]

With the army increasingly asking for air support for its operations, the Indian Air Force had by now shifted its focus to close support and interdiction operations. In this, the targeting of Pakistani railways was at the top of its priorities. It was no surprise that the Pakistan Air Force had also done its pre-war preparations and carried out extensive cross-border photo recce sorties a month before the outbreak of the all-out war. Most of these were carried out by No. 5 Squadron, PAF. Early on in the war, PAF had focused on the Suleimanki-Fazilka sector from where Pakistan's 2 Corps was to launch its main offensive.

In preparation for the same, PAF Mirages had conducted photo recce missions along Ferozepur-Kot Kapura, Ferozepur-Fazilka and Fazilka-Muktasar railway networks, as well as in the general area of Ferozepur and Sri Ganganagar, for the latest disposition of forces.

The photo-reconnaissance in the sector was being carried out by the Indian Air Force, also with the No. 222 Squadron, IAF, playing a key role in this. Several missions were launched against the rail network by the Sukhois in this sector. During one such mission, a train was targeted at Chistain Mandi on 5 December and the engine was destroyed by a direct hit. During another tactical reconnaissance mission by No. 3 Squadron, IAF, in the same area, Flt Lt A.V. Pethia made two attacks against a train and destroyed it in face of heavy AA fire. As he made another attack to try and silence the Pak AA guns, his Mystére was hit by enemy ground fire and crashed.[23]

During the interdiction missions against the Pakistani railway network, the sections specifically and repeatedly targeted were Sialkot-Shahdara, Jhelum-Lahore, Lahore-Sahiwal, Shahdara-Lyallpur, Kasur-Arifwal, Mandi Sadiqganj-Samasatta and Bahawalpur-Lodhran. Lack of low-level radar cover meant that there was hardly any warning of these raids available to Pak air defences. But even if the railway sections had been under the radar cover, it would have not mattered much as these target areas had no AAA defences to protect them and were at the mercy of the largely absent PAF. It was as if the IAF had a free run during these interdiction missions. Some of the railway stations like Wazirabad and Kasur were repeatedly attacked by IAF which claimed to have incurred severe damage. The claim was understandably denied by Pakistan.[24]

> The damage incurred on these trains was, however, inconsequential. Neither was any army movement impeded nor were any vital supplies interdicted.

On 16 December, the day Pakistani forces surrendered in East Pakistan, No. 26 Squadron, IAF, carried out one of the last interdiction raids. It was carried out against Narowal railway station by a four-ship mission during which a Sukhoi was shot down by Pakistani AAA.[25]

> On 16 December, Wg Cdr R.K. Batra, the Sqn Ldr, led a four-aircraft bombing mission to the railway yard at Narowal. Flt Lt T.S. Dandass, a classmate of mine from Delhi, was No. 2, Flt Lt Ravish Malhotra was No. 3, with me as No. 4. The mission was flown late in the afternoon, and visibility conditions were poor. The aircraft was heavily loaded and it was to be a steep glide attack from 4.2 km height to give greater accuracy as the intent was to destroy the Narowal rail yard, a prime interdiction target.
>
> Due to navigational error, the formation drifted left of the track and when we pulled up the target was displaced well to our right. The speeds had dropped during the pull-up and we were lazily turning right to get into attack mode when

the sky was filled by anti-aircraft fire. Despite our altitude, the ack-ack shells were bursting around and above us. The barrage of fire came from Chinese-built quads. We rolled into the attack through the ack-ack fire and went into steep dive individually.

Being the last, I saw No. 1 pulling out after bomb release and No. 2 in the dive. A few seconds later No. 2's aircraft appeared to continue in the dive till it impacted the ground. I saw the huge ball of fire followed by a plume of smoke. By now I had achieved release conditions. Bombs were released and I pulled out of the dive.

Later, when the formation was gathering up the leader asked for check-in on the radio. All but No. 2 checked in but the time was not right for me to volunteer any information as the images were still fuzzy in my mind. On landing, I related what had happened. I could not confirm an ejection as I did not see any. Later it was conjectured that the aircraft could have taken a direct hit on the cockpit disabling the pilot.

In the south, Indian Air Force operated almost with impunity as it faced no opposition in the air. Pakistani AA defences were too thinly spread out to be of any consequence. In any case, most of the railway nodes were without any AAA defences. On the Landhi-Khanpur section and, between the Mirpur Khas-Naya Chor section, nine railway stations were repeatedly targeted, with particular emphasis on the important junctions of Mirpur Khas and Rohri; the latter was attacked as many as five times.

These interdiction missions were often subjected to intense anti-aircraft fire and the IAF aircraft were repeatedly hit and damaged. On the second day itself, Flt Lt Pradip Vinayak Apte's HF-24 was hit while attacking a goods train being unloaded at Dhornaro railway station. Earlier, he had observed a vehicle convoy moving towards the railway station and attacked it with front guns. Thereafter, he turned towards the goods train and attacked it despite the concentrated ground fire. As he was making the third pass, his aircraft was hit and damaged by the AA fire. Apte tried to get back to the base that was about 100 miles away but he had to abandon the aircraft en route and did not survive the crash.[26]

In another interdiction mission on 5 December, Sqn Ldr Vishnu Narain Johri of No. 120 (ad hoc) Squadron operating from Nal, spotted a train at Bahawalnagar. As he was attacking the train, his Mystére was hit by AA fire but Johri continued with the attack and destroyed several tanks. After pulling out of the attack, he found the port wing of his aircraft on fire but he managed to bring the crippled aircraft back to base safely.[27]

On another occasion, Indian Air Force used the An-12 transport aircraft for a bombing raid against a railway station. One Pakistani source acknowledges that nineteen trains, including two 'special military' type, were attacked on the above-mentioned sections, while several track segments between Reti and Khanpur were damaged.[28]

The railways were targeted by PAF as well and, in one of the earlier raids, a B-57 attacked a concentration of tanks and vehicles and followed it up with several strafing passes on a stationary train on 7 December in what was to be the only daytime raid by the B-57 during the war. The oil tanks at Barmer were attacked by a solitary T-33 of No. 2 Squadron, PAF, during the night of 7/8 December.[29]

The railway station was defended by an ADA troop but failed to prevent the PAF from inflicting damage to the oil tanks.[30] It was the timely action by Sri Krishna Sharma, the driver of the train, which prevented further damage and destruction as he de-coupled the unharmed train wagons and moved the train to a safe distance from the railway station to avoid the fire from spreading. Sharma was awarded the Shaurya Chakra for his act of bravery.[31]

The interdiction missions petered off after the initial effort as the focus shifted towards close support to the army. It was much later, on 14 December, that PAF launched one of its biggest strikes against the Indian rail network as a 9-ship composite formation of 4 F-86Fs and 4 T-33s, escorted by a lone F-86E and, covered on top by 2 F-104s, struck three trains laden with POL and explosives near Naya Chor. In the same mission, a convoy was struck and many vehicles destroyed.[32] The next day PAF carried out an attack on the Mukerian railway station. It was a four-ship mission to attack the Bhangala railway station on the Jalandhar-Pathankot railway line but no rolling stock was found at Bhangla and it was decided to attack further south along the railway line. The four Mirages carried out a single-pass dive attack with two 750-lb bombs each and claimed to have damaged a number of trains. This was the first and only interdiction mission flown by the PAF Mirages.[33]

The other targeted railway stations were in the Chor sector and included Vasarwah and Munabao. Pakistan Air Force carried out a total of 24 sorties (including 5-night sorties by B-57 and C-130) against railway stations or rail segments, most of which were claimed to be satisfactory.[34]

It was almost towards the end of the war that IAF recommenced raids on economic targets. On 14 December, four Hunters from Jaisalmer carried out a rocket attack on Sui natural gas plant in north Sindh at 1258 hours. Though no opposition was faced by the Hunters, the gas plant was only partly damaged.[35]

The same day, Su-7s of No. 222 Squadron, IAF, carried out short-term interdiction missions against railway rolling stock, marshalling yards, bridges and convoys, and tactical photo-reconnaissance sorties were mounted to continuously monitor the battlefront. The squadron's war diary reads:[36]

> 14 December: Rail traffic between Kasur to Pukhpattan and Montgomery attacked: goods trains, locomotives, railway junctions, bridges and marshalling yards hit. All rail traffic paralysed.

It was good that it was the sturdy Su-7 that was largely used for the interdiction missions as Chattopadhyay notes:[37]

> Opposition from enemy air was limited to a fleeting gun or missile interception attempts by MiG-19s and Sabres, without any loss, but the Su-7s ran the full gauntlet of heavy ground fire. The Pakistani air defence system was based on the Chinese model, with multi-barrel 37 mm cannon, plus concentrated machine gun and small arms fire.
>
> Being a relatively large aircraft and continuously exposed, the Su-7 was certainly vulnerable to such concentrated air defence, and many aircraft were recovered to base 'peppered', some having sustained extensive damage to wings and fuselage. But for its ruggedness, far more Su-7s would have been written off. Losses were commensurate with the scale of effort, if not below it.

The arrival of ADA troops from the east by now meant that the defences at the railway network could be strengthened. One of the ADA troops deployed for this task was the troop of 48 AD Regiment commanded by 2nd Lt B.S. Chhetri. With the need to cover a large number of assets, here too, the troop was split into three sections of two guns each of which one section was deployed to cover Munabao railway station while a section was deployed on a train with one gun mounted on a KF wagon in front of the engine and the second gun on another wagon at the end of the train. The third section was used to augment the ADA troop already deployed at Khokhrapar railway station.[38]

It was just coincidental that these were not raided by the PAF after the arrival of the additional troops though the rail line between Jallandhar and Pathankot was attacked on 15 December with the PAF targeting Dasuya and Mukerian railway stations.[39]

The IAF had kept the interdiction missions going with the railway network given special treatment. Lack of effective ground defence by Pakistan ADA meant that IAF could occasionally use its, too, for these tasks. These missions were not always smooth sailing as it happened on 14 December when the An-12s of No. 44 Squadron, IAF, were bombing the Rohri marshalling yard. As the aircraft was being subjected to heavy ground fire, the release units of one of the An-12s failed to function electrically and manually. It was only when Flt Lt S. Balasundaram opened up the jacks of the release mechanism that the load could be dropped over the target.[40]

One of the more important economic targets attacked by the IAF towards the end of the war was the Sui natural gas plant. Four Hunters from Jaisalmer carried out a rocket attack on the natural gas plant in north Sindh at 1258 hours on 14 December but could only partly damage the plant even as they faced no opposition.[41] The next day, three An-12s attacked the gas plant in the evening, each An-12 dropping eighty 500-lb bombs. The raid was mounted from Bareilly with Jodhpur used as the staging airfield. In the failing light, the An-12s were not able to hit the target though the cooling plant suffered considerable damage.[42]

The last of the raids against strategic targets was mounted by Canberras on 15 December as five of them attacked Karachi harbour at 2100 hours, including the naval establishment at Manora.[43] A revisit was paid on the next day with Pakistan claiming to have shot down a Canberra by AA fire over Karachi.[44]

With this, the interdiction and strategic missions came to an end, aptly with the strikes on Karachi from where it had started on 4 December. Without an effective radar cover or any warning system in place over the widely dispersed and vulnerable assets, both the ADAs were hard-pressed to defend against committed attacks and it was always a challenge to score hits against attacking aircraft, leave aside achieve any kills. Not surprisingly, the losses of both air forces to AAA during interdiction and strategic strike remained low.

## NOTES

1. Vice Admiral G.M. Hiranandani, *Transition to Triumph: Indian Navy 1965-1975*, Spantech & Lancer, New Delhi, 2009, p. 302.
2. Maj Gen Shaukat Riza, *Izzat-o-Iqbal: History of Pakistan Artillery 1947-1971*, School of Artillery, Nawshera, 1980, p. 453.
3. Prasad and Thapliyal, op. cit., p. 220 and Malcolm Browne, 'More Air Strikes', *New York Times*, 5 December 1971, accessed on 22 January 2020 at https://www.nytimes.com/1971/12/05/archives/more-air-strikes-pakistanis-report-11-enemy-bases-are-being-bombed.html
4. 'The D Day of 4 December 1971', *Indian Aerospace Defence News*, accessed on 18 September 2020 at https://it-it.facebook.com/IADnews/posts/must-read-yno1the-d-day-of-04-dec-1971-indo-pak-war-laungewala-the-battle-as-the/1002001266544595/
5. Sushant Singh, 'December 4, 1971: When Navy Got Credit for IAF's Strikes on Karachi Oil Tanks', *Indian Express*, 4 December 2015, accessed on 12 April 2020 at https://indianexpress.com/article/explained/december-4-1971-when-navy-got-credit-for-iafs-strikes-on-karachi-oil-tanks/
6. Prasad and Thapliyal, op. cit., p. 220.
7. Tufail, op. cit., pp. 128-9.
8. Ibid., pp. 129-30.
9. Hiranandani, op. cit., p. 304.
10. Citation for the Vir Chakra awarded to Naik Dhondy Ram Bhonsade can be accessed at https://www.gallantryawards.gov.in/awardee/1880
11. Prasad, op. cit., p. 220.
12. Jagan Pillarisetti, 'When Lightning Strikes!', *Bharat Rakshak*, 2 April 2015, accessed on 12 April 2020 at http://www.bharat-rakshak.com/IAF/history/1971war/1276-20-squadron.html#gsc.tab=0
13. Tufail, op. cit., p. 86.
14. 'Anti-Aircraft Fire in Bombay', *New York Times*, 7 December 1971, accessed on 16 March 2020 at https://www.nytimes.com/1971/12/07/archives/antiaircraft-fire-in-bombay.html
15. Michael Patrao, 'Memories of 1971', *Deccan Herald*, 15 March 2019, accessed on 11 April 2019 at: https://www.deccanherald.com/opinion/right-in-the-middle/memories-of-1971-723280.html

16. Jagan Pillarisetti, 'When Lightning Strikes!', *Bharat Rakshak*, 2 April 2015, accessed on 11 April 2019 at http://www.bharat-rakshak.com/IAF/history/1971war/1276-20-squadron.html#gsc.tab=0
17. Kaiser Tufail, 'Air Defence in the Northern Sector', *Aeronaut*, accessed on 19 March 2019 at http://kaiser-aeronaut.blogspot.com/2011/02/air-defence-in-northern-sector-1971-war.html
18. Prasad, op. cit., p. 216.
19. Riza, op. cit., p. 457.
20. *The Report of the Hamoodur Rehman Commission of Inquiry into the 1971 War*, University of Michigan Press, 2000, p. 237.
21. Citation for the Vir Chakra awarded to BHM Babu Mall can be accessed at https://www.gallantryawards.gov.in/awardee/1701
22. Prasad and Thapliyal, op. cit., p. 217.
23. Pethia was awarded the Vir Chakra for his bravery. The citation can be accessed at https://www.gallantryawards.gov.in/awardee/180
24. Tufail, op. cit., p. 85.
25. Air Marshal Narayan Menon, 'Recollections of the 1971 War', *Indian Defence Review*, vol. 24, no. 4, 4 October-December 2009, 10 December 2019, accessed on 20 February 2020 at http://www.indiandefencereview.com/spotlights/recollections-of-the-1971-war/
26. Flt Lt Apte was awarded the Vir Chakra posthumously. Gazette of India, 29 July 1972, No. 92, Pres/72, dated 18 July 1972 refers. It can be accessed at https://twdi.in/node/3519
27. Johri was awarded the Vir Chakra. The details can be accessed at https://twdi.in/node/3981
28. Tufail, op. cit., p. 95.
29. Ibid., pp. 114-15.
30. Lt Col B.S. Chhetri, *Meandering into Memories*, Purboyon Publishers, Guwahati, 2020, p. 100.
31. The citation can be accessed at https://www.gallantryawards.gov.in/awardee/3542
32. Tufail, op. cit., p. 115.
33. Kaiser Tufail, 'Mirages at War', *Defence Journal*, May 2009 issue, and *Shaheen* – Journal of the Pakistan Air Force, vol. 60, accessed at http://kaiser-aeronaut.blogspot.com/2009/05/
34. Kaiser Tufail, 'Sundry Air Support', *IBlogspot*, accessed on 20 February 2020 at http://kaiser-aeronaut.blogspot.com/2010/06/sundry-air-support-1971-war.html
35. Prasad and Thapliyal, op. cit., p. 221.
36. R. Chattopadhyay, 'Sukhoi-7 BMK: A Whale of a Fighter', *Bharat Rakshak*, 26 July 2015, accessed on 11 June 2019 at http://www.bharat-rakshak.com/IAF/aircraft/past/1306-sukhoi-7.html#gsc.tab=0
37. Ibid.
38. Chhetri, op. cit., pp. 99-100.

39. Prasad and Thapliyal, op. cit., p. 219.
40. Balasundaram was awarded the Vayu Sena Medal (Gallantry). The citation is available at Gazette of India dated 7th October 1972, No. 108, Pres/72, dated 23rd September 1972.
41. Prasad and Thapliyal, op. cit., p. 221.
42. Ibid., p. 211.
43. Ibid., p. 221.
44. Ibid., p. 220. Prasad refers to the claim in 'History of PAF 1947-1984' but there are no corroborating accounts of this claim nor is it included in the 'official' list of IAF losses.

# CHAPTER 9

# Looking Back

Pakistan carried out pre-emptive strikes on Indian airfields at dusk on 3 December. Unlike the strikes during the previous war in 1965, these raids by PAF failed to cause any worthwhile damage or achieve anything. Many reasons have been put forth, by both sides, to explain the failure of these strikes to achieve any of the objectives. As per one Pakistani account, Aftab Alam leading the strike against Pathankot could not find his target, even though the Doppler navigation system fitted in the Mirages had very high accuracy.[1]

One reason why the Pak pre-emptive strikes failed to achieve their objective is that the Pakistan Air Force did not press home the attacks and just went through the motions – executing the attacks at high speed thereby compromising with accuracy. This was ostensibly to keep the aircraft safe from Indian AAA and minimize attrition. Another reason, as mentioned by some analysts, is that the strikes were more to instigate and provoke IAF to retaliate and, thereafter, take on the IAF over its own (Pak) territory from a position of advantage. As hostilities had already started in the east with the Indian Army making regular forays into Pak territory, there is some merit in this assumption and is borne out by Air Commodore Mansoor Shah of PAF in his book *The Gold Bird*:[2]

> An interesting rationale for the initial strikes has been elaborated in his book, *The Gold Bird* by Air Cdre Mansoor Shah, who was the assistant chief of air staff (operations) during the war. Shah claims that these strikes were meant to provoke IAF into retaliating against PAF bases, which were the only well-defended target sets in the country. He goes on to state that it was important to keep the IAF's attention focused on the bases or else, it might have switched to countrywide interdiction of lines of communications, where the PAF was defenceless.

To add to their woes, PAF raids largely missed their targets:[3]

> Of the 130 sorties flown by B-57, T-33 and C-130, forty per cent were reported by the aircrew – in all candour – to be unsuccessful, either due to armament malfunctions, or, because the targets could not be located and bombs were dropped in general target vicinity on 'dead reckoning'.

The main reason for the failure of the PAF pre-emptive strikes was also the preparations done by India in anticipation of such a strike. Following the 1965 War, the IAF and the army went about refining their drills and procedures and also built-up a robust air defence network. The radar network was upgraded by inducting additional radars and re-siting additional radars at Amritsar, Uttarlai and Ahmedabad. A careful study of the existing air defence network revealed a few shortcomings. These were:[4]

- Inadequate radar cover at a medium and high level,
- Large gaps in low-level radar cover,
- Lack of suitable airborne interception radars and air-to-air missiles for low-level interception by fighters, and
- Lack of adequate radar-controlled AD guns and surface-to-air missile systems.

These shortcomings forced the IAF to evolve the base air defence concept that gave the nominated air bases autonomous control over the deployed aircraft and AD weapons. The other measures taken were redeployment of radars, having dedicated squadrons of MiG-21s and Gnats placed under the ADDCs for air defence and re-siting the SAGW squadrons to cover the four major areas, viz., Delhi, Adampur (Jallandhar), Halwara (Ludhiana) and Chandigarh-Ambala areas. In the east, one SAGW squadron was deployed near Calcutta.[5]

To improve the low-level detection capability, visual observation posts and flights (later called MOPs and MOUs) were formed and integrated into the overall air defence network, and also with the base AD organization. The railways were also integrated into the observers' network and proved to be of invaluable service. While the MOPs and MOFs have generally been credited with providing timely warnings, the contribution of civilian observers has largely gone unnoticed. The exemplary contribution of A.S. Cheema, an assistant station master at

Gurdaspur railway station in Punjab, is illustrative. He was responsible for the low-level reporting of PAF aircraft in the area and, during the period of 3 to 17 December, made over 100 observation reports, 90 per cent of which were passed on within 30 seconds of the detection to the control centre. As many as 21 of the reports related to actual PAF raids on Pathankot. In one instance, the warning resulted in a successful interception by the IAF, preventing an attack over Gurdaspur.[6]

Some actions were taken at the local level to enhance the air defence set-up, e.g., at Halwara, the radar of the GCA (ground-controlled approach) was integrated into the BADC as the base air space radar. Additionally, S-1000, a 3-D radar, installed on the airfield for field trials was linked up to the BADC as a standby to the base radar.[7]

These measures all added up to make for a better air defence network than what existed in 1965. But these were not all that was done. The IAF had carried out organizational changes as well, the boundaries of IAF commands and their duties were redefined. The Western and Eastern Air Commands were made responsible for air defence of the areas, as per boundaries of the army commands. The Central Air Command that was looking after large areas of Uttar Pradesh up to the border of Bengal in the east and up to the borders of Delhi, Punjab and Haryana in the west was made responsible for bomber operations and maritime air support. The responsibility of air defence was now only with the Western and Eastern Air Commands. This enhanced the efficiency of the air defence.[8]

The Territorial Army AD regiments were all embodied by October 1971 and were deployed at their locations much before the start of operations, except one battery of 103 AD Regiment that was deployed by 1 December 1971.[9] Gole, in *The Air Operations of December 1971: Reflections of an Air War*, mentions that with the declaration of Exercise Cactus Lily in August 1971, the ADA started getting deployed at the airfields, radar stations and other installations. Both the IAF and ADA carried out joint exercises with the ADA regiments practising drills and procedures for aircraft recognition and control of AD weapons but 'on the declaration of war, all the regular AD regiments were moved to the forward army formations leaving the airfields to the mercy of the Territorial Army AD regiments who were still being embodied'.

This may have happened at one odd airfield but, at all other locations, the AD regiments were embodied in time and were at their locations, as per their tasking.

The allotment of ADA resources was more balanced, with six ADA regiments in the east and seventeen AD regiments deployed along the western border. The remaining were on VP/VPs in the depth areas. The overall allotment may have been balanced but the detailed allocation left much to be desired. While it is understandable that overall emphasis was on *air defence*, the allocation to the IAF bases and installations did not leave very many ADA batteries available for the field formations. In this, too, the allotment seems to be done on an ad hoc basis, depending on the 'demand of field formations' rather than on any appreciation of the air threat and the requirement of ADA resources.

The *History of Army Air Defence* mentions that 'Indian field forces increased their demand after the Boyra incident'.[9] It implies that the was no planning for air defence and, thereby 'demand', earlier. One reason could be that the formations may have been relying on the IAF to ensure AD. It is a different thing that the IAF itself was relying on ADA for low-level AD of not only its bases but also of the SAGW squadrons.

The sub-allotment of ADA by the formations was also against all laid-down norms of employment of the ADA resources. They were deployed in singles and twos, and at times set tasks that did not warrant allotment of AD guns. To wit, the 9 Infantry Division in the east asked for and was given, ADA guns as it was witnessing a heated exchange of fire with the Pakistani troops. One of the AD guns was deployed with the headquarter company of an infantry battalion in July 1971 and stayed with it for well over six months. The AD guns can be and are used in direct firing roles but this can only be their secondary responsibility and should not be their primary role, especially when there was a paucity of ADA resources.

The drawbacks in the ADA planning came to the fore when an AD battery was moved from the east to Agra after the first strikes by PAF during the night of 3/4 December. The battery moved on 4 December by air and rail. As the radars could not be taken by air, they were transported by rail, and, as a result, the battery was deployed at the Agra airfield without its radars. It is not known if this was a 'contingency plan' or not, but it does reveal the lack of detailed planning for the ADA, i.e. need to move a battery after the first air raid means the due application was not done while appreciating the threat and the need of ADA. Similarly, an AD brigade headquarters was moved from east to Bharatpur to take over the responsibility of ADA in the Southern Command. There were many such examples and they all reveal a disconnect between the higher commanders and ADA commanders and advisers.

It was not as if the Pakistan ADA did not have any drawbacks or problems but there appears to have been a better understanding of the employment of ADA. Pakistan had only one AD brigade, i.e. the 3rd AA Brigade and it was responsible for the air defence of the Pakistan Air Force installations and the naval dockyard at Karachi, while the AA regiments allotted to the field formations were directly controlled by them. Only one LAA regiment was allotted for East Pakistan. To augment the regular AA regiments, Pakistan raised AA Mujahid companies and they were meant to provide air defence to static installations in the rear under command logistic areas.[10]

In 1971, Pakistan had 99 AA batteries, including Mujahid AA companies, though the requirement had been assessed to be of a total of 342 AA batteries. The details of the requirement were as follows:[11]

| *LAA* | *Requirement* |
|---|---|
| Field Army | 64 Batteries |
| Important Installations | 171 Batteries |
| PAF | 85 Batteries |
| Navy | 7 Batteries |
| Total | 327 LAA batteries |
| HAA | |
| PAF Bases | 9 Batteries |
| Centres of civil population & industries | 6 Batteries |
| Total | 15 HAA Batteries |
| Grand Total | 342 AA Batteries |

The requirement of LAA batteries for the field army was as follows:

| *Formation* | *Requirement* |
|---|---|
| 12, 18, 23, 33 Infantry Division and Northern Area (one regiment each) | 20 Batteries |
| 1, 2 and 4 Corps (two regiments each) | 24 Batteries |
| Armoured Divisions (one regiment each) | 8 Batteries |
| Army Reserve | 12 Batteries |

Pakistani air defences were activated from July onwards with AA regiments getting deployed. The PAF also mobilized well in time with all elements getting deployed but, surprisingly, there was no collective exercise or training of all elements carried out to test the readiness of AD and iron out the problems, if any. The radar cover was inadequate, especially in East Pakistan, as it had only one low-level radar located at Mirpur. The mobile observation units of PAF in East Pakistan had been withdrawn in March 1971 itself, leaving a void in the early warning network.

The allocation of its AA batteries by the Pakistan Army followed a different pattern as compared to India. The field army was allocated 59 AA batteries against a requirement of 64 LAA batteries, whereas the PAF was allotted 33 LAA batteries only, with the Navy getting just one LAA battery. All the six available HAA batteries were allotted to the PAF, Navy and Karachi area. The emphasis was thus on defending the field army and not the air force bases and installations. It is thus not surprising that IAF lost more aircraft while carrying out CAS than while counter-air operations.

The batteries and troops were largely employed as integrated sub-units though at times they were employed in ones and twos. This was more in East Pakistan where 6 LAA Regiment was the only AA regiment that was available. Another measure taken to meet the shortfall of AA resources was the creation of an ad hoc AA battery for deployment at Chittagong. There was only one instance of an ad hoc AD troop being created by an Indian AD regiment in the western sector while the AD troops were often sub-allotted as sections (two guns each) in the field formations in the east. These may have given the impression of the formation (or a unit) having been provided AD but it was more of a 'notional' protection than anything else.

The related problem of control and reporting (C&R) arrangements for these ad hoc troops and sections was never addressed, with visual detection and recognition being the only 'control' arrangement available. How reliable and effective these arrangements were can only be speculated now, as they were never tested, with the PAF practically being grounded in the east.

Even at sites that had well established C&R arrangements, they failed at times. The more common problem was that information on enemy air raids was not provided to the ADA in time. This was a common problem for ADA deployed in depth and on strategic targets. The lack of early warning (EW) cover over Pakistani economic targets was exploited well by the IAF as it carried out a number of successful strikes against targets like the Attock oil refinery, Mangla Dam and Sui natural gas plant beside the strikes on Pakistani railways network. With no radar or EW cover, the AA defences at these sites were always caught by surprise and were not able to put up a worthwhile AA defence.

Even at places where a C&R system existed, there were occasional problems due to break in communications or miscommunication. One of the first such incidents occurred at Hashimara well before the start of the war, on 14 November 1971. The local warning radar of the AD battery deployed at the airfield picked up a track around 1710 hours and the information of the same was passed on to the base operations room for verification. The base ops could not confirm the identity of the track as the communications between it and the SU had broken down. The AD guns were on a 'high' state of readiness and in 'guns free' status. They had the ammunition loaded and were ready to fire. At the last moment, the communications with the SU were restored and the identity of the track was confirmed as 'friendly' – a C119 Packet on an unscheduled flight from Guwahati. The control orders were changed to 'guns tight' and a mishap was averted.

Timely and accurate information of 'own' tracks was not always passed on to the ADA troops, especially those with the field formations, and this resulted in some close calls for the ADA. One such incident occurred on 7 December when the gun area defended by the 65 AD Battery was strafed by IAF aircraft.[12]

On 7 December around 1300 hrs, while I was in our gun area, an Indian Air Force mission comprising five Su-7 and one MiG-21, appeared in our area about which we did not have any advance information. All the five Sukhois kept hovering over

> us for some time and, suddenly to our horror, they started diving and strafing over us. All of us jumped and took shelter in nearby trenches and gun pits. They dropped one 1,000-pounder bomb which landed in between our two AD guns creating a huge crater and covering our nearby guns with mud and slush.
>
> We used the 'Delta 5' net to contact Artillery Brigade but were told that there was no IAF mission in our area at that point in time and we have probably mistaken an F-6 aircraft of Pakistan as 'SU-7'. The Su-7s had, meanwhile, blown up two Kraz vehicles loaded with ammunition.

Captain Arvind Nautiyal took the rather unusual step of firing a single gun at the Sukhois to 'scare them away. Thankfully, the aircraft went back, without further damage either to the own troops of the aircraft.

The problem of not being provided timely information was faced even by the ADA troops at airbases and radar stations. At Amritsar SU, two IAF aircraft being ferried from Pathankot were once picked up by the ADA troop and no information of any 'friendly' track had been passed on by the SU to the troop. As the aircraft suddenly appeared overhead, it was only the presence of mind of the troop commander that the AD guns did not open up as the control orders were still 'guns free'. Having recognized the aircraft as friendlies, Lt Sandhu immediately ordered 'hold fire', thus preventing any accident.[13]

The accidental shooting down of own aircraft was averted because of an effective control exercised over the AD guns by commanders at all levels. As a result, there were no incidents of fratricide involving Indian ADA. It was not so with the Pakistani AAA as it shot down one of its aircraft on 7 December when Sqn Ldr Cecil Chaudhry of No. 18 Squadron, PAF, was hit by its own AAA, near Zafarwal. On 8 December, the PAF suffered another loss when Flt Lt Afzal Siddiqui's F-6 was shot down by Pakistani AAA while he was chasing an IAF SU-7 aircraft. These were the aircraft lost, though there were many more incidents of PAF aircraft being hit by friendly fire.

It was not only in the tactical battle area that these accidents occurred, as the Pakistani AAA is known to have fired at own aircraft while deployed at airfields too. As the B-57s returned from their first raid on Agra on the night of 3/4 December, one of the B-57s, flown by Flt Lt Mazhar Bukhari with Flt Lt Nasim Khan as navigator, 'barely survived a mistaken AAA barrage on recovery at Rafiqui'.[14]

Flt Lt Javed Latif had a similar experience on 4 December as he was on cockpit standby at Risalewala. As he was intercepting the Sukhois on their second raid, his aircraft was hit by 'friendly' fire and damaged. Thankfully for him, the aircraft was under control and Latif managed to get back safely.

Similar accidents may have been prevented at IAF bases with better fire discipline by the ADA troops and strict control over fire orders by the BADC or the base ops, but it did create unintended problems. The ADA troops were generally issued with 'guns tight' to ensure the safety of their own aircraft. While this is understandable, maintaining the 'guns tight' even when there were no friendlies in the air during an air raid or when it was known that the 'aircraft is not own' only went to degrade the performance of the ADA. Two instances would suffice.

First, on the night of 3/4 December, Halwara was raided by the PAF. The airfield had two ADA batteries, one each of the radar controlled L/70 and the L/60 deployed for its protection and with the 'raiders' having been picked up, adequate warning was available. There were no friendlies in the air and yet the AD guns were not allowed to open up. The following account by the COO is quite revealing:[15]

Barnala alerted us about the likelihood of a threat just short of eleven thirty. Two tracks at low level had been picked up. It was possible that Halwara could be their target. The aircraft were painting well and they were flying quite low. It was felt that MiG-21 Type 77 would not be effective against such a target. The Archers, though refueled and ready, were not launched.

By now, my Visual Observation Posts and Mobile Observation Posts had come alive. The first local call came from the civil defence control room Ludhiana. Two aircraft had flown over the town and had turned south. Quite obviously they were trying to follow the canal to reach Halwara from the east. This was an expected technique and I had saturated that approach with VOPs. I kept on getting a second to second report of where the planes were. At 2338 hrs., Barnala declared Halwara as threatened and I sounded the air raid siren.

*I ordered 'guns tight' for the AD Arty units* (*emphasis added*).

I was now under a threat. No friendly aircraft were airborne within my airspace. It should have been logical therefore to place the guns free.

I had no inclination of disclosing the location of the airfield. The airfield was well camouflaged and concealed. Night visibility was not very high. Hence, 'guns tight' was a better option.

By 2342 hours, the hostile aircraft entered my defended zone. They obviously had not spotted the airfield. Soon they realized that they had missed the airfield.

They turned around and went back to Ludhiana. All this drama was being picked up by all my sensors deployed.

After reaching Ludhiana a second time, the aircraft turned around and followed the canal once again and approached the airfield from the east. They must have spotted the prominent bend in the canal a bit late. They threw in a left turn to come to the airfield, but they were late and missed the airfield a second time. All this was happening perhaps because they were flying really, and I mean really low. They continued circumnavigating the airfield and at one stage turned quite hard to align themselves with Runway 13. The first aircraft came overhead at about 20 degrees to the runway and dropped its bombs. It was so low that its bombs did not explode. The L-60 guns opened up and the L-70s followed. The aircraft remained very low, below the missile cover and made a getaway.

Wing Commander Sen was clear that it 'should have been logical, therefore, to place the guns free' but as he had no inclination of disclosing the location of the airfield, he did not allow the guns to open up. The B-57s came in low and dropped their bombs and managed to get away as the guns were allowed to fire much too late. Incidentally, the SA-2s for which the order was 'sky is clear' failed to engage the low flying B-57s. Also, the MiG-21 Type 77 stationed at the base were 'not suitable' for intercepting the B-57s at night and could not be used.

A perfect opportunity existed for the radar-controlled AD guns to have taken on the B-57s but was denied due to the overcautious approach taken. At Sirsa, the situation was different, but with similar results. The airfield had an ADA battery deployed and, with the war having started the previous day, was fully prepared to take on any PAF raiders. In this case, it was the confusion at the base ops that resulted in the PAF B-57s not being engaged.[16]

It was the evening of 4 Dec. 1971 and I was on duty at the improvised makeshift 15 Ft high Air Traffic Control Tower. Around 2030 hrs., I had only two MiG from the base airborne, which were expected to re-join around 2100 hrs. I was admiring the crescent moon in a cloudless sky, when, in the background of the moon I spotted the outline of an aircraft at quite a distance. Fixing my gaze I reconfirmed within myself that what I saw was right. Sure enough, the aircraft kept closing in and instinctively I said that it had to be an enemy aircraft approaching from the 'west' as no other known traffic was expected from that direction.

I promptly informed the base commander, late Air Cmde K.K. Malik, then Wg Cdr on the hotline. In utter disbelief, he uttered, 'impossible! (as no radar had informed about any intruder)'. Keeping my gaze fixed at the aircraft, I directed all the ATC personnel, except the ops clerk, to take shelter in the respective trenches, and time and again kept reporting to the base cdr about the approaching aircraft urging him to act.

Lo and behold, at 2033-34 hrs the intruder arrived overhead and, very cunningly, dropped delay fuse bombs during this inbound run, one of which fell a few yards away from my tower. Soon afterwards the first bomb explosion was heard and, a few seconds later, I saw the same aircraft going back in the same direction from where it had approached dropping many more live bombs.

The incident finds mention in Air Chief Marshal P.C. Lal's memoirs where he also notes that the ADA guns were ordered 'guns tight' even though it was known that B-57 was 'not ours'.[17]

It is also worth noting that the ADA shot down three B-57s on 5-6 December. Even during the previous war, it was only the ADA that had shot down the B-57s and there should have no doubts about their capability to take on these aircraft. One of the reasons for keeping 'guns tight' was that the AD fire gave away the location of the target and, in fact, helped the raiding aircraft. There may be some truth in this supposition but even in the case where ADA was not allowed to open up, the raiding aircraft did manage to identify the targets in most of the cases and inflict damage on the airfields.

Another factor that cannot be overlooked is the effect of intense AA fire as the aircraft comes in for a bombing run or for strafing. In one account after another, it is mentioned that the aircraft failed to deliver its payload accurately in face of hostile AA fire. The choice of the payload and weapon delivery tactics was also dictated by the ADA present at the intended target. About the PAF raids on Indian airbases, Tufail mentions:[18]

The shallow dive angles dictated by AAA avoidance tactics had also worked against deeper bomb penetration ... one-quarter of the 32 planned bombing and strafing sorties were unsuccessful, any pretence about the significant success of the first strikes was rather misplaced.

As the presence of ADA hindered the strikes, the aircraft at times directly attacked the gun positions to suppress them. During the first air encounter at Boyra in November 1971, the PAF F-86 Sabres were first engaged by the ADA troop present in the salient and one of the Sabres turned on the AD guns in an attempt to silence them:[19]

Four ground-scrambled Gnats, of Dum Dum, based No. 22 Squadron, were able to sneak in and bounce the F-86 formation. At that time, the leader, Wing Cdr Choudhry, was attacking a AAA battery that was noticed to be firing at them.

Later during the IAF raids on Tezgaon, the only opposition faced by the Indian aircraft was from the Pakistani AA guns deployed at the airfield. The AA fire was very intense and in the second raid of the day, the AA gunners managed to shoot down Flight Lieutenant S.G. Khonde's Hunter. The aircraft crashed east of the runway barely fifty yards from the gun that had claimed it.[20]

It was hit in the cockpit and crashed 50 yards from the gun position in the vicinity of the ammunition pit. The gun commander went around pulling and kicking the aircraft shouting, 'My gun, my gun'. Fortunately, a fire truck came up within minutes and saved the situation.

The Hunter was shot down by a gun of 21 LAA Battery, PA. It also hit another Hunter, flown by Flying Officer V.K. Arora. As he found his aircraft being targeted, Arora, in turn, attacked the AA gun position itself, destroying it with his front guns. The Pakistan Army, however, maintains that the gun was strafed and the entire detachment was injured, but the gun was not damaged.[21]

At Tezgaon, the IAF reportedly used napalm on 5 December against the AA guns in order to suppress them.[22] This suppression of enemy air defence (SEAD) missions did not succeed much as the AAA remained operational all throughout. Even in the west, the SEAD missions were not very successful though it was PAF that largely carried them out. The main target of PAF, as in the previous war, was the Amritsar radar. The other high priority for PAF was the radar at Faridkot. PAF had planned to neutralize them in the first wave and the F-104s, which were earmarked for air defence of the southern sector while based at Masroor, were reportedly held back at Sargodha for two days especially for these radar strikes.[23]

A pair of F-104s each carried out a strafing attack on the two radars at 1710 hrs. on 3 December. The PAF claimed to have hit the antenna of Faridkot radar. The Amritsar radar was also attacked, with both pilots claiming to have hit the antenna; but only some damage to the communication equipment was acknowledged by the IAF. The PAF was using a locally developed radar homing device, fitted on an F-104 (tail no. 56-804). The radar was soon back on air and was revisited by PAF but it remained operational all throughout. According to PAF, the Amritsar 'radar busting' project came to a halt at midday on 5 December, when the specially-equipped F-104 flown by Sqn Ldr Amjad Hussain was shot down by ADA.[24]

The raids by PAF, however, continued with the radar being subjected to a total of twenty-nine enemy attacks. The radar 'stopped functioning only once. Even on that one occasion, the disruption of power supply and damage to the equipment was rectified in about half an hour.[25]

The Indian efforts towards SEAD were comparably more successful. The radars targeted by IAF were at Badin and Sakesar. The Badin radar was first attacked on 4 December and had suffered serious damage, putting it out for a day. Before the next strike, two MiGs from Jamnagar first carried out a PR mission of the radar complex on 12 December which was followed by four MiGs attacking the radar with bombs. The result of the raid could not be ascertained and it was decided to pay the radar a re-visit the next day. The next day, during the mission in the morning using 57 mm rockets, one MiG was hit by the AA fire and damaged. It was next decided to use the more powerful S-24 rockets in the next mission, but before the aircraft could be loaded with the new ammunition, the Western Air Command ordered the squadron to carry out one more urgent strike. During this strike, the IAF lost a MiG to AAA. The damage to the radar was not ascertained.

The fate of the strike against the radar at Sakesar was all too similar. Two Hunters and one Su-7 were lost during the mission even as one of the antennas of radar was claimed to have been hit and the radar put off for some time. The radar was defended by 20 LAA Battery of 53 LAA Regiment, PA, which claimed to have hit all the Indian aircraft. These missions were still more effective than the IAF efforts to try and locate the radar at AR-1 radar at Mirpur in East Pakistan. As this was the only PAF radar in the east, IAF was keen to destroy it or at least disable it. But it failed to locate the radar despite repeated efforts to do so.

Both sides faced similar problems during the SEAD missions. Though the FPS-20 radars were easier to locate due to their large antennas, the IAF never managed to destroy them or put them off the air for a long enough time. The Badin radar, though, had its performance downgraded after the first IAF strike but it remained operational none the less. The other radars were not only difficult to locate but difficult to target as well. The antennas were hit at times but they were soon repaired with marginal efforts. As such, the SEAD missions never really succeeded.

The effectiveness of other missions was related to the presence of the ADA. This was especially true of the IAF interdiction campaign against Pakistan's railway network. Tufail mentions as much.[26]

> The IAF had a free hand in its interdiction campaign against the railway network, along with a few attacks against targets of strategic importance. Lack of low-level radar cover meant that intruders came in completely unobserved and unmolested by interceptors. Shortage of AAA assets resulted in these target areas being unguarded, leaving the attackers with little to worry about during weapon delivery.

It was as if 'the IAF felt free to attack at leisure. The absence of interceptors and AAA only made the interdiction campaign uncomplicated and effortless'.[27]

The IAF carried out strikes against strategic targets as well, but these were seen more as 'as an attempt to further stretch the already-thinned Pakistani air defences' as it did not go beyond the strikes against Mangla Dam, an oil refinery and the natural gas plant, with the results of the raids not very clear. Interdiction of the railway system may have been seen as a far more lucrative exercise, due to the complete absence of any sort of defences. Given the deployment pattern, the IAF was opposed by Pak AAA more in the tactical battle area, rather than during counter-air or interdiction missions. The majority of IAF losses also occurred during the CAS missions. While the IAF may claim that it was indicative of its greater emphasis on air support to the army, it was really the presence of Pak AAA that was the reason for greater losses.

Before the bean count of losses and hits, it would be worthwhile to look at the effect of the ADA on air operations. There are two aspects to it – the effect on the conduct of air operations and the number of aircraft destroyed or hit. Tiwary, in *IAF in the Wars*, mentions that 92 per cent of all IAF strike aircraft suffered hits or damage from ground fire.[28]

In the east, a large number of aircraft being hit by ground fire meant that the IAF had to change its tactics and advise the pilots not to fly at excessively low levels and avoid taking risks. In the west, the air defences were denser with a larger presence of AAA in the tactical battle area with the risk of getting hit from ground fire very real and it could not be wished away. On the first day itself, 13 out of 16 Sukhois of No. 26 Squadron, IAF, had small arms bullet damage.[29]

The same was experienced by all striking aircraft but it was not the AAA alone that posed a threat as small arms, AA machine guns and even tank main guns were used rather effectively against the striking aircraft. One of the aircraft damaged by the fire from a tank main gun was Wing Commander Suresh's Hunter at Longewala.[30]

> During a gun attack, one of the tanks whose main gun was pointing towards me fired a shell. Although the shell did not hit me, the flash and dust blinded me and my aircraft just fell out of control. I hit a sand dune at 420 knots and I am living to tell the tale. During those fleeting moments, I remembered my entire life. As the dust cleared, I found myself flying very low but the aircraft was just about controllable.

The tank's AA machine guns were very effective against low flying aircraft as Flt Lt Apramjeet Singh found out as Chhamb. His MiG-21 was shot down by a tank of 22 CAV of Pakistan Army.[31]

> The pilot had brought the plane down to treetop level and I could see his white helmet. I could also see from the tracers that the bullets were hitting the target. However, at the back of my mind, I somehow felt that this was doomsday for me. One short burst from his 30 mm cannon or a salvo of rockets and I would be blown into smithereens. Luckily, I got him first, because he pulled the plane straight up and ejected when he had gained enough height.

There is an instance of wire-guided missiles having been used to shoot down a MiG-21 in the Shakargarh sector on 10 December though other sources attribute the loss to an F-86. If true, it would be a first.[32]

The large number of aircraft being hit by ground fire resulted in a review of tactics and the weapons being used. The result was adopting weapons that may not have been ideal against the intended target but was used to keep the aircraft safe. Wing Commander Sen mentions that the CAS aircraft changed over from using rockets to bombs even though 'a bombing attack is less accurate than a rocket attack' but it was preferable as 'it kept the aircraft further away and reduced the chances of a hit from ground fire'.

For the last two days, we had been facing a lot of small arms fire in the close-support role. Our repair load was running high. We had also lost two aircraft on 4 December. With Kuruvilla's ejection this morning it became imperative that we relook at this business of close support with rockets and guns.

The only option we had was to change our weapon of attack to bombs. We could use bombs instead of rockets to attack ground targets. Inherently, a bombing attack is less accurate than a rocket attack. However, the lethality of a 500 kg bomb was much higher than that of a salvo of rockets. Our boys were generally more proficient in rocketing rather than bombing. At the same time, a bombing attack kept the aircraft further away from the target and reduced the chances of a hit by ground fire. A changeover from rockets to bombs was therefore not a straightforward decision. For the afternoon wave of attacks, we tried the bomb option for three pairs. The results seemed satisfactory. Perhaps tomorrow onwards we would use bombs more regularly.

The forced changes in tactics and weapons loads meant a degradation of airstrikes. This was a major role played by the ADA in influencing air operations and keeping their own field forces safer from the enemy air. It was not that PAF did not face such ground fire. The small arms fire was equally damaging to the PAF aircraft. One of the recorded instances of small arms fire shooting down a PAF aircraft is of 10 December when a Gorkha battalion claimed an F-6 though it was later verified as having been shot down by an ADA Troop.[34]

One of the advancing battalions being the 7$^{th}$ Bn, 11 Gorkha Rifles Regiment. On 10 December, the advancing column of 7/11GR reached an area called Pul Bajaun, when the PAF put in an appearance. MiG-19s came over and strafed the positions of Indian troops. one of the Gorkha riflemen, Lance Naik Dhan Bahadur Rai, replied back with his 7.62 mm light machine gun. It was an act of defiance, and incredibly, the spectators on the ground saw the MiG-19 burst into flames as bullets found their mark. The PAF pilot. Flt Lt Wajid Ali Khan, ejected and was picked up by the Gorkha troops. Wajid Ali became a PoW for the rest of the war. One of the rare occasions where a jet was bought down by a small arms fire.

As with the IAF, the tactics were changed by PAF also to avoid the ADA fire. During the raids on Indian airbases, PAF found that these changes degraded their performance.[35]

It led the PAF to resort to conventional iron bombs which would bounce off the runway and explode above the surface, causing more blasts and fewer breaches. Also, delivery from shallow dive angles to avoid exposure to anti-aircraft artillery (AAA) made the bombs skip off the surface even farther and, whatever cratering that occurred was repaired overnight.

In case the ADA was not present or was not in adequate numbers, the attacking aircraft had an easier run during weapons delivery.[36]

Shortage of AAA assets resulted in these target areas being unguarded, leaving the attackers with little to worry about during weapon delivery, and the absence of interceptors and AAA only made the interdiction campaign uncomplicated and effortless.

While the ADA may have scored enough hits and forced a change in the weapons loads and weapon delivery tactics, the real test was in shooting down enemy aircraft. In this case, the data available is not very clear with conflicting claims. India claimed a total of 75 Pak aircraft of which 50 were on the western front.[37]

The majority were claimed to have been destroyed on the ground during IAF raids on Pakistani air bases, with as many as 23 thus destroyed. The 'ground fire' accounted for 15 PAF aircraft with 12 claimed by the IAF in air-to-air combat. In the east, PAF lost 22 aircraft to include 19 F-86 Sabres and three RT-33s. Of these, 13 were destroyed on the ground by the PAF to prevent them from falling into Indian/Bangladeshi hands while three aircraft (one transport and two light aircraft) were destroyed on the ground during IAF raids.[38]

The thirteen aircraft were planned to have been destroyed by demolition charges but, as Tezgaon air base was surrounded by Indian troops before the aircraft could be destroyed, the aircraft was damaged by using crowbars and hammers. Five of the F-86s were later recovered and used by the newly formed Bangladesh Air Force.[39] Pakistan never confirmed the number of aircraft lost during the war with exaggerated claims of its own about IAF aircraft shot down. One of the few sources to give any information about the PAF losses is Kaiser Tufail's book, *In the Ring and On its Feet*, which mentions a total of 27 aircraft lost in combat by PAF during the war, with 13 destroyed on the ground by PAF itself. These 27 include the loss of two F-86 Sabres during the battle of Boyra on 22 November 1971. The maximum number (ten), as per Tufail, were lost by PAF in air-to-air combat, while eight aircraft were shot down by AAA. As against the 23 claimed by IAF to have been destroyed on the ground during air raids, Tufail admits to a loss of seven aircraft only, with two aircraft lost in combat-related accidents.[40]

There is thus a major variation between the Indian claims and the losses admitted by Pakistan. The details are also muddied with conflicting claims and classification of losses to AAA as 'technical losses' at times. While the nature of 'ground fire' not clear at times, it is difficult to identify the exact source – whether it was a small arms fire of AAA fire though Tufail attributes all losses to AAA. Taking the figures given in the official history of the war, more PAF aircraft were lost to ground fire than to the IAF. Considering the figures given by Tufail, an almost equal number of PAF aircraft were shot down by IAF and AAA.

The IAF lost a total of 71 aircraft during the war, 56 in enemy action and 15 in flying accidents. A total of 52 aircraft were lost by the IAF on the western front with 19 lost in the east.[41]

The IAF lost 16 aircraft in air-to-air combat in the west with Pakistani AAA accounting for 24 aircraft. The losses to AAA were a higher proportion in the east, with 10 losses as compared to 3 in air combat. A number of losses, classified as 'accidents or technical losses', were due to damage inflicted by ADA fire and should rightly be included in losses to ADA.

The fact that the losses to ADA were higher than to the enemy air force remains underappreciated with the contribution of ADA not getting the recognition it derives. However, the overall contribution of ADA was not in inflicting losses or damage on the enemy but also in helping maintain a favourable air situation, especially over the tactical battlefield. Even at the air bases, the ADA complemented the interceptors in holding off the raiding aircraft and, at times, acted as the only line of defence, especially during the night raids.

One reason for overlooking the contribution of ADA, of both sides, during the War of 1971 is the lack of published material on the subject. Hopefully, it will be corrected as more accounts of the war are published but it will be wise to remember Admiral Arun Prakash as the history is written:[42] 'Sensible nations ensure that history is not replaced by mythology.'

## NOTES

1. Sajjad S. Haider, *Flight of the Falcon; Demolishing the Myths of India-Pak Wars 1965 & 1971*, Vanguard Books, Karachi, 2010, p. 138.
2. Mandeep Singh, *Anti-Aircraft Artillery in Combat 1950-1972: Air Defence in the Jet Age*, Pen & Sword, Barnsley, 2020.
3. Kaiser Tufail, *In the Ring and on its Feet*, p. 58.
4. C.V. Gole, 'The Air Operations of December 1971: Reflections of an Air War', *Vayu*, vol. VI, 1991, pp. 15-17.
5. Ibid.
6. Apar Singh Cheema was awarded the Shaurya Chakra for his contributions to the war effort. The citation can be accessed at https://www.gallantryawards.gov.in/Awardee/apar-singh-cheema
7. Wing Commander Sen, *Hectic Days in Halwara-3: ... and Wings Clipped!* 30 March 2010 accessed at https://tkstales.wordpress.com/2010/03/30/hectic-days-in-halwara-3-and-wings-clipped/
8. Lal, *My Years with the IAF*, pp. 173-5.
9. 'History of Army Air Defence', published by Army Air Defence Association, New Delhi.
10. Riza, *History of Pakistan Artillery 1947-1971*, pp. 452-3.
11. The Report of the Hamoodur Rehman Commission of Inquiry Into the 1971 War, University of Michigan Press, 2000, pp. 248-54.
12. Interview with Captain Arvind Nautiyal.
13. Interview with Colonel H.S. Sandhu.
14. Tufail, op. cit., p. 56.
15. Wing Commander T.K. Sen, 'Hectic Days at Halwara: The Enemy Shows up' accessed at https://tkstales.wordpress.com/2010/04/04/hectic-days-in-halwara-4-the-enemy-shows-up/
16. Wg Cdr Divakar Chaudhri, Sirsa's War, *Bharat Rakshak*, 23 August 2011 accessed at http://bharat-rakshak.com/IAF/History/1971War/1095-Sirsa-War.html#gsc.tab=0
17. Lal, op. cit., p. 270.
18. Kaiser Tufail, 'PAF on the Offensive', *Defence Journal*, Aug.-Sep. 2011 accessed at http://kaiser-aeronaut.blogspot.com/2011/08/paf-on-offensive-1971-war.html
19. Kaiser Tufail, 'The Last Stand', *Defence Journal*, Nov 2012 accessed at http://kaiser-aeronaut.blogspot.com/2012/10/the-last-stand-air-war-1971.html
20. Riza, op. cit., p. 365.
21. Ibid.
22. Kaiser Tufail, 'The Last Stand', *Defence Journal*, Nov 2012 accessed at http://kaiser-aeronaut.blogspot.com/2012/10/the-last-stand-air-war-1971.html
23. Tufail, *Air Defence in the Northern Sector* accessed at http://kaiser-aeronaut.blogspot.com/2011/02/air-defence-in-northern-sector-1971-war.html
24. Tufail, *In the Ring and on its Feet*, p. 60.

25. Wing Commander Gandharva Sen, the CO of the radar unit was awarded the Vayu Sena Medal (Reference: Gazette of India dated 7th October 1972, No. 108, Pres/72, dated 23rd September 1972).
26. Tufail, *In the Ring and on its Feet*, pp. 84-5.
27. Ibid.
28. Tiwari, *IAF in the Wars*, p. 215.
29. Air Marshal Narayanan Menon, 'Flying the Sukhoi-7 in Operation Cactus-Lily', *Bharat Rakshak* 16 June 2017 accessed at http://www.bharat-rakshak.com/IAF/History/1971War/1135-Narayanan-Menon.html#gsc.tab=0
30. Wg Cdr Suresh, 'Battle of Longewala - 5th and 6th December', *Bharat Rakshak*, 12 accessed at http://www.bharat-rakshak.com/IAF/history/1971war/1282-kukke-suresh.html#gsc.tab=0
31. Gp Capt Apram Jeet Singh, 'Mission to Chhamb', *Bharat Rakshak*, 16 June 2017 accessed at http://www.bharat-rakshak.com/IAF/History/1971War/1089-Chamb.html#gsc.tab=0
32. Flt Lt K.K. Mohan was killed in action after being hit by a wire-guided missile near Shakargarh. Air Marshal Narayan Menon, 'Recollections of the 1971 War', *Indian Defence Review*, vol. 24, no. 4, 4 October-December 2009, 10 December 2019 accessed at http://www.indiandefencereview.com/spotlights/recollections-of-the-1971-war/
33. Wing Commander T.K. Sen, 'Hectic Days at Halwara: The Enemy Shows up' accessed at https://tkstales.wordpress.com/2010/05/20/hectic-days-in-halwara-9-on-to-day-three/
34. Lance Naik Dhan Bahadur Rai was awarded the Vir Chakra. (Indian Air Force Trivia Page accessed at http://jaganpvs.tripod.com/trivia01.htm). The claim was however awarded to 29 AD Regiment after verification. Citation for the Vir Chakra accessed at https://www.gallantryawards.gov.in/Awardee/dhan-bahadur-rai
35. Kaiser Tufail, 'Mirages at War', *Defence Journal*, May 2009 accessed at http://kaiser-aeronaut.blogspot.com/2009/05/
36. Kaiser Tufail, *Air Defence in the Northern Sector*, accessed at http://kaiser-aeronaut.blogspot.com/2011/02/air-defence-in-northern-sector-1971-war.html
37. Prasad and Thapliyal, op cit., p. 237.
38. Ibid., p. 368.
39. Tufail, *In the Ring and on its Feet*, pp. 150-1.
40. Ibid., p. 192.
41. Prasad and Thapliyal, op cit., p. 236.
42. Admiral Arun Prakash, 'Did IAF win the 1971 war? Pak scholar says no. Ex-Indian Navy chief says debate with facts', *The Print*, 20 February 2018 accessed at https://theprint.in/opinion/iaf-win-1971-war-pak-scholars-say-no-ex-indian-naval-chief-debate-with-facts/36740/

# APPENDICES

APPENDIX A

# Indian Air Defence Artillery: Order of Battle

## FORMATIONS

| *Formation* | *Commander* | *Location* | *Area of Responsibility* | *Remarks* |
|---|---|---|---|---|
| 312 (I) AD Brigade | Brig. Prem Singh Gill | Shillong | Assam | Moved to Bharatpur in Dec. 1971 and took over the responsibility of south Rajasthan, Gujarat and Maharashtra |
| 322 (I) AD Brigade | Brig. Kailash Chander | Delhi | Punjab and north Rajasthan | |
| 332 (I) AD Brigade | Brig. A.S. Mann | Ambala | Punjab | |
| 342 (I) AD Brigade | Brig. E. Coelho | Panagrah | West Bengal | |

## REGIMENTS

| *Regiment* | *Commanding Officer* | *Location* | *Weapon System* | *Remarks* |
|---|---|---|---|---|
| 19 AD Regiment | Lt Col Sardul Singh | Jorhat | L/70 | |
| 25 AD Regiment | Lt Col S.P. Roy | Kanchrapara | L/70 | |

| | | | |
|---|---|---|---|
| 26 AD Regiment | Lt Col K.K. Vohra | Delhi | L/70 |
| 27 AD Regiment | Lt Col H.W. Saldhana | Jallandhar | L/70 |
| 28 AD Regiment | Lt Col Rajendar Singh | Tezpur | L/70 |
| 29 AD Regiment | Lt Col D.S. Sukarchakia | | L/70 |
| 45 AD Regiment | Lt Col T.K. Bose | Kaluchak | L/70 |
| 46 AD Regiment | Lt Col Krishan Singh | Oodlabari | L/60 |
| 47 AD Regiment | Lt Col Y.P. Malhotra | Panagarh | L/70 |
| 48 AD Regiment | Lt Col P.R. Ratra | Guwahati | L/60 |
| 49 AD Regiment | Lt Col Ajit Singh | Pathankot | L/70 |
| 50 AD Regiment | Lt Col H.S. Brar | Jhansi | L/60 |
| 103 AD Regiment (TA) | Lt Col P.K.U. Menon | Bombay | L/60 |
| 104 AD Regiment (TA) | Lt Col D.R.N. Kapur | Ambala | L/60 |
| 105 AD Regiment (TA) | Lt Col Wadhawan | Jallandhar | L/60 |
| 107 AD Regiment (TA) | Lt Col Gopal Singh, VrC | Calcutta | L/60 |
| 126 AD Regiment (TA) | Lt Col Mahender Kumar | Delhi | L/60 |
| 127 AD Regiment (TA) | Lt Col K.B.S. Bhinder | Jodhpur | L/60 |
| 128 AD Regiment (TA) | Lt Col S.B.S. Chima | Madhopur | L/60 |
| 129 AD Regiment (TA) | Lt Col D.S. Kahlon | Delhi | L/60 |
| 130 AD Regiment (TA) | Lt Col D.D. Sachdev | Guwahati | L/60 |
| 131 AD Regiment (TA) | Lt Col B.N. Sharma | Siliguri | L/60 |
| 140 AD Regiment (TA) | Lt Col J.N. Kakra | Ambala | L/60 |
| 144 AD Regiment (TA) | Lt Col A.K. Singla | Delhi | L/60 |
| 151 AD Regiment | Lt Col E.R. Tullett | | L/60 |
| 152 AD Regiment | Lt Col N.P. Sachar | Bharatpur | L/60 |

APPENDIX B

# Pakistan Air Defence Artillery

FORMATION

3 AA Brigade

REGIMENTS

41 HAA Regiment
52 HAA Regiment
5 LAA Regiment
6 LAA Regiment
13 LAA Regiment
19 LAA Regiment (SP)
20 LAA Regiment
29 LAA Regiment (SP)
43 LAA Regiment
36 LAA Regiment
58 LAA Regiment
74 Composite LAA Regiment
75 LAA Regiment

INDEPENDENT BATTERIES

45 Independent LAA Battery
310 Independent LAA Battery

*Notes:*

1. According to the 'Report of the Hamoodur Rehman Commission of Inquiry into the 1971 War', Pakistan had a total of 99 AA batteries including 62 regular and 37 Mujahid AA batteries. Of the regulars, there were 6 HAA batteries and 56 LAA batteries.
2. HAA and LAA regiments had three and four batteries each respectively.
3. The designation of two HAA and three LAA regiments, not listed above, is not known.

APPENDIX C

# Indian Air Force Losses

Indian Air Force lost a total of 75 aircraft during the war.

*Loss by Type.* The breakdown of losses as per the type of aircraft is as follows:

| *Type* | *East* | *West* | *Total* |
|---|---|---|---|
| MiG-21 | 2 | 6 (2) | 8 |
| Sukhoi-7 | 1 | 18(1) | 19 |
| Hunter | 12 (3) | 11(2) | 23 |
| Canberra | 1 | 4 (1) | 5 |
| Gnat | - | 3 (2) | 3 |
| Mystére IVa | - | 5 (2) | 5 |
| HF-24 | - | 4 | 4 |
| Vampire | - | 1 | 1 |
| Alize (Navy) | - | 1 | 1 |
| Dakota | 1 (1) | - | 1 |
| AOP (Army) | - | 1 | 1 |
| Helicopters | 2 (2) | 2 (1) | 4 |
| TOTAL | 19 (6) | 56 (11) | 75 (17) |

*Note:* Figures in parenthesis are operational accidents.

*Loss by causes.* The majority of losses were due to ground fire to include AD artillery and small arms. The losses to Pakistan Air Force were only 20 aircraft of which 2 were destroyed on the ground during Pakistan Air Force raids. The details of the aircraft lost, both in east and west to various causes are as follows:

| *Type of Loss* | *East* | *West* | *Total* | *Percentage* |
|---|---|---|---|---|
| Anti Aircraft /Ground Fire | 10 | 26 | 36 | 48 per cent |
| Air-to-Air Combat | 3 | 15 | 18 | 30 per cent |

| | | | | |
|---|---|---|---|---|
| Destroyed on Ground | - | 2 | 2 | 2 per cent |
| Undetermined (Possible air combat) | - | 2 | 2 | 1 per cent |
| Accidents | 6 | 11 | 17 | 22 per cent |
| TOTAL | 19 | 56 | 75 | |

*Losses to AD Artillery/Ground Fire*
Eastern Sector

| *Date* | *Aircraft* | *Sqn* | *Name of the Pilot* | *Location* | *Remarks* |
|---|---|---|---|---|---|
| 4 Dec. 71 | Sukhoi-7 | 221 | Sqn Ldr V. Bhutani | Tezgaon | AAA |
| 4 Dec. 71 | Hunter | 37 | Sqn Ldr A.B. Samanta | Tezgaon | AAA |
| 4 Dec. 71 | Hunter | 37 | Fg Off S.G. Khonde | Tezgaon | AAA |
| 4 Dec. 71 | Hunter | 7 | Flt Lt A.R. Da Costa | Lal Munir Hat | AAA-crashed |
| 4 Dec. 71 | Hunter | 7 | Sqn Ldr S.K. Gupta | Baghdogra AFB | Ejected at base |
| 6 Dec. 71 | MiG-21 | 4 | Sqn Ldr Rao | Guwahati | AAA |
| 7 Dec. 71 | Hunter | - | - | Dum Dum | Ejected at base |
| 10 Dec. 71 | Hunter | - | - | Lal Munir Hat | Pilot ejected |
| 12 Dec. 71 | MiG-21 | 28 | Sqn Ldr K.J.S. Gill | Agartala | Ejected |
| 15 Dec. 71 | Canberra | 16 | Fg Off B.R.E. Wilson | Kurmitola | |

Western Sector

| *Date* | *Aircraft* | *Sqn* | *Name of the Aircrew* | *Location* | *Remarks* |
|---|---|---|---|---|---|
| 4 Dec. 71 | Sukhoi-7 | 101 | Flt Lt Gurdip Singh | - | |
| 4 Dec. 71 | Sukhoi-7 | 222 | Flt Lt P.N. Saksena | - | |
| 4 Dec. 71 | Sukhoi-7 | 108 | Flt Lt D.R. Natu | Halwara | |
| 4 Dec. 71 | Sukhoi-7 | 32 | Flt Lt M.S. Grewal | Shorkot | |
| 4 Dec. 71 | Hunter | - | - | - | |
| 4 Dec. 71 | HF-24 | 220 | Flt Lt P.V. Apte | Nayachor | Dharnaro RS |
| 4 Dec. 71 | HF-24 | 220 | Flt Lt J.L. Bhargava | Nayachor | |
| 5 Dec. 71 | Canberra | 5 | Flt Lt S.K. Goswami (Pt)<br>Flt Lt S.C. Mahajan (Nav) | - | Crashed near Khushab |

| | | | | | |
|---|---|---|---|---|---|
| 5 Dec. 71 | Mystére | 3 | Flt Lt A.V. Pethia | Bhawal-nagar | |
| 5 Dec. 71 | Sukhoi-7 | 32 | Flt Lt V.V. Tambey | Shorkot AFB | |
| 5 Dec. 71 | MiG-21 | 29 | Flt Lt Harish Singhji | Suleimanke | |
| 5 Dec.71 | Sukhoi-7 | 26 | Sqn Ldr D.S. Jafa | E of Lahore | |
| 5 Dec. 71 | Canberra | 35 | Flt Lt S.C. Sandal (Pt) Flt Lt K.S. Nanda | Masroor | |
| 6 Dec. 71 | Sukhoi-7 | 222 | Fg Off K.C. Kuruvilla | Jassar-Bridge | |
| 6 Dec. 71 | Sukhoi-7 | 101 | Flt Lt J. Bhattacharya | Chhamb | |
| 8 Dec. 71 | MiG-21 | 45 | Sqn Ldr Denzil Keelor | Chhamb | |
| 8 Dec. 71 | Hunter | 7 | Wg Cdr B.A. Coelho | Suleimanke | |
| 8 Dec. 71 | Mystére | 3 | -- | Haveli | |
| 9 Dec. 71 | Sukhoi-7 | 32 | Flt Lt N. Shanker | NW Amritsar | |
| 9 Dec. 71 | HF-24 | 10 | Sqn Ldr A.V. Kamat | Hydera-bad | At Kotri |
| 10 Dec. 71 | Hunter | 27 | Sqn Ldr M.K. Jain | Chhamb | |
| 10 Dec. 71 | Sukhoi-7 | 26 | Flt Lt Dilip Parulkar | Zafarwal | |
| 10 Dec. 71 | Sukhoi-7 | 108 | Flt Lt S.K. Chibber | Mdi Sdiqganj | |
| 11 Dec. 71 | Canberra | 5 | Flt Lt R.D. Naithani | | |
| 13 Dec. 71 | Mystére | 3 | Sqn Ldr J.D. Kumar | Haveli | |
| 13 Dec. 71 | MiG-21 | 47 | Wg Cdr H.S. Gill | Badin | |
| 16 Dec. 71 | Sukhoi-7 | 26 | Flt Lt T.S. Dandass | Narowal RS | |

APPENDIX D

# Pakistan Air Force Losses

*Total Losses*

| | *East* | *West* | *Total* |
|---|---|---|---|
| PAF Aircraft Lost in Air Combat | 5 | 5 | 10 |
| PAF Aircraft Lost to AA Fire | 0 | 9 | 9 |
| PAF Aircraft Lost in Accidents | 0 | 2 | 2 |
| PAF Aircraft Destroyed in IAF Attacks | 0 | 8 | 8 |
| PAF Aircraft Destroyed by Self | 13 | 0 | 13 |
| TOTAL PAF aircraft | 18 | 24 | 42 |
| Non-PAF Aircraft Lost in IAF Raids | 4 | 2 | 6 |
| Non-PAF Aircraft | 1 | 2 | 3 |
| TOTAL aircraft (All) | 23 | 28 | 51 |

*Loss by Aircraft Type*

| *Ac Type* | *East* | *West* | *Total* |
|---|---|---|---|
| F-86 Sabre | 16 | 12 | 28 |
| F-104 Starfighter | 0 | 3 | 3 |
| MiG-19 (F-6) | 0 | 4 | 4 |
| T-33 | 2 | 0 | 2 |
| B-57 Canberra | 0 | 5 | 5 |
| Miscellaneous | 5 | 4 | 9 |
| TOTAL | 23 | 28 | 51 |

*Losses to AD Artillery* (according to PAF)

| *Aircraft* | *Sqn* | *Pilot* | *Remarks* |
|---|---|---|---|
| B-57 Canberra | 7 Sqn | S/L Khusro (KIA),<br>S/L Peter Chisty (KIA) | Jamnagar |
| B-57 Canberra | 7 Sqn | S/L Ishfaq Hameed (KIA),<br>F/L Zulfiqar Ahmed (KIA) | Bhuj |

| | | | |
|---|---|---|---|
| B-57 Canberra | 7 Sqn | F/L Javed Iqbal (KIA),<br>F/L G.M. Malik (KIA) | Amritsar |
| F-104 Starfighter | 9 Sqn | S/L Amjad Hussain (PW) | Amritsar |
| MiG-19 (F-6) | 11 Sqn | F/L Wajid Ali Khan (PW) | Marala |
| F-86 Sabre | 18 Sqn | S/L Cecil Choudhry | Own AAA near Chhamb |
| F-86 Sabre | 26 Sqn | F/L Fazal Elahi (KIA) | Chhamb |
| MiG-19 (F-6) | 25 Sqn | F/O Shahid Raza (KIA) | Shakargarh |
| F-6 | 23 Sqn | Flt Lt A.J. Siddiqui | Own AAA near Chhamb |

APPENDIX E

# Gallantry Awards: Indian Air Defence Artillery

*Vir Chakra*

1. BHM Babu Mali, 129 AD Regiment (TA)
2. Hav. K. Mahalakshmaiah, 45 AD Regiment
3. Hav. T. Ramaswamy Chettiar, 27 AD Regiment
4. Hav. M.V. Gopalakrishanan, 27 AD Regiment
5. Hav. K.K. Gopalakrishanan Nair, 27 AD Regiment
6. Hav. Bal Bahadur, 29 AD Regiment
7. Hav. Ajmer Singh, 105 AD Regiment (TA)
8. Hav. Uttam Jawalge, 151 AD Regiment
9. L/Hav. Kans Raj, 128 AD Regiment
10. Nk Dhondi Ram Bhansode, 129 AD Regiment (TA)
11. L/Nk Shreepati Singh, 26 AD Regiment
12. Gnr Bhadreshwar Pathak (Posthumous), 29 AD Regiment
13. Gnr R. Armugam (Posthumous), 151 AD Regiment

*Shaurya Chakra*

1. Maj V.D. Sharma, 26 AD Regiment

*Sena Medal*

1. Col K.K. Pandey, 49 AD Regiment
2. Lt Col A.K. Sinha, 49 AD Regiment
3. Capt S.N. Dharamadhikari, 129 AD Regiment
4. Capt R.C. Dabral, 45 AD Regiment
5. Capt H.S. Sandhu, 27 AD Regiment
6. Capt Amarvir Singh, 49 AD Regiment
7. Nb Sub Rati Ram, 26 AD Regiment

8. Nb Sub Jagir Singh, 45 AD Regiment
9. Nb Sub Sardara Singh, 29 AD Regiment
10. BHM Rampal Singh, 126 AD Regiment
11. Hav N.J. George, 45 AD Regiment
12. Hav Hira Singh, 29 AD Regiment
13. Hav M.S. Thomas, 45 AD Regiment
14. Hav M. Nagalingam, 45 AD Regiment
15. LHav Sita Ram, 144 AD Regiment
16. Nk Soban Singh, 29 AD Regiment
17. LNK Pritam Singh, 126 AD Regiment

APPENDIX F

# Gallantry Awards: Pakistan Air Defence Artillery

A total of 67 gallantry awards were won by Pakistani AD artillery personnel. The details are:

| | |
|---|---|
| Sitara-e-Jur'at | 21 |
| Tamgha-i-Jurat | 25 |
| Imtiazi Sanad | 21 |
| Total | 67 |

Some of the known awardees are:

*Sitara-e-Jur'at*

Lt Col Mohammad Afzal
Major Fahim Durrani
Captain Mohammad Anwar
Lieutenant Atta Mohammad

*Tamgha-e-Jurat*

Havildar Mohammad Latif
Havildar Mohammad Iqbal
Havildar Mohammad Aslam
Naik Mohammad Yousaf
Lance/Naik Abdul Rashid
Gunner Abdul Ghafoor

# Bibliography


Bajwa, Major General Kuldip Singh, 'Battle of Longewala', *Journal of the United Service Institution of India*, vol. CXXXVIII, no. 574, October-December 2008.

Bajwa, Farooq, *From Kutch to Tashkent: The India Pakistan War of 1965*, Pentagon Press, New Delhi, 2014.

Bowman, Martin W., *Cold War Jet Combat : Air to Air Jet Operation 1950-1972*, Pen and Sword Books, Barnsley, 2016.

Candeth, Lt Gen K.P., *The Western Front*, Allied Publishers, New Delhi, 1984.

Chakravorty, B.C., *History of the Indo-Pak War 1965*, History Division, Ministry of Defence, Government of India, New Delhi, 1992.

Chhetri, Lt Col B.S., *Meandering into Memories*, Purboyon Publishers, Guwahati, 2020.

Dean, Judy, 'An Easy War in the Royal Artillery (pt. 2)', *BBC WW2 People's War*, 26 May 2005.

File No. 601/2093/WD War Diary of Headquarters 9th AA Brigade, RA, maintained by History Division, Ministry of Defence, New Delhi.

File No. 601/2290/WD, War Diary of 1st Indian HAA regiment maintained by History Division, Ministry of Defence, New Delhi.

Fricker, John, *Battle for Pakistan: The Air War of 1965*, Allan Printing, Shepperton, Surrey, UK, 1979.

Fricker, John, 'Postmortem of an Air War', *Air Enthusiast*, May 1972.

Gole, Air Marshal C.V., 'Reflections on an Air War: The Air Operations of December 1971', *Vayu* VI/91, New Delhi, 1991.

Hai, Kutub, *The Patton Wreckers*, Times Group Books, New Delhi, 2015.

Haider, Sajjad S., *Flight of the Falcon: Demolishing the Myths of India-Pak Wars 1965 & 1971*, Vanguard Books, Karachi, 2010.

Hiranandani, Vice Admiral G.M., *Transition to Triumph: Indian Navy 1965-1975*, Spantech & Lancer, New Delhi, 2009.

Hussain, S.S., *History of the Pakistan Air Force 1947-82*, PAF Press, Karachi, 1982.

Jagan Mohan and Samir Chopra, *Eagles Over Bangladesh, The Indian Air Force in the 1971 Liberation War*, HarperCollins, New Delhi, 2013.

Jagan Mohan, P.V.S. and Samir Chopra, *The India-Pakistan Air War of 1965*, Manohar Books, Delhi, 2005.

Khan, Yasmin, *India at War: The Subcontinent and the Second World War*, Oxford University Press, 2015.

Khanna, Col R.B., *1971: The Sappers War*, published by Engineer-in-Chief, Army Headquarters, New Delhi, May 1995.

Lal, Air Chief Marshal P.C., *My Years with the IAF,* Lancer Publications, New Delhi, 1986.

Lehl, Maj. Gen. Lachhman Singh, *Victory in Bangladesh*, Natraj, Dehradun, 1991.

Menon, Air Marshal Narayan, 'Recollections of the 1971 War', *Indian Defence Review*, Issue vol. 24.4 Oct.-Dec. 2009, 10 Dec. 2019.

Mullick, B.N., *My Years with Nehru: The Chinese Betrayal,* Allied Publishers, New Delhi, 1972.

Nayar, K.K., *Amar Jawan,* India Book House, New Delhi, 1997.

Nordeen, Lon O., *Air Warfare in Missile Age*, Smithsonian Books, 2010.

Partition of Personnel and Units of Armed Forces, 'Fourth Meeting of Partition Council, Allocation of Armoured Corps and Infantry Units, Partition Proceedings', vol. 5, p. 44. http://shodhganga.inflibnet.ac.in/bitstream/10603/14220/8/08_chapter%204.pdf, accessed on 3 January 2020.

Peter, Davies, *F-104 Starfighter Units in Combat*, Osprey Publications, Oxford, 2014.

Potter, William C. and Harlan W. Jencks, eds., *The International Missile Bazaar: The New Suppliers' Network*, Westview Press Inc., Boulder, 1994.

Prabhala, S., K.V. Koshy and S. Krsihnan, *Inside the Solid State: The Story of Bharat Electronics* Westland, Chennai, 2014.

Pradhan, R.D., *1965 War: The Inside Story – Defence Minister Y.B. Chavan's Diary of India-Pakistan War*, Atlantic Publishers, New Delhi, 2007.

Prasad, Bisheshwar, *Expansion of the Armed Forces and Defence Organization, 1939-45*, History Division, Ministry of Defence, Government of India, New Delhi ( Reprinted and Distributed by Pentagon Press, New Delhi), 2012.

Prasad, S.N. and U.P. Thapliyal, *India-Pakistan War of 1971,* Natraj, Dehradun.

———, *The India-Pakistan War of 1971: A History*, Natraj Publishers, New Delhi, 2014.

Riza, Maj Gen. Shaukat, *Izzat-o-Iqbal: History of Regiment of Artillery 1947-1971*, School of Artillery, Nawshera, 1980.

Routledge, N.W., *History of the Royal Regiment of Artillery: Anti-Aircraft Artillery, 1914-55*, Brassey's, London, 1994.

Sandhu, Major General A.J.S., *Battleground Chhamb: The India Pakistan War of 1971*, Manohar Books, New Delhi, 2018.

Singh, Amarinder and T.S. Shergill, *The Monsoon War: Young Officers Reminisce*, Roli Books, New Delhi, 2015.

Singh, AVM M.M., 'With Gnats in Peace and War', *Vayu* II/9, New Delhi, 1991.

Singh, Colonel Mandeep, *Baptism under Fire: Anti-Aircraft Artillery in India Pakistan War 1965*, Vij Publications, New Delhi, 2017.

———, *Anti-Aircraft Artillery in Combat, 1950-1972: Air Defence in the Jet Age*, Pen & Sword, Barnsley, 2020.

Singh, Major General Lachhman, *Indian Sword Strikes in East Pakistan*, Vikas Publishing House, New Delhi, 1979.

Singh, Maj Gen Sukhwant, *Defence of the Western Border* (vol. 2), Vikas, New Delhi, 1981.

———, *General Trends, India's Wars Since Independence*, Vikas Publishing House, New Delhi, 1982.

Singh, Pushpindar, *Journal of an Air War, Air Enthusiast*, April 1972.

Singh, Pushpinder and Ravi Rikhye, *Fiza'ya, Psyche of the Pakistan Air Force,* Himalayan Books, New Delhi, 1991.

Smith, Jeff M., 'A Forgotten War in the Himalayas', *Yale Global Online*, 14 September 2012, accessed on 5 June 2021 at https://yaleglobal.yale.edu/content/forgotten-war-himalayas

Subrahmanyam, K., 'Arms and Politics', *Strategic Analysis*, January 2005, vol. 29, issue 1, accessed on 18 July 2021 at http://www.idsa.in/strategicanalysis/ArmsandPolitics_ksubrahmanyam_0305

Sukumaran, R., 'The 1962 India-China War and Kargil 1999: Restrictions on the Use of Air Power', *Strategic Analysis*, vol. 27, no. 3, July-September 2003, Institute for Defence Studies and Analyses, New Delhi, 2003.

Tiwary, Air Commodore A.K., *Attrition in Air Warfare*, Lancer International, New Delhi, 2000.

The Report of the Hamoodur Rehman Commission of Inquiry into the 1971 War, University of Michigan Press, 2000.

Tufail, Kaiser, *In the Ring and on its Feet: Pakistan Air Force in India-Pakistan War 1971*, Ferozsons, Lahore, 2018.

Wahab, Abdul A.T.M., *Mukti Bahini Wins Victory: Pak Military Oligarchy Divides Pakistan in 1971*, Colombia Prokashani, Dacca, 2004.

Werrell, Kenneth, *Archie to SAM: A Short Operational History of Ground-Based Air Defense*, Air University Press, Maxwell AFB, Alabama, 2005.

Zimmerman, David, 'Information and the Air Defence Revolution, 1917-40', *Journal of Strategic Studies,* vol. 27, issue 2, 2004.

# Index